THE SEASONS

THE SEASONS

Philosophical, Literary, and Environmental Perspectives

Edited by

LUKE FISCHER and DAVID MACAULEY

SUNY
PRESS

Published by State University of New York Press, Albany

For information, contact State University of New York Press, Albany, NY
www.sunypress.edu

Library of Congress Cataloging-in-Publication Data

Names: Fischer, Luke, editor. | Macauley, David, editor.
Title: The seasons : philosophical, literary, and environmental perspectives /
    Luke Fischer and David Macauley.
Description: Albany : State University of New York, [2021] | Includes
    bibliographical references and index.
Identifiers: LCCN 2021009169 (print) | LCCN 2021009170 (ebook) | ISBN
    9781438484259 (hardcover : alk. paper) | ISBN 9781438484242 (pbk. : alk.
    paper) | ISBN9781438484266 (ebook)
Subjects: LCSH: Human ecology and the humanities. | Seasons.
Classification: LCC GF22 .S43 2021 (print) | LCC GF22 (ebook) | DDC
    304.2/5—dc23
LC record available at https://lccn.loc.gov/2021009169
LC ebook record available at https://lccn.loc.gov/2021009170

10 9 8 7 6 5 4 3 2 1

Contents

Contents

Illustrations

Acknowledgments

David Macauley would like to thank Penn State University, Brandywine for support during work on this book. He received valuable assistance and intellectual friendship from Troy Paddock, Luke Fischer, Eric Orts, Richard Odabashian, and Howard Macauley. He would also like to acknowledge the constructive responses he received after presenting talks to the Renaissance Society at the University of Chicago, the Geo-aesthetics Society at Towson University in Maryland, the Becoming-Elemental Conference at Concordia University in Montreal, and the International Association for Environmental Philosophy in Philadelphia.

Luke Fischer would like to thank David Macauley for first suggesting that we co-edit a volume on the topic of the seasons. This idea came about after he (Luke) presented a paper on the seasons at the "Geo-Aesthetics in the Anthropocene" conference at the University of Maryland in 2010. At the time David was completing his book *Elemental Philosophy*, and there were significant points of interconnection between our respective research. In 2011 David Macauley, Craig Holdrege, and Luke Fischer presented a panel on the seasons (moderated by James Hatley) at the International Association of Environmental Philosophy conference. The presentations at these two conferences, as well as more recent exchanges with a number of scholars, have sparked valuable conversations for which he is grateful. He would also like to thank Jeffrey Hipolito and Dalia Nassar for their feedback and interest in this project.

We would both like to thank the academic journals *Transformations* (www.transformationsjournal.org) and *Environment, Space, Place* (published by the University of Minnesota Press) for permission to use and revise several articles for the present volume. The following articles first appeared in *Transformations* 21 (2012): Jo Law, "The Almanac Projects: Modeling the

Seasons through the Material World"; Joseph Ballan, "Seasonal Affective Order: Rhythmanalysis and Mesology of Circumpolar Religion" (in the present volume the title has been changed to "Seasonal Affective Order: The Passage of Sense in Circumpolar Religion"); Rod Giblett, "The Seasons: Homage to Henry David Thoreau" (in the present volume the title has been changed to "The Nature and Culture of the Seasons: Homage to Henry David Thoreau"). The following articles first appeared in *Environment, Space, Place* 5, no. 1 (Spring 2013): John Charles Ryan, "Toward a Phen(omen) ology of the Seasons: The Emergence of the Indigenous Weather Knowledge Project"; Tom Bristow, "Climatic Literary Geoinformatics: Radical Empiricism, Region, and Seasonal Phenomena in John Kinsella's *Jam Tree Gully* Poems" (in the present volume the title has been changed to "The Decolonized Pastoral: Kinsella, Thoreau, and the Seasons"). The following articles first appeared in *Environment, Space, Place* 6, no. 1 (Spring 2014): Luke Fischer, "A Poetic Phenomenology of the Temperate Seasons" (in the present volume the title has been changed to "A Poetic Phenomenology of the Seasons"); Alphonso Lingis, "Arctic Summer." David Macauley's article "The Four Seasons and the Rhythms of Place-Based Time" first appeared in *Environment, Space, Place* 10, no. 2 (Fall 2018).

We would like to thank Andrew Kenyon and Michael Rinella at SUNY Press in particular for their assistance, encouragement, and patience in seeing this book through to its completion. We would also like to thank the production editor, Ryan Morris, and the copy editor, Heather Grennan Gary. Finally, we extend our appreciation to the contributors to this volume and to the reviewers of a draft of the manuscript.

Introduction

Thinking through the Seasons

LUKE FISCHER AND DAVID MACAULEY

No one, to my knowledge, has observed the minute differences in the seasons . . . A book of the seasons, each page of which should be written in its own season and out-of-doors, or in its own locality wherever it may be.

—Henry David Thoreau, *Journal*, June 11, 1851

The Role and Relevance of the Seasons

We are living in a time in which we are likely more alienated from seasonal rhythms than in any other period of history. During long winter nights, we switch on electric lights and thus, as it were, artificially extend the day. Through indoor heating and air-conditioning, we sequester ourselves from the bitter cold of winter or the oppressive heat of summer. Modern technology enables us to control the temperature of our homes, shops, public buildings, and transport vehicles. This seeming ability to separate ourselves from the environing atmosphere is, in a deeper sense, a dangerous illusion. The fluorocarbons used in air-conditioning, for instance, are released into the environment and in turn contribute to global climate change. Ironically, when we cool ourselves in this manner we promote the further warming of the atmosphere. Of course, humans have always sought ways to cool their dwellings in summer and warm them in winter. Gas heating, for example, has replaced the hearth. The shady courtyards and fountains of Arabic architecture were actually very effective in providing cool sanctuaries in the summer. But these earlier forms of temperature regulation involved a closer connection to the elements—wood, fire, water, and the courtyard's exposure to the outdoors—than those of modern technology.

Our apparent ability to detach ourselves from the climate—through the production of artificial micro-climates—is emblematic of wider problems connected with Western subjectivity and the unfolding ecological crisis. Through the assumptions of modern philosophy and the growth imperatives of our economic systems, we have thought and acted as though we human beings can exist separately from the natural world. Nature has been conceived as a realm that is radically divided from human experience and self-consciousness, and humans have treated the environment as a mere resource for industry and the manufacture of commodities. In the current era of the Anthropocene, we are—all too slowly—becoming aware that human life is dependent on and interdependent with the earth's dynamic, interconnected, and fragile ecosystems; that our exploitation of natural resources is unsustainable; and that human activity is adversely affecting the entire biosphere.

In the context of our modern global economy, we can shop at supermarkets where mangoes and strawberries—transported from thousands of miles away—are available on the shelves in the middle of winter. Whereas many small-scale and organic farmers continue to collaborate with seasonal cycles and there are environmental limits to what can be grown in a particular region at particular time of year, most of us now reside in cities and large towns where we are typically disconnected from the rhythms of agrarian life. Moreover, industrial agriculture is largely mediated by modern technologies and the capitalist economy; short-term yields and the maximization of profits are prioritized, rather than a sustainable collaboration with natural cycles.

Reflecting on these issues, environmentalist Bill McKibben opines, "The seasons don't matter to most of us anymore except as spectacles. In my county and in many places around this part of the nation, the fair that once marked the harvest now takes place in late August, while tourist dollars are still in heavy circulation." He asks rhetorically, "Why celebrate the harvest when you harvest every week with a shopping cart?"[1]

Modern forms of transportation not only convey goods and produce across great distances, they also enable individuals to travel to the other side of the earth within a day. Travelers who fly from one hemisphere to another experience a disruption from the geographical specificities and continuities of seasonal change; they also experience a complete reversal of the seasons themselves. Such occurrences remind us that the earth's two hemispheres exist in a polar relationship to one another, but they also bring about a rupture in the sense of seasonal time, while plane travel exacerbates global warming.

Particular cultural imaginaries can be sources of seasonal alienation as well. In Australia, where I (Luke) grew up, there is confusion that derives from a displaced European conception of the seasons. In the process of colonization, a European model of the four seasons was imported to a hemisphere and applied to ecologies where it does not fit.[2] Aboriginal cultures that became deeply attuned to ecological nexuses across Australia over tens of thousands of years have discerned between two and nine seasons. Moreover, the symbols associated with specific holidays often relate to seasons in the Northern Hemisphere and are incongruous with Australian seasons; for example, many Christmas songs and symbols invoke winter imagery that is misplaced in the summer months of December and January in Australia (though more fitting seasonal adaptations to Christmas in summer have also emerged).

In the rural East Coast of North America where I (David) grew up, the seasons have tended historically to be marked by relatively clear and even dramatic transformations. In my youth, I associated certain family tasks with the reliable arrival of distinct periods of the year: raking leaves and chopping wood in autumn; shoveling snow in winter; preparing the garden or cleaning out the house in spring; and cutting grass or picking strawberries and blueberries in summer. There seemed to be a larger unwritten but trustworthy calendar that told me the appropriate or "pre-appointed" time for ice skating on the frozen ponds and sledding on the snow-ballasted hills (winter); hiking the newly thawed stream and waterfalls near our scouting retreat (spring); swimming in and canoeing on the tributaries of the Susquehanna River (summer), or camping out when the nights were cooler and the leaves changed color (autumn). As I glance back now, I believe these recollections are not mere wistfulness on my part—a painful search for a lost home, as the word *nostalgia* suggests. Rather, there were (and still are) larger rhythms and deeper ecological changes at work. I mention these experiences because seasonal disruption has been occurring at a faster rate over the last several decades, and our human senses are often able to pick up on warning signals. It is, moreover, to these ancient, enduring, and increasingly altered rhythms that we should arguably be attending.

In this vein, the essayist and novelist Pico Iyer speculates that the seasons can lead us to appreciate "an order higher than ourselves, or nation, or ideology" insofar as they "rescue us from our private winters and admit us to a larger rhythm, as unanswerable as the dawn." They help us to see processes that are "more universal than New Year" but "more flexible than moons."[3] They encourage us to understand transitions and to accept the idea that there are some things that should remain beyond our reach to alter in a significant way.

Anthropogenic climate change is not only disrupting our individual and cultural senses of the seasons but also the seasons themselves. Record high temperatures are occurring in diverse regions. We experience "summery" days in fall, spring, and even winter. We experience unprecedented heat waves in summer. Such temperature shifts affect times of plant growth, flourishing, and fruition, the lives and migration patterns of animals, and human behavior and activities—we swim at the beach or eat lunch on the balcony on a "winter's" day. One telling marker of climate change is the occurrence of "unseasonal" phenomena within a particular season.[4] A discomfiting trend in many locations around the planet is the emergence of frequent flooding during traditional dry seasons. In Australia, an increasing number of bushfires (wildfires) occur not only in summer, but also in spring and winter. The most devastating bushfires ever recorded in Australia began in June (winter) 2019 and peaked in December 2019 and January 2020. The fires burned close to 19 million hectares and destroyed almost 6,000 buildings. At least thirty-four people and 1.25 billion animals were killed (over 3 billion animals were impacted by the fires).[5]

Human existence is entangled with, and responsive to, seasonal phenomena even in our endeavors to escape from the weather by means of technology (air conditioning and heating, for example). And despite our relative alienation from the seasons, they continue to inform our lives in significant ways, from agricultural produce (locally grown fruit and vegetables tend to be fresher and riper) to holidays and festivals, to calendars of all kinds, to sporting activities, and to fashion. Moreover, in our time of climate change and seasonal alienation, attending to the seasons could both better our understanding of the natural environment and contribute toward healing our estrangement from it. As literary critic Lawrence Buell puts it, "seasonal representations tease us toward awareness of ourselves as environmental beings," and reflections upon seasonal change can serve "to make ourselves more aware of how phenomena signify and how, beyond that, even our suburbanized, attenuated lives are subtly regulated—maybe even constituted—by the elements," including "bees . . . trees, clouds, humidity, heat, light."[6]

It is not only modern Western culture and society that are relatively alienated from the seasons but also Western philosophy in the course of its history. Whereas the seasons have historically played a crucial role in poetry, literature, art, religion, myth, and the life-worlds of human societies, they have been scarcely thematized within Western philosophy. While the discrepancy between the presence of the seasons in poetry and their absence from philosophy might appear as striking on first consideration, this discrepancy is not merely accidental. Seasonal phenomena affect our moods, sensibilities, and modes of embodiment, which have always been concerns of poetry and art.

Philosophy, by contrast, has tended to pursue disembodied forms of thought and dispassionate ("affectively neutral") rationality. Thus, the absence of the seasons from philosophical reflection is hardly surprising. In its engagement with pre-theoretical modes of experience and embodiment, and in its emphasis on the primordial significance of moods, phenomenology opens up a significant philosophical approach to the seasons that can redress their historical neglect (as a number of essays in the present volume illustrate).[7] The Japanese philosopher Watsuji Tetsuro authored a pioneering phenomenological study in this regard, in which he explicates how "climate"—including the seasons—is integral to our self-comprehension as human beings.[8] At the same time as revealing their philosophical significance, phenomenological investigations of the seasons bring about a transmutation of philosophical thinking such that it comes nearer to poetic modes of being and writing.

It is perhaps even more surprising that the seasons have been relatively neglected within environmental thought. Environmental philosophy has, for example, given far more attention to place and space than to seasons and seasonality. However, just as space lacks a crucial dimension when regarded in abstraction from time, considerations of place and environmental regions are prone to abstraction and reification if they are not characterized in relation to seasonal time. While there has been a growing interest in "deep time," especially in terms of mapping how past changes in climate might inform prediction of the imminent effects of anthropogenic climate change, there has been less attention to cycles of seasonal time.

By situating places in seasonal time, we become aware of the inherent dynamism of places and are less inclined to objectify them. Our attention is drawn to the environment not as a static entity but as an unfolding process. Rather than seeing the environment in terms of inert nouns, we come to appreciate places as verbal manifestations of seasonal time. Just as Heidegger came to speak of the "thinging" of things and the "worlding" of the world, an attention to seasons reveals the "placing" of place, the "environing" of the environment, and the "naturing" of nature, in which the verbal dimension of being takes precedence over the substantive.[9] The regularities, patterns, and features of a place come to resemble the waves and ripples in a river that are dynamically maintained and transformed within the flux of time. At the same time, in attending to the temporality of nature, human subjectivity becomes attuned to the environment. Rather than the opposition of subject and object—a discrete observer and an external place—there emerges a participatory relation between human temporality and the "placial" manifestations of seasons. Humans and other-than-human beings together take part and take place in seasonal time. Contemplation of the seasons is one significant way toward overcoming our alienation from the environment.

The premise of this volume is that philosophy, environmental thought, ecocriticism, and the environmental humanities can all benefit greatly from a deeper attentiveness to seasons and seasonality. This collection of essays begins an exploration of the seasons—the canonical "four seasons" commonly associated with temperate regions as well as the more-or-less-than four seasons identified by various cultures across the earth—focusing in particular on contributions that engage philosophical ideas and literary texts in relation to subjects such as climate, locality, affect, culture, ecology, natural change, and time.

Through an engagement with the seasons, we hope to generate interest in and attention to a range of questions and controversies that are relevant to philosophers, geographers, literary critics, and environmentalists, among others. What exactly is a season, and how might it be understood ontologically, metaphysically, or historically? Are the seasons the same as they were in former eras given rapid rates of ecological and climatic change? How do they play a role in our cultural imaginations, everyday life, and creative pursuits? In what ways do the seasons relate to or influence our senses of time, geographical place, and embodiment? What might they reveal about the elemental world or notions of the cold, the hot, the wet, and the dry? How do winter, spring, summer, and fall affect our use of language, psychology, views of the land, and social or political practices?

In these and other ways, conceptions and cycles of the seasons offer us sensuous alternatives or more specific supplements to the abstract notion of "nature," and they open up new modes of envisioning sustainability and responding to ecological challenges.

Seasonal Complexity and the Need for Interdisciplinarity

What are the seasons and how do they arise? While the seasons are at once natural and cultural phenomena, it is helpful to begin to answer this question by limiting our focus to the physical dimensions of the seasons. Even in relation to this restricted focus, the seasons exhibit a complexity and fluidity that can only be understood through an interdisciplinary approach that draws on various sciences.

In the first instance, the seasons result from the relative relationship between the sun and the earth in the latter's yearly orbit. Due to the axial tilt of the earth in its orbital plane, for almost half of the year the Northern Hemisphere leans toward the sun and is exposed to longer, more direct, and more intense periods of sunlight in the earth's diurnal rotation. (At the same time, of course, the Southern Hemisphere leans away from the sun and experiences the opposite seasons.) As the days grow longer and the nights grow shorter in the Northern Hemisphere, the days grow shorter and nights grow longer in the Southern Hemisphere. The greatest extremes in the discrepancy between night and day occur in the North and South Poles respectively—also a result of the earth's axial tilt.

There are periods around the solstices in the Arctic Circle and Antarctic Circle when the sun never sets and respectively when the sun never rises—periods of extended night and extended day. At the North Pole, for example, there can be six months of polar day in a single year. The least amount of change occurs at the earth's equator, where the length of day and night are almost equal throughout the year. In terms of the purely astronomical relationship between the earth and the sun, there are no distinct seasons at the equator (there are often two seasons with regard to weather, a dry and a wet season), and there are four seasons in the Northern and Southern Hemispheres marked by the summer and winter solstices—when each of the hemispheres is respectively most tilted toward and away from the sun (around June 21 and December 21)—and the vernal and autumnal equinoxes when day and night are virtually equal in length in both hemispheres (around March 20 and September 22).

While the astronomical relationship between the earth and the sun is the central underlying factor of seasonal change, seasons can by no means be limited to the relative duration and intensity of day and night that results from this dynamic relationship. And while the dates of solstices and equinoxes can be accurately determined, they are not the only factors influencing the transition to a new season. Even if one only introduces the additional factor of temperature, there is already, for example, a discrepancy between the longest day and the hottest day. Due to what is known as "seasonal lag"—the gradual time in which it takes the atmosphere to warm or cool as a result of longer or shorter days—the warmest days and coldest days of the year tend to occur about a month after the summer and winter solstices.

In addition to the above factors, the temperatures and weather in a particular region are affected by altitude, topographies, built-environments, cloud cover, winds, land masses, water bodies, ocean temperatures that are influenced by cycles such as the El Niño and La Nina, and vegetation. Thus, there are wide differences in temperatures and weather even in areas that share the same latitude. In addition to daylight, air temperature, and weather, the seasons are manifest in the specificities of flora in a given region and their particular responses to light, warmth, and water (or its absence). Animals likewise respond to light, warmth, vegetation, water, and each other. In other words, a season is marked by a great confluence and complexity of factors.

We notice the emergence of spring in the thawing of a frozen lake, the presence of ducklings, newly sprouting leaves, unfolding flowers, longer days, increasing warmth, and so on. Seasons recur but not in an identical fashion; they possess a coherent complexity, a symphonic integrity, but not one that is mathematically determinable or strictly regular. Any mapping of the seasons (such as by almanacs) can be no more than a rough musical score; any actual occurrence of the seasons will play itself out in an individuated fashion and with much improvisation. It could even be said that each of the four seasons—to stick with this model for the present purposes—in fact contains a great multiplicity of seasons; each species of plant and animal in a given region has its specific seasonal cycles: different flowers blossom and fruit at divergent times, and different species of animals mate, lay their eggs, and migrate at distinct times.

The seasons involve ecological relationships of intersecting and divergent cycles and time scales. In this respect, any given season is an unfolding polyphony of numerous seasonal cycles. Skunk cabbages put forth leaves and flowers in the pre-spring, long before many plants, and thus draw insects earlier than other vegetation.[10] In the mild winters in much of Australia, a variety of plants flower. In short, a season is a dynamic complex of astronomical, ecological, and meteorological factors. The complexity involved in understanding the seasons thus requires—like other environmental topics—interdisciplinary approaches.

However, understanding the seasons calls for more than the synthesis of various scientific disciplines. The seasons are deeply entwined with culturally specific factors such as calendars (solar, lunar, and lunisolar), nomadic and sedentary modes of life, myths, religious holidays and ceremonies, art, literature, and poetry. Seasons influence our behavior and psychology (for some autumn and winter incite a particular form of depression—"seasonal affective disorder"), and they are imbued with symbolic meanings. Seasons can thus be described as integrated phenomena of "natureculture"; understanding them requires interdisciplinary approaches that not only incorporate various physical sciences but also the humanities and social sciences—anthropology, sociology, psychology, art history, literary studies, religious studies, and philosophy, among others.

Seasons as Natureculture:
Poetry, Literature, Art, and Myth

Many religious calendars and festivals—whether pagan, polytheistic, or monotheistic—are closely aligned with seasonal time. In ancient Greece, the myth of Demeter and Persephone offered a rich narrative of seasonal change, vegetative life, and cycles of death and rebirth. Persephone is forced to spend time in the underworld with Hades during the winter months and is reunited with her mother, Demeter, in spring. The myth played a central role in the initiation rites of the Eleusinian Mysteries, in which (according to some theories) the one who was initiated attained eternal life and joined the immortal company of the gods. In Judaism, Passover was originally a spring festival in which pilgrims traveled to the Temple in Jerusalem and made offerings of the "first fruits of the barley." Easter, which takes place around the same time as Passover, is dated in accordance with the first full moon that follows the spring equinox in the Northern Hemisphere. In the tradition of Easter eggs, vernal manifestations of fertility become symbols of Christ's death and rebirth—the eggs represent the empty tomb of Jesus (discovered by Mary Magdalene, to whom the resurrected Christ appears as a "gardener" [John 20:11–15]). Christmas closely follows the winter solstice in the Northern Hemisphere—the "light of the world" is thus, for Christians, born on the earth as the daylight increases. In India, Hindu calendars identify six seasons (*Ritu*), which are closely tied to numerous religious festivals, as well.

The seasons have similarly played a central role in diverse literary traditions. In the poetic genre of haiku—which grew out of Zen Buddhism in

Japan and the earlier form of the renga—each three-line poem traditionally suggests a particular season. To offer two examples, here is an evocation of spring by a founder of the genre, Matsuo Bashō (1644–1694):

> the old-lady cherry
>   in bloom: a remembrance
>   of her old age
> [*ubazakura* / *saku ya rōgo no* / *omoiide*][11]

And here is a more recent one by the African American writer, Richard Wright, which elicits a Buddhist theme:

> I am nobody:
>   A red sinking autumn sun
>   Took my name away.[12]

Through the use of a specific "season word" (*kigo*), poets are able to link their sensual surroundings to the period of the year and open the listener's mind to the beauty of everyday but extraordinary phenomena. In the Japanese art form of haiga, painted images that evoke the seasons are often integrated with haiku written in calligraphy, too. The image and words complement and enrich one another. These artforms draw attention to diverse ways in which human experience is entwined with the events of seasonal time.

Many English-language poets have thematized and celebrated the seasons. The prologue of Chaucer's *Canterbury Tales* (c. 1400) opens with a depiction of spring as the time in which people like to start off on a pilgrimage:

> Whan that Aprill with his shoures sote
> The droghte of Marche hath perced to the rote,
> And bathed every veyne in swich licour
> Of which vertu engendred is the flour;
> Whan Zephirus eek with his swete breeth
> Inspired hath in every holt and heeth
> The tendre croppes, and the yonge sonne
> Hath in the Ram his halfe cours y-ronne,
> And smale foweles maken melodye,
> That slepen al the night with open yë
> (So priketh hem Nature in hir corages):

Than longen folk to goon on pilgrimages,
And palmers for to seken straunge strondes,
To ferne halwes, couthe in sondry londes . . .[13]

[When April with his sweet showers has
pierced the drought of March to the root,
and bathed every vein in such moisture
as has power to bring forth the flower;
when, also, Zephyrus with his sweet breath
has breathed spirit into the tender new shoots
in every wood and meadow, and the young sun
has run half his course in the sign of the Ram,
and small birds sing melodies and
sleep with their eyes open all the night
(so Nature pricks them in their hearts):
then people long to go on pilgrimages,
and palmers long to seek strange shores
and far-off shrines, known in various lands . . .]

Chaucer places human behavior and psychology in a continuum with the vernal stirrings of vegetative and animal life. As the fowls sing and the flowers emerge, nature incites the hearts of humans to commence a journey on foot. The religious and cultural practice of pilgrimage is depicted in a way that suggests parallels to animal migration. Today, many people still make intentional journeys to witness seasonal events and phenomena: the changing colors of leaves, salmon returning home to spawn, or cherry blossoms bursting into view.

Shakespeare invokes the seasons throughout his sonnets and plays, too, including *The Winter's Tale*, *As You Like It*, *The Tempest*, and *Love's Labour's Lost*. He refers to spring "when proud pied April" has placed "a spirit of youth in everything"; compares a lover to a day in summer whose "lease hath all too short a date"; speaks of "teeming autumn" which bears "the wanton burden of the prime, / like widow'd wombs after their lord's decease"; and writes of the "freezings I have felt" and the "dark days seen" in the barren of winter.[14] In *A Midsummer's Night's Dream*, he alludes to how "the seasons alter":

hoary-headed frosts
Fall in the fresh lap of the crimson rose,
And on the old Hiems' thin and icy crown

An odorous chaplet of sweet summer buds
Is, as in mockery, set. The spring, the summer,
The childing autumn, angry winter, change
Their wonted liveries, and the mazed world,
By their increase, now knows not which is which.[15]

Here, Shakespeare suggests, perhaps presciently, that the seasons have all changed places due to vengeful winds, "contagious fogs," and rising waters, and that this "progeny of evils" results from human actions—"our debate, from our dissension; / We are their parents and original."[16]

John Keats, in his "To Autumn," famously describes autumn as the "Season of mists and mellow fruitfulness" and concludes with an evocation of the "gathering swallows [that] twitter in the skies,"[17] about to begin their 6,000-mile migration from England to South Africa. The seasons, too, have long been linked closely with the periods of human life in the associations of spring with birth, summer with growth and development, autumn with maturity or decline, and winter with death. In his poem, "The Human Seasons," Keats draws a strong analogy between the phases of human life and the four seasons as follows:

Four Seasons fill the measure of the year;
    There are four seasons in the mind of man:
He has his lusty Spring, when fancy clear
    Takes in all beauty with an easy span:
He has his Summer, when luxuriously
    Spring's honied cud of youthful thought he loves
To ruminate, and by such dreaming high
    Is nearest unto heaven: quiet coves
His soul has in its Autumn, when his wings
    He furleth close; contented so to look
On mists in idleness—to let fair things
    Pass by unheeded as a threshold brook.
He has his Winter too of pale misfeature,
Or else he would forego his mortal nature.[18]

At the same time as connecting the seasons with the stages of life, Keats' poem builds on a long tradition of associating the seasons with specific states of mind ("seasons in the mind of man"). The passion of youth is identified with spring, summer involves a maturation of thought, autumn is a time of quietude and greater detachment from the world, and the winter of old age is aware of the imminence of death.

In pre-modern cosmology and physiology, the four seasons, the four humors (temperaments), the four elements, and the four bodily fluids were often regarded as interconnected. While authors differed on the precise correlations—whether, for example, winter is earth (thus melancholic) or water (thus phlegmatic) and so forth—they shared a sense of the deep interconnectedness of human embodiment, psychology, and seasonal characteristics.[19] One widespread schema was as follows:

> winter—phlegmatic—water—phlegm
> spring—sanguine—air—blood
> summer—choleric—fire—yellow bile
> autumn—melancholic—earth—black bile

Hippocrates, for example, argued that the seasons could help to predict if the coming year will be "healthy" or "unhealthy" based upon specific and detailed observations about elemental heat, rainfall, winds, dryness, and the like in relation to the human body. He observed that "changes of the seasons are especially liable to beget diseases, as are great changes from heat to cold or cold to heat in any season."[20] Deep connections were thus found or forged between the human and the universe, the microcosm and the macrocosm, and the human dispositions and the four seasons.

Similar kinds of ties between affects and seasons continue to be drawn—though less systematically than in ancient and medieval humoral theory—by writers, artists, and filmmakers, even if they no longer directly inform approaches to science and medicine. Keats identifies autumn with a "mellow" and "idle" mood. George Eliot, in a letter from 1841, describes the "melancholy" of autumn as follows:

> Is not this a true autumn day? Just the still melancholy that I love—that makes life and nature harmonise. The birds are consulting about their migrations, the trees are putting on the hectic or the pallid hues of decay, and begin to strew the ground, that one's very footsteps may not disturb the repose of earth and air, while they give us a scent that is a perfect anodyne to the restless spirit. Delicious autumn! My very soul is wedded to it, and if I were a bird I would fly about the earth seeking the successive autumns.[21]

Many early naturalists attuned themselves, in turn, to the poetic and mythological romance with the seasons. Thoreau's first known work was an essay entitled "The Seasons," composed when he was only eleven or twelve years old. In the piece, he inquires, "Why do the Seasons change? And why / Does Winter's stormy brow appear? / It is the word of him on high, / Who rules the changing varied year."[22] Thoreau's love of winter, spring, summer, and fall developed more fully in later works, especially his *Journal*. Echoing, altering, and expanding upon the well-known lines in Ecclesiastes, Thoreau observes:

> There is a season for everything, and we do not notice a given phenomenon except at that season, if indeed, it can be called the same phenomenon at any other season. There is a time to watch the ripples on Ripple Lake, to look for arrowheads, to study rocks and lichens, a time to walk on sandy deserts; and the observer of nature must improve these seasons as much as the farmer his . . . We must not be governed by rigid rules, as by the almanac, but let the season rule us.[23]

Thoreau reminds us that we have to be attentive to the specificities of a season in its actual unfolding. While a season is manifest in recognizable patterns, its manifestations are not strictly regular or predictable.

The seasons are one of many natural rhythms, including the pulse of circulation, the oscillation of breathing, the ebb and flow of tides, and the 25,772-year period of the Great Year (the rotation of the earth's axis). Given the importance of rhythm, recurrence, and variation, as well as affect, to the artform of music, it is not surprising that the seasons have been explored in rich and evocative ways in various musical genres, from the late medieval round "Sumer is icumen in" to Gershwin's "Summertime," from Vivaldi's *Four Seasons*, Schubert's *Winterreise*, to Stravinsky's *The Rite of Spring*. There are also countless children's songs that address and celebrate the seasons and weather, and through which children learn about the phenomena that express seasonal change (for example, "Five Little Ducks," "I Like the Flowers," "Colchiques dans les prés," "Alle Vögel sind schon da," "Schneeglöckchen Weißröckchen," and the Arabic song "Al Fousoul al Araba'a" [*The Four Seasons*] by Elias Rahbani).

The seasons have been important as both a setting and a topic for films. The South Korean film, *Spring, Summer, Fall, Winter . . . and Spring*, tells the story of a monk who dwells on an island monastery in the middle of a lake and helps to heal the sick. The film links the outer world of changing seasons with the inner lives of the characters, particularly the aging monk, who becomes a kind of *bodhisattva* or Buddha-figure himself, passing into the embracing cycles of the biological world. Eventually, he becomes self-less and "no one" (like a *sannyasin* or an ascetic in Hinduism) rather than a distinct "someone" with a clear identity and self, as he is dissolved into the very processes of seasonal change and extinguished in a conflagration on the lake. Each of the seasons is tied tacitly to one of the Four Noble Truths in Buddhism: spring becomes the time of *dukkha* (suffering); summer explores *tanha* (bodily desires and the cause of suffering); fall announces a cure in the form of *nirvana* (liberation from the finite remains of the self); and winter is positioned as the treatment for the pains of existence (the eightfold path).

In David Hockney's recent video artwork, *The Four Seasons, Woldgate Woods (Spring 2011, Summer 2010, Autumn 2010, Winter 2010)*, four screens respectively show footage of a narrow road through the Woldgate Woods in East Riding of Yorkshire, England, in one of the four seasons, highlighting how much the manifestations of a place are transformed by seasonal time. Hockney's video art recalls Claude Monet's *Haystacks*, twenty-five paintings that render the "same" stack of harvested grain during different seasons, weather, and times of day.

The seasons have been a perennial theme in the visual arts, from Greek and Roman depictions of the Horae as goddesses to Giuseppe Arcimboldo, who in the sixteenth century imaginatively created portrait heads composed of vegetables, flowers, fish, and fruit to portray both the cycles of the four seasons and the four elements. Thus, his "Spring" painting is made entirely of flowers while "Winter" is assembled out of tree roots. In cobbling together these profiles, Arcimboldo not only shows a fascination with the grotesque, the imperial, and the surreal, but also reveals a close aesthetic kinship between humans and the encompassing natural world.

The contemporary artist Andy Goldsworthy works closely with seasonal time, especially as it is tethered to or emergent from unique places. He uses ice, stone, sticks, snow, light, and soil that is marked and transformed by the revolving wheel of the year to show how the seasons disappear, endure, or sequester themselves underground or out of sight. One of his "earth works" involved creating and transporting thirteen one-ton snowballs (which he kept refrigerated for months) into the busy streets of London on a warm summer night. When the city awoke the next morning, people were treated to the fascinating sight of his "sculptures" and offered a charming, if evanescent, link to a different seasonal time and place: the vanished winter and the distant outlying countryside. As the great balls of snow melted over the next five days, their interiors revealed a colorful and textured mix of feathers, barbed wire, stones, wool, seeds, pinecones, and branches, much to the delight of the public.[24]

The above reflections offer just a few examples of the perennial appeal and significance of the seasons for myth, poetry, literature, and art, which, at the same time, bring into relief their striking absence from philosophical discourse. These reflections also serve to elaborate further ways in which seasons defy any neat boundaries. We apprehend the seasons not only through synthesizing various natural-scientific perspectives, but also through the creative and interpretative practices embodied in diverse genres, media, and cultures. Ultimately, the task of understanding the seasons calls for interdisciplinary approaches that draw on the natural sciences, the humanities, and the creative arts.

The essays in the present volume explore many examples of the seasons as phenomena of an integrated "natureculture" as well as cases in which nature and (seasonal) culture exist in a discordant relation. Our use of the term "natureculture" here can thus be regarded as both descriptive and prescriptive. Descriptive in that culture and seasonal phenomena are always, to some extent, entwined. Prescriptive in that modern Western societies are characterized by a historically unprecedented degree of discord—and its devastating ecological consequences—between human culture and the environment. In the latter respect, there is an urgent need for creative reintegrations of nature and culture.

Philosophical, Literary, and Environmental Perspectives

Each of the essays in this volume reveals the seasons in a fresh vocabulary and illuminating way. The contributors explore the seasons from interdisciplinary and cross-cultural perspectives that shed new light on their significance for philosophy, environmental thought, ecology, aesthetics, poetics, and post-colonial studies. Synopses are provided under the headings of the sections in which they appear.

Environmental Time

One fundamental issue at the very heart of questions about the seasons involves the nature of time and how different conceptions or experiences of it affect our interactions with the environment. While all of the essays in this collection consider time in some respect, David Macauley's and Craig Holdrege's essays are exemplary entry points into this topic. Macauley's essay draws attention to the way in which the seasons shed light on large-scale questions about temporality, whereas Holdrege's essay highlights how each species has a unique manner of participating in and contributing to seasonal time.

In "The Four Seasons and the Rhythms of Place-Based Time," Macauley examines the perennial idea of the four seasons in relation to notions of place and time. He also shows the philosophical and environmental importance of emphasizing the periods of winter, spring, summer, and fall. After clarifying the Western view of a season, he considers the seasons in the Eastern world. He then identifies and articulates different views and scales of seasonal time in relation to place, including ideas associated with repetition, *kairos*, *chronos*, and mythic temporality. Macauley looks in turn at possible challenges to the four-seasons model and discusses seasonal disruptions and discontinuities. He concludes by setting forth the values of a seasonal framework in terms of both providing an alternative to the idea of "nature" and contributing to sustainable living, noting the roles of seasonal festivals, storytelling, gardening, food preparation, the elements, walking, and everyday aesthetics.

In "The Seasons Embodied: The Story of a Plant," Holdrege shows that plants are highly context-sensitive organisms. One of the key contexts in which they are embedded is the rhythmical transformation of seasons. Our idea and experience of the seasons—including what they can reveal to us as we interact with the rest of nature—is greatly influenced by changes in plant life such as the colors of fall foliage. Plants embody and express the qualities of the seasons. Holdrege applies a Goethean phenomenological method in order to follow and participate in the life histories of plants, thus permitting us to gain a more subtle and specific understanding of the very meaning of the time of the seasons. In particular, Holdrege examines and portrays skunk cabbage (*Symplocarpus foetidus*), an unusual wetland plant that is the first plant to flower in the northeastern part of the United States. As Holdrege vividly illustrates, this plant both gives expression to and, in unique ways, helps to usher in the spring.

PHENOMENOLOGY AND POETICS

As discussed earlier, one valuable approach to understanding seasonality is through the philosophical field of phenomenology, which explores the central structures of experience and phenomena as they appear in the world. As many recent philosophers have shown, there are interesting affinities between phenomenological and ecological thought or perception. In "A Poetic Phenomenology of the Seasons," Luke Fischer draws on the phenomenology of Maurice Merleau-Ponty, key ideas in the writings of the poet and scientist Johann Wolfgang von Goethe, a phenomenological conception of affects, and poems that address the seasons to outline a poetic phenomenology of the four seasons often associated with temperate regions. He aims to unite a poetic sensibility for seasonal phenomena with a structured phenomenological approach. In doing so, he presents the seasons as a meaningful polyphony in which human beings also participate. Fischer gives a non-reductive account of how the human experience of the seasons is closely connected to natural seasonal phenomena and indicates ways in which we can deepen our understanding of, and participation in, the seasons.

Paola-Ludovika Coriando's essay, "Hölderlin, Heidegger, and Seasonal Time" focuses on the late Heidegger's thinking of the four-foldness of the world (as earth, sky, mortals, and divinities) and Hölderlin's "latest" poems. Written during the long period of his mental derangement, these poems primarily thematize the seasons. In the context of this conversation between thinking and poetry, Coriando demonstrates that the everyday experience of the cycle of the seasons should not be merely regarded as a subtopic of phenomenological philosophy but rather as a primary philosophical concern. Coriando contrasts the dispositional attunement to the seasons that is reflected in Heidegger and Hölderlin with the alienation from the seasons that characterizes the technological mindset of modernity and with the rationality of classical Western philosophy, which, in its striving for an objective knowledge that is "emotionally neutral," has failed to bring to light the fundamental significance of seasonal experience. Coriando concludes her essay with some indications of how philosophy might transform itself in connection with a deeper appreciation of the seasons.

In "Toward a Phen(omen)ology of the Seasons: The Emergence of the Indigenous Weather Knowledge Project," John Charles Ryan argues that the Western calendar insufficiently accounts for the seasonal subtleties and the multiple notions of time in Australia. Working with the recent proposal to revise the four-season model, he tracks the Western calendar in Europe and its institutionalization in Australia. Ryan explores the Indigenous Weather Knowledge Project as a partnership between Aboriginal communities and the Bureau of Meteorology, one that can potentially preserve and promote knowledge of the endemic seasons of regions in Australia. He further examines the six-season Nyoongar calendar of the southwest of Western Australia. The calendar is premised upon meteorological conditions and ecological time—as well as upon the obtainment of food, the maintenance of cultural knowledge, and the performance of ceremonies. Ryan suggests that through the union of phenomenological—experiential, sensory, place-based, actual—and phenological—cognitive, visual, enumerative, digital—approaches, the native seasons of Australia can be better appreciated in their true depth and extent.

ANTHROPOLOGY AND THE ARCTIC

"To restore any place," observes ethnobiologist Gary Nabham, "we must also begin to re-story it, to make it the lesson of our legends, festivals, and seasonal rites."[25] Toward this end, two essays in the volume engage the often-overlooked polar regions in relation to the seasons.

In "Arctic Summer"—composed in a mixed-genre style like a vivid travel diary interspersed with philosophical and anthropological reflections—Alphonso Lingis evocatively explores the Scandinavian Arctic and the changing of the seasons, which the Sámi experience as eight in number. Visitors to this region find summer in the valleys and find winter both in the mountains and in the permafrost underfoot. As Lingis reveals, summers spent in motion encourage us to understand the very force of movement and both our sedentary and nomadic instincts. The seasonal migrations of reindeer and the periodicity of lemming years invite comparison with human movements. Lingis shows how an understanding of seasonal places and displacement, including rock paintings in Alta, Norway, and the Esrange Space Center in Kiruna, Sweden, extend the span of our own historical comprehension—from humans assembled at the foot of a retreating glacier 7,000 years ago to recent travel beyond the earth itself.

Joseph Ballan likewise looks at polar regions. In "Seasonal Affective Order: The Passage of Sense in Circumpolar Religion," he points out that in Inuit society, there exists a rhythm between their collective religious life in winter and their more profane life in summer. In this rhythm, changes in the natural world are wedded to alterations in social and emotional life. In a classic study of seasonal changes among the Inuit, Marcel Mauss and Henri Beuchat investigate this relationship between natural conditions and cultural distributions. These researchers revealed a close connection between extreme seasonal changes in nature and the patterns of human social and religious life in circumpolar regions. Focusing on these issues, Ballan provides some needed revisions to Mauss and Beuchat's ideas by reconsidering social morphology in light of recent ethnographic and historical research and the theoretical contributions of Henri Lefebvre and Augustin Berque. Taken together, Lefebvre and Berque offer a way of understanding how physical changes in the environment assume meaning and affective qualities for both individuals and communities.

Everyday Aesthetics

As noted earlier, the seasons have long been linked with artistic representations and ideas about beauty. Forms of aesthetic engagement both give expression to and facilitate our understanding of the seasons. Jo Law's "The Almanac Projects: Modeling the Seasons through the Material World" investigates the almanac as a medium or forum for engaging and enacting a vital materialist practice. In the process, she addresses a number of key environmental questions: What elements should we include in our considerations of climate, weather, and the seasons? What possibilities open up when we view weather and the seasons from non-human perspectives? And what are the results of these new ways of thought? Law draws upon Jane Bennett's conception of "vital materialism" in reflecting upon the seasons as human and non-human assemblages of activity. She also offers her own almanac projects as a creative engagement with both living and non-living worlds that participate in seasonal changes. Law argues that the medium of the almanac possesses the potential to make visible an inclusive ecology that helps to articulate our multi-dimensional experiences of the seasons.

In "The Cycle of Seasons: The Temporal Structure of Fashion," Yvonne Förster explores the temporality of fashion and its ever-changing character, which is perhaps the only constant and continuous dimension of it. In her view, fashion is marked by the changing of the seasons and the sense of anticipation tied to these transformations. Förster contends that the phenomenal qualities associated with spring, summer, autumn, and winter do influence local developments in fashion, but the industry is now global in scope so that at the larger scale, every season is, in some sense, present at all times of the year. Thus, one must be critical about the way in which the seasons are defined. Förster also considers the relationship of seasonal qualities to social and cultural contexts. This relationship is the basis of the anticipatory character of fashion famously formulated by Walter Benjamin, whose theory she takes up. In short, Förster investigates the basic temporal aspects of fashion such as seasonal changes, the relation of anticipation and memory, and the connections between temporality and eternity.

Decolonizing Literature

As a number of essays in this volume make clear, the seasons are influenced and mediated by the particular cultures that experience or evoke them. The ceremonies, festivals, food, art, religions, and music of cultures in North and South America, Asia, Africa, Europe, and Australia vary widely in this regard. In certain contexts, such cultures can also be out of touch with the endemic specificities of seasonal change.

In "The Nature and Culture of the Seasons: Homage to Henry David Thoreau," Rod Giblett argues that all cultures have seasons and an understanding of annual cycles, especially periods devoted to growing, gathering, and hunting. However, the distinct number or nature of these seasons, along with their physiological and psychological affects, varies widely from culture to culture. In the view of Giblett and other writers, the four-season cycle of spring, summer, autumn, and winter is a European cultural construct. From this perspective, the four seasons were imposed on the climates of Australia, which were inappropriately described as "Mediterranean" or "temperate," and they supplanted indigenous seasons—six in the instance of some Australian Aboriginal groups. Giblett charts the colonization of the seasons in Australia and calls for their decolonization. In an extensive appraisal of Western writing about the seasons, he presents James Thomson's poetry as emblematic of the traditional European conception of the seasons, and Thoreau's writing as an example of a decolonizing approach. For Giblett, the seasons play a crucial role in contemporary discussions of culture and ecological politics. In an era of anthropogenic changes to the environment, the seasons are being regularly unsettled. Rather than speaking of "climate change" or "global warming," Giblett proposes "seasonal dislocation" or "seasonal disruption" as more precise and poetic ways to characterize these phenomena.

In "The Decolonized Pastoral: Kinsella, Thoreau, and the Seasons," Tom Bristow continues the cultural discourse on the seasons. He discusses John Kinsella's *Jam Tree Gully Poems* and their close attention to elemental water (often sparse), heat, and time, as well as to interactions between humans and animals. In its engagement in a cross-cultural conversation with Thoreau's classic work, *Walden*, Kinsella's poetry evinces a form of international localism. In Bristow's reading, Western notions of the seasons are invoked so as to bring into relief the sub-seasons within the seasons themselves, which serve as more localized markers of change. In emphasizing the displacement of inherited notions of the seasons, while at the same time engaging with the specificities of the rural environment of Jam Tree Gully, Western Australia,

Kinsella decolonizes traditional pastoral modes of writing and develops a form of "anti-pastoral." In Bristow's interpretation of the dynamic interplay between poetic consciousness and environmental conditions, he draws on William James' pragmatism and Gaston Bachelard's understanding of the material imagination.

❧◦৶

While by no means comprising an exhaustive account of the infinitely rich topic of the seasons, the essays collected in the present volume make a strong case for the significance of the seasons to our daily lives, scientific understanding, diverse cultural practices, and politics. They illustrate ways in which inquiry into the seasons can extend environmental thought, philosophy, anthropology, cultural studies, and literary criticism. In addition, we hope that the volume serves to stimulate the germination, florescence, and fruition of further research in the cross-disciplinary field of seasonal studies.

Notes

1. Bill McKibben, *The End of Nature* (New York: Anchor Books, 1989), 69.
2. See the essays by John Charles Ryan and Rod Giblett in this volume.
3. Pico Iyer, *Tropical Classical: Essays from Several Directions* (New York: Alfred A. Knopf, 1997), 294–296.
4. For further discussion of the pertinence of the seasons in conceiving "climate change," see Rod Giblett's essay in this volume.
5. "2019–20 Australian bushfire season," https://www.wwf.org.au/what-we-do/bushfires/bushfires#gs.7txqmo, accessed January 7, 2021.
6. Lawrence Buell, *The Environmental Imagination* (Cambridge, MA: Harvard University Press, 1995), 249–251.
7. See the essays in this volume by Paola-Ludovika Coriando, John Charles Ryan, and Luke Fischer.
8. Watsuji Tetsuro wrote his book *Climate and Culture: A Philosophical Study*, trans. Geoffrey Bownas (New York: Greenwood Press, 1988 [1961]) following a stay in Europe and his encounter with Heidegger's philosophical thought in the period of *Being and Time* (1927). He was of the view that *Being and Time* gave too little attention to the "climatic," spatial, and social dimensions of human existence, which his work *Climate* (*Fudo*) sought to remedy. The seasons are a crucial aspect of his central concept of climate.
9. See, for example, Martin Heidegger, "The Thing," in *Poetry, Language, Thought*, trans. Albert Hofstadter (New York: Harper & Row, 1971), 163–82.

10. See Craig Holdrege's essay in the present volume.

11. *Bashō's Haiku: Selected Poems of Matsuo Bashō*, trans. David Landis Barnhill (Albany: State University of New York Press, 2012), 19.

12. Richard Wright, *Haiku: The Last Poems of an American Icon*, ed. Yoshinobu Hakutani and Robert L. Tener (New York: Arcade Publishing, 2012), haiku no. 1.

13. Geoffrey Chaucer, *The Canterbury Tales*, selected, ed. and trans. A. Kent Hieatt and Constance Hieatt (New York: Bantam Books, 1990), 2–3.

14. William Shakespeare, *The Sonnets*, ed. William Burto (New York: Penguin Random House, 1999), Sonnets 98, 18, and 97.

15. Shakespeare, *A Midsummer Night's Dream*, ed. Wolfgang Clemen (New York: New American Library, 1963), Act II, Scene I, lines 107–114, p. 59.

16. Shakespeare, *A Midsummer Night's Dream*, lines 115–117.

17. John Keats, "To Autumn," *John Keats: The Complete Poems*, ed. John Barnard (London: Penguin Books, 1988), 434.

18. *John Keats: The Complete Poems*, 232.

19. For further discussion of the seasons, elements, and humors, see the essays in the present volume by Rod Giblett, David Macauley, and John Charles Ryan. See also David Macauley, *Elemental Philosophy: Earth, Air, Fire, and Water as Environmental Ideas* (Albany: State University of New York Press, 2010).

20. G. E. R. Lloyd, ed., *Hippocratic Writings*, trans. J. Chadwick and W. N. Mann et al. (London and New York: Penguin Books, 1983), 213.

21. George Eliot, "Letter to Miss Lewis, Oct. 1, 1841," in *George Eliot's Life, as Related in Her Letters and Journals*, vol. 1., ed. J. W. Cross (Boston: Houghton Mifflin Co., 1908), 71.

22. Henry D. Thoreau, "The Seasons," cited in Ronald A. Bosco, *Nature's Panorama* (Amherst: University of Massachusetts Press, 2005), xix.

23. Henry David Thoreau, *The Journal of Henry David Thoreau*, Vol. XII, ed. Bradford Torrey and Francis Allen (Boston: Houghton Mifflin, 1949), entry of April 24, 1859, 159–160.

24. See Andy Goldsworthy, *Midsummer Snowballs* (New York: Harry N. Abrams, 2001).

25. Gary Nabham, *Cultures of Habitat* (Washington, DC: Counterpoint, 1998), 319.

ENVIRONMENTAL TIME

1

The Four Seasons and the
Rhythms of Place-Based Time

David Macauley

In spring, hundreds of flowers, / In summer, refreshing breeze. / In autumn, harvest moon, / In winter, snowflakes accompany you. If useless things do not hang in your mind, / Every season is a good season.

—Wumen Huikai, Zen Buddhist monk (1183–1260 CE)

Sowing the Seasons into Place

In recent decades, environmental philosophers have made great strides in understanding and drawing attention to the significance of ecological issues related to place and emplacement. By contrast, questions concerning time have been subordinated or neglected all too frequently. And, yet, conceptions of place and time are intertwined at a deep experiential and ecological level. One way to respond to and help rectify this imbalance is to focus on the perennial but often overlooked notion of the seasons—winter, spring, summer, and fall, as well as wet and dry periods—as a lens and framework through which to engage and grasp different senses and scales of place-based time from the geological, biological, and historical to the more sensual, mythical, and qualitative modes of temporality that compete, dovetail, or co-exist in specific locations. In what follows, I examine the contested notion of a season and argue that, despite some limitations, a seasonal perspective not only enables us to yoke place with time in concrete and sensuous ways, but it is valuable for encouraging sustainable environmental practices that range from gardening and the arts to storied residence in the land and an awareness of elemental and affective dimensions of the encompassing world.

Historically, the seasons have been tethered to times of planting, growth, harvests, hunting, reproduction, migration, and hibernation, together with cultural celebrations, ceremonies, and festivals. In fact, the word *season* derives from a division of time allotted to "sowing" of the soil—from the Latin, *sationem*, a "sowing." The seasons thereby have provided a semblance of temporal place-bound order, regularity, and predictability for a host of human activities that have helped to root or relate many societies to the returning rhythms of the more capacious earth.

The seasons offer us both a profound, other-than-human viewpoint on time in addition to affording us more sensuous and evanescent surface outcroppings of emplaced beauty through the cadences of changing colors, sounds, temperatures, textures, and smells. Thus, many naturalists in the West invoke the seasons as an organizing principle for their meditations: Henry Thoreau (*Walden*), Annie Dillard (*Pilgrim at Tinker Creek*), Henry Beston (*The Outermost House*), Joseph Wood Krutch (*The Twelve Seasons*), John Muir (*My First Summer in the Sierras*), Edward Abbey (*Desert Solitaire*), Aldo Leopold (*Sand County Almanac*), Edwin Teale (*Circle of the Seasons*), and James Thomson (*The Seasons*), among them.

Thoreau and Dillard, for example, each arrange major works, *Walden* and *Pilgrim at Tinker Creek* respectively, around this thematic. In one, we get a male voice, a stable body of water (Walden Pond), and a discourse on the *oikos* (both economy and ecology); in the other, we encounter a female persona, a kind of theodicy and negative theology, and the flow of time along a moving stream (as opposed to more stationary pond). In both cases, the passing seasons of winter, spring, summer, and fall figure prominently. The trope of seasons, with its emphasis on temporal cycles and more internal principles of change coupled with outward manifestations of that change in biology and beauty, contrasts to a great extent with that of environmental treatments of excursions (pilgrimages, walks, travel explorations) and their accent on outer or exterior geographical movement conjoined frequently with philosophical and psychological transformation of human individuals.[1]

The Notion of the Season

What, we might ask initially, is the meaning of a season? Briefly and most basically, it is a division of the year based on changes in weather (especially precipitation, humidity, and temperature); ecology (plant and animal activity in particular); and the amount or intensity of sunlight that appears on a daily basis. Changes in these phenomena trigger and contribute to other processes or events that help to define and give voice to the individual seasons: bird migrations, hedgehog hibernation, the blossoming of flowers, the dormancy of plants, ice formations or thaws, color loss or gain in leaves, and the transformation of the Earth's albedo from brown to white, white to green, or green back to brown. More broadly, the seasons result from the revolution of the Earth around the sun, and specifically the tilt of the axis relative to the plane of its revolution. The astronomical aspects of the seasons become apparent during periods of the solstice and equinox.

In temperate zones, there are four calendar-based seasons of the vernal, estival, autumnal, and hibernal, otherwise known as spring, summer, fall and winter, although some ecologists increasingly employ a six-season model that includes pre-spring (pre-vernal) and late summer (serotinal) along with the canonical four. In tropical areas, we find a three-way division, typically constituted of hot, cool, and rainy. In some locales, the seasons are marked by distinct and recurring events—hurricanes, monsoons or torrential rains, floods, and wildfires—which underscore the force of elemental phenomena, especially airy wind, moving water, and transfiguring fire. These agents of change, in turn, generate the division between wet and dry seasons because the amount of precipitation varies more greatly than the average temperature.

Sightings of particular species of animals and plants or even individual beings—birds or mammals—are often omens or concrete emblems of the passage of seasonal time: the sleepy or awakening bear at the opening of his cave; the seals and whales arriving en masse to the craggy rocks off the shoreline, the swallows returning each year to San Juan Capistrano, the salmon making their way home to spawn through the chilly, fast-moving waters, or the honking geese in a V-shaped formation overhead. We learn to recognize and celebrate the signs: crocuses popping their tiny heads out of the thawing earth to herald a timorous spring; apples fruiting in autumn; bees diligently pollinating; or sunflowers stretching their golden heads toward the azure sky in summer.

We recognize spring with our attendant senses: when we smell the earthy scent of soil that microbes, known as Streptomyces, release chemically as they warm, or when we hear the whistles and trills of a succession of songbirds like the pine warbler or red-winged blackbird as they migrate back into our air spaces. There are also visual cues provided by animals, who serve as seasonal "indicator species" of a sort: when gray whales return from their 10,000 mile migrations in spring to California and Mexico; when newly-hatched and hungry inchworms dangle or drop from trees along the eastern coast of the United States; when fox pups emerge from their dens to explore and play; when baby robins break forth from their blue eggs; and when the browns of autumn and the whites of winter give way to the greens of March and April. Plants, too, have their own circadian clocks and rhythms: they sense when daylight waxes through photoreceptors in their leaves, telling themselves—and, by extension, informing us—that it is time to flower.[2]

Punxsutawney Phil, the famous groundhog who is ignominiously uprooted each February in western Pennsylvania, is a popularized notion of this time-tested phenomena in that he is thought either to portend the arrival of spring or, alternately, the extension of winter, depending upon whether he sees his shadow. The film *Groundhog Day* invokes the animal in a humorous and occasionally philosophical way in making connections with both place and temporality through implicit reference to Nietzsche's notion of "eternal recurrence of the same." (The main character in the film is trapped in time and location, bound to witness and relive an endless repeating cycle of activity.)[3]

The *Farmer's Almanac* is one cultural register of seasonal change that has been particularly useful to farmers and gardeners. Through the years, it has claimed that there are distinct signs of a harsh impending winter that can be detected by observant ears and eyes: thicker than normal corn husks; early arrival of the snowy owl; heavy and frequent fogs during August; mice eating ravenously into the home; insects marching in a straight line rather than meandering; muskrats burrowing holes high on the riverbank; a narrow orange band in the middle of the woolly bear caterpillar that warns of heavy snow; and fat and fuzzy caterpillars, which presage bitter cold.

The seasons, then, clearly involve the centrality of weather, an under-appreciated phenomenon within philosophy, despite a near universal interest outside of it. Annie Dillard thus declares: "There are seven or eight categories of phenomena in the world that are worth talking about, and one of them is weather."[4] We could speculate as to other "categories," though it is likely that many of them are concerned with the seasons themselves: food, fertility, reproduction, growth, and death, among them.

A season, however, is also increasingly a cultural concept with ragged edges. We now speak of sports seasons, television seasons, holiday seasons, and even shopping seasons. The seasons, then, are surely constituted in part by and through geography, history, and society as well as the material conditions found in given natural places. Within Hindu culture, there are six seasons (*Ritu*) that include *Vasanta* (spring), *Greeshma* (summer), *Varsha* (monsoon), *Sharad* (autumn), *Hemanta* (pre-hibernal), and *Shishira* (winter). Thus, we may need to view the seasons broadly or figuratively, at least if we wish to break out of rigid organic or essentialist formulations.

The East

In the Eastern world, we find seasonal poetry and artful haiku, which has been described poignantly as "a pebble thrown into the pool of the listener's mind" and as "a hand beckoning, a door half-opened, a mirror wiped clean." As the Zen scholar R. H. Blyth once remarked, "It is a way in which the cold winter rain, the swallows of evening, even the very day in its hotness, and the length of the night become truly alive, share in our humanity, speak their own silent and expressive language."[5] Haiku is traditionally composed in seventeen restrained but often lightning-like syllables and offered to the tempos and themes of the appropriate period of the year. It customarily contains a *kigo* ("season word") that is associated with one particular season (*ki*), a literary device that aids in the economy and identity (imagery, feelings, locale) of the poem along with the shared Japanese culture.

There is a vast litany of *kigo*—including plum blossoms, snow, deer, pumpkins, and the harvest moon—upon which a poet can draw either from memory or from a book called a *saijiki*. Spring is associated with skylarks, frogs, and cherry blossoms; summer is evoked by cicada, wisteria, and southern winds; autumn is revealed by crickets, persimmon, and colored leaves; and winter is signaled by oyster, fallen leaves, and icicles, among many other respective *kigo*. Well-crafted haiku point to the significance of sensible things as a conduit through which to understand seasonality, along with the power of grasping that which is complex through the nuances of particularity—*what*, *where*, and *when* are conjoined in a flickering sketch and delightful epiphany.

Bashō, an itinerant Japanese poet in the seventeenth century, is the most famous master of the art. As he wandered the countryside, he penned many lines that concentrated on seasonal phenomena. He celebrated the first quarter of the year with memorable images such as the following: "Spring too, very soon! / they are setting the scene for it—plum tree and moon." And he reprised these Zen telegrams with panegyrics to fall and the other seasons. For example: "On a withered branch / A crow has alighted / Nightfall in autumn." And "In a cowshed, mosquitos buzzing darkly—lingering summer heat."[6]

In a like vein, Dōgen, an acclaimed Buddhist, marshaled the four seasons into a tranquil whole: "Flowers in spring, / cuckoos in summer, / moon in autumn, / snow in winter / serene and cool."[7]And Ryōkan, another well-known Japanese figure, even delivered a seasonal poem as he lay dying: "For a memento of my existence / What shall I leave (I need not leave anything) / Flowers in the spring, cuckoos in the summer / And maple leaves / In the autumn."[8] In fact, we might imagine his corpse as the unstated "memento" or *memento mori* for the season of winter.

There are many other reflections upon seasonal renewal, continuity, and impermanence in the East. For instance, Zen Buddhists may counsel that you are ready to die when you have experienced the fullness and fecundity of all four seasons. In Japan, a tradition dating from the early eighth century celebrates seasonality in both rural and urban contexts. The four seasons are represented in gardens, flower arrangements, kimonos, the tea ceremony, poetry, screen painting, Noh performances, and multiple annual observances. These expressions extend to seasonal greetings (*aisatsu*), poetic seasonal almanacs (*saijiki*), and popular linked verse (*haikai*). By the early 1800s, the Japanese almanac contained more than 2,600 seasonal topics (*kidai*) that embraced an encyclopedic array of subjects ranging from astronomy to botany and geography and assembled into an entire worldview organized around the seasons themselves. As Haruo Shirane has shown, a "secondary nature" began to flourish as an idealized sense of harmony with the environing world precisely as a more primary relationship with this world was vanishing.[9] Historically speaking, the cherry blossom serves as the very symbol of Japanese beauty and represents "seasonality at its most sublime" in an "aesthetic of evanescence."[10] However, in contemporary society "when cherries are forced to blossom all the time, the fragile beauty of fleeting time" becomes more absent of meaning.[11]

Kinds of Time

One approach to addressing the seasons is to draw upon the ideas and insights of natural historians, environmental philosophers, and Continental theorists. We can rely upon this work as a way of elucidating cyclical rhythms and repetitions of seasonal and corporeal lived time so as to account for both the geological and historical continuities—the deep sense of time generated by the revolution of the Earth, and concomitantly the seasons, as well as the discontinuities increasingly caused by humans. In the process, we could—given proper time—articulate conceptions of measure, flow, pace, recurrence, duration, and periodicity in order to comprehend and clarify the tempos of the seasons and their ties to what Edwin Way Teale has termed the "the rounded year."[12]

PLACING TIME

First, the seasons help to emplace or "placialize" time, which is not tantamount to "spatializing" it—that is, encompassing it within the frame of a clock, watch, sundial, hourglass or calendar. When time is treated in terms of space and portrayed figuratively as an arrow aimed in a single direction or as a linear string with extension (*res extensa*), it is often forcibly squeezed or violently stretched (as the fabled Greek Procrustes did to his guests so as to make them fit his bed) and theoretical problems rapidly ensue. By comparison, place-based time is less of an abstraction. The seasons bound and locate temporal continuity and change within a geographical context, climactic setting, or ecological area (e.g., "gardens" are physically and etymologically *enclosures*). Time is particularized, given shape and form both as a concrescence (or coalescence) and in local, more atmospheric ways. The budding or progressively denuded magnolia trees in a park or campus quad embody it; the squirrels anxiously gathering or burying nuts evoke and express it; the fruiting pumpkins or ripening strawberries in a farmer's field articulate it in their engaging colors, sizes, and scents; the migrating caribou or spawning salmon communicate it as moving emissaries or ambassadors of a place. And humans dancing, singing, harvesting, cooking, and eating— especially during seasonal festivals—celebrate this kind of time when they offer a place to itself through rituals, play, and performances.

The seasons, in turn, leave marks and create traces of their presence and passing, signatures in effect of time. This occurs in tree rings, in fossils, in sidewalk cracks, and in mounds of leaves. It occurs in lengthening shadows crawling up and down a city street. The year is held—even memorialized—in the land, in the scape and shape of the ever-proliferating surface of the earth. And this, the syntax of time, so to speak, is what we learn to decipher or "read." If we liken individual plants and animals to the black tufts of letters alighting on a page, particular places become like words;

ecosystems emerge as sentences or paragraphs; and the seasons appear as something like chapters of the evolving and revolving year in the great text of the environing world—the "Book of Nature," as it used to be called.

REPETITION AND RHYTHM

Secondly, the notions of repetition and rhythm are integral to the idea and perhaps even identity or ontology of the seasons. Spring, summer, autumn and winter clearly recur and repeat themselves in some fashion. We witness a revolving and recycling wheel of time with recognizable portents and hallmark signs. But the autumn of 2021 in a given place is not exactly equivalent to the autumn of any previous year. The air will be slightly cooler or warmer; the amount and frequency of precipitation will be different; the colors of flora will vary; and fauna will appear in greater or less numbers. Repetition, while often serving as a defining mark of an entity or process, need not be construed as sameness or self-sameness. Repetition with difference provides a twist and deepens, in turn, our encounters with the phenomenal world. Here we might even ask: Is this seasonal "twist" somewhat like a Möbius strip, wherein movement along a looping inside path subtly and slowly changes, eventually becoming an outside as one follows its course?

Gilles Deleuze, for example, suggests a model of repetition as a system of relations that resembles a spiral—as opposed to a simple circle—making possible new formations and metamorphoses rather than merely duplicating singularities and existing patterns or, alternatively, subsuming particulars under a universal—what he terms "bare repetition."[13] In this view, repetition is related to a unique series of events or objects, and there is a relevant distinction between a "qualitative order of resemblances," which is represented by the image of a cycle, and a "quantitative order of equivalences," which finds its symbol in equality.[14] A season, too, is a *haecceity* (this-ness), a relation of movement and rest with individuality—like a singular happening—that should nevertheless not be construed as a discrete subject, substance, or thing.[15] If we apply such thinking to spring, summer, autumn, and winter, we discover that there is continuity but also change, commonality as well as a testament to difference between seasonal comings and goings.

Experientially, a sense of enchantment and a hint of the sensuous are bound up with encounters of repetition. We take delight and comfort in the presence of discernable patterns, colors, textures, sounds, and smells. But we are charmed by surprises that break the stability and disrupt the familiar so as to interject wonder, awe, or curiosity into the world and our routines.[16]

To this extent, when seasonal predictability is upended, we become suddenly engaged: warm days in the dead of winter; snowfall in late spring; a solar eclipse that brings darkness to the day; unexpected hailstorms; or a night sky replete with shooting stars. Our aesthetic appreciation of seasonal change might be expressed by or related to the beauty we recognize in a serpentine line, as in the undulating curves, coils, or spirals that can be found visually in seashells, meandering streams, handcrafted wooden furniture, and decorative fashion, or the hips and lips of the human body. In this perspective, beauty is a midpoint or productive tension between variety and uniformity, too little change (monotony or boredom) and too much alteration (exhaustion or overstimulation). If this idea is applied more conceptually—as one might do to songs or paintings—it can be said that we seem to enjoy a regularity and order to the seasons, but we also appreciate some, though not too much, deviation from the norm so as to make matters (levels of precipitation, sunlight, temperature, humidity) interesting to us.

Like repetition, rhythm involves flux and flow. It expresses time in terms of a musical movement that is punctuated with cultural or biological significance. Here we can draw a distinction between endogenous and exogenous rhythms, tying these changes to the fluctuations of light, shadow, and darkness. Endogenous rhythms persist even when the environment fails to significantly change. By contrast, exogenous rhythms are linked to the physical changes in the environment and do not continue when external conditions remain constant. The seasons appear to possess both aspects in an intertwined or chiasmatic way: there are internal or immanent (endogenous) rhythms that drive the seed into the fruit in summer or fall, for example, as well as more externally expressed (exogenous) rhythms of plants and animals that respond to, for example, elemental changes in light, temperature, water, wind, and soil. Our own circadian rhythms, too, are tied closely with the seasons in their connections especially to ambient light, which synchronizes our internal "clocks"—waking us up or triggering hunger pangs—and perhaps even providing a sense of internal time consciousness.

A related way to grasp the seasons is through the oscillating and rhythmic polarities of expansion and contraction. Spring and summer can be understood in terms of the progressive waxing of elemental light and heat as the days grow longer and warmer. By contrast, the solar energy of autumn and winter slowly wanes, and we witness a marked "closing down" of earthly activity with the onset of increasing darkness, cooling, and freezing. In the first two seasons, animals who migrate, hide, or hibernate slowly re-appear and alight; life moves from below ground to the surface and sky. The more interiorized and intimate world—embodied in the cloistered bird nest, bear cave, rabbit hole, or human house—of winter expands and gives way to more exuberant displays outside. Colors brighten; pace quickens; movement becomes more pronounced. Relying creatively upon Merleau-Ponty's notion of "sensible ideas" (which encourages us to see the year as a great symphony), phenomenological descriptions of seasonal "moods" (which we internalize and express ourselves) as well as Goethe's conception of *Steigerung* or intensification—which permits us to see winter, spring, summer, and fall as a differentiated whole or polyphony, Luke Fischer explains the seasonal process insightfully by way of references to poetry and an analogy that can be found in a series of contractions and expansions in plant morphology and metamorphosis, specifically what occurs in the developments of the leaves, petals, pistil, stamen, seed, and fruit.[17]

Kairos and Chronos

In addition to placializing time, rhythmic repetition, and the dynamics of expansion and contraction, we need to make multiple distinctions within the notion of time itself. One is between *kairos* (καιρός) and *chronos* (χρόνος), two Greek terms for representing time. Whereas *chronos* refers to sequential or chronological time, *kairos* signifies a less determinate time, a period or extended moment in which something unique or special may occur. It is a kind of intermezzo, interstice, or in-between place of time. It is a temporal opportunity for the making or taking, a time to be appreciated or seized, as in possessing good timing. *Chronos* is quantitative in nature; *kairos* is qualitative. Interestingly, in both ancient and modern Greek, *kairos* can mean "weather," a phenomenon connected intimately with the seasons (the plural, καιροι, means "the times") while in Latin, *tempus* may refer equally to weather and time as well, with *tempestas* meaning "season of the year" and coming to be used as bad weather or a storm (tempest).

Gardens are places informed deeply by seasonal time and by *kairos*. We plant after the last frost, not on April 15, for example. We actively look for and even seize the chance to harvest before the fruit or vegetables wither and die on the vine. Marcus Aurelius hints at a notion of *kairos* in his *Meditations*: "Everything which is in tune with you, O Universe, is in tune with me. Nothing which happens at the right time for you is early or late for me. Everything, O Nature, which your seasons produce is fruit to me."[18] We find kairological time as well in the biblical book of Ecclesiastes: "For everything its season, and for every activity under heaven its time."

The passage proceeds to indicate, more particularly, that there is "a time to be born and a time to die; a time to plant and time to uproot."[19] In other words, there are proper, appointed, or allotted times that are marked off by the seasons, an insight acknowledged too by Shakespeare: "At Christmas I no more desire a rose, / Than wish a snow in May's new-fangled mirth; / But like of each thing in season grows."[20]

SCALES OF TIME

Building upon these distinctions, we can delineate other dimensions of lived time that help to illuminate the notion and experience of the seasons. Time is admittedly one of the most complex subjects we can conceivably investigate, and there are a host of subtle differences between subjective, objective, and intersubjective time; between biological and cultural time; and between physical and metaphysical time, among other conceptions. While traveling through rural India, for example, I discovered that in Hindi one word, *kal*, means both "yesterday" and "tomorrow"; one word, *parson*, means both "the day after tomorrow" and "the day before yesterday"; and one word, *atarson*, means both "three days hence" and "three days ago." As with the Hindi word *namaste*, which can be used as either a greeting (hello) or a leave-taking (goodbye), such a linguistic and cultural perspective may assist in orienting us toward a larger sense of temporal continuity, even reversibility, and perhaps the idea, experience, or glimpse of wider expanses of interconnected moments or overlapping periods—dare we say the vantage known as *sub specie aeternitatis* ("from the perspective of the eternal")? It can indicate that some events, processes, and entities are slow to unfold and develop in perceptual ways, even when we concede that all phenomenal things do undergo flux and change (Heraclitus's *panta rhei*, or "all things flow"). In some respects, the seasons have been like this historically, at least until very recently.

"One swallow [bird]," Aristotle famously noted, "does not a summer make."[21] Nor does one flower mean spring, we might add. Patterns must emerge; a season comes into focus gradually, protractedly through time, per-haps in the manner a pointillist Seurat painting is unified and disclosed to our senses, or in the way a pixilated television image comes into coherence. One season slowly passes away, but it survives insofar as it is retained in the next as a modicum of warmth or wetness, for example, or through the persisting shape, structure, location, and form of tree branches. As Charles Dickens poetically noticed, the March days of spring are often times "when the sun shines hot and the wind blows cold: when it is summer in the light, and winter in the shade."[22] This is a passing away that endures, a "flowing permanence" we might say, something that suggests a notion of "duration" (*la durée*) and a spectrum of change, stability, and continuity. This is also an instance (though not an instant) of relational time rather than an example of absolute or discrete Newtonian time.

MYTHIC TIME

Finally, when the seasons cross into the cultural sphere—or even the geological realm—they might enter near-mythic or deep time (*duratio permanens*). This is the place where Plato speaks of time as "a moving image of eternity"—a "time" in effect outside of conventional or mundane ideas of change. In this regard, the critic Northrop Frye, who has examined poetry and literature to discover archetypal patterns, motifs, and symbols, argues that mythically spring is linked most closely with comedy, summer with romance, autumn with tragedy, and winter with irony and satire; he develops these points through an analysis of the Bible, works by Shakespeare, ancient Greek plays, and a wealth of classical poetry.[23] Metaphorically, spring, too, entails an upward or rising movement (as the word "spring" suggests) while autumn is associated with a downward or falling movement (as the word "fall" implies). These cyclical and cosmological symbols are, in turn, associated as well with complex connections to innocence (e.g., rising happiness or humor) and experience (e.g., a tragic "fall" of the hero), along with the four periods of the day (morning, noon, evening, and night) and the four periods of life (youth, maturity, age, and death).

Grappling with the senses of natural time, Annie Dillard writes, "Yesterday, I set out to catch the new season, and instead I found an old snakeskin." Knotted in a loop without beginning or end, the snakeskin becomes an image of lived eternity, an *Ouroborus*—the snake consuming its own tail, the unending and continuous loop of time itself. "Time," she speculates, "is an ascending spiral if you will, like a child's toy Slinky. Of course, we have no idea which arc on the loop is our time, let alone where the loop itself is, so to speak, or down whose lofty flight of stairs the Slinky so uncannily walks."[24]

Within Zen Buddhist thought and some Eastern conceptions of the seasons, we might ultimately pass with the winter, spring, summer, and fall into the realization of "no time," the experience or recognition that temporality is in some significant sense a splendid illusion, that the "now" is an expansive co-presence of place and time because the past is no longer here and the future is not yet arrived. This is where we encounter *Ensō*, the Japanese image and concept of the "circle" that also suggests emptiness. Empty but exquisite, we might suggestively say.

Here, the fluid interplay of the seasons gives way to focused periods of play—the Dionysian days of festivals, carnivals, and commemorations marking the ostensible passing of time, and even the subjective surpassing of time itself into the realm of the ever-enduring. Here, too, we meet up with paradoxical, provocative, and poetic ideas: Heraclitus' proclamation, "Eternity [αἰών] is a child at play," along with the Hindu notion of "Lila," an aesthetic conception of the universe at creative play with itself, manifesting forms and engaging in a kind of unending game of cosmic hide-and-seek, appearance and disappearance. Thus, we find seasonal festivals of all kinds throughout the world. Fire festivals such as May Day, the summer solstice, and the Celtic Samhain (Halloween) promote growth of crops and health of livestock. There are celebrations marking the death of winter, the first dew of spring, the first frost, or the first caterpillar of the New Year. These examples can be multiplied easily: The Kayapo people of Brazil have seasonal ceremonies tied to agriculture, hunting, and fishing cycles. The Ainu people of Japan hold festivals to welcome the first salmon, an animal who is linked with their own identity. And in the European Alps, the return of cattle in autumn from mountain pastures to their barns in the valley is celebrated as Almabtrieb.

All of this suggests that we might reasonably speak of time as fundamental to the seasonal world itself because it is "borne and offered not only by things but also, above all, by the elementals."[25] As Heidegger claimed, "Time first shows itself in the sky, that is, precisely there where one comes across it in directing oneself naturally according to it, so that time even becomes identified with the sky."[26] Time is "the element in which we exist," Joyce Carol Oates notes succinctly. As a primordial feature of the ever-changing realm of appearance, Oates writes, "we are either borne along by it or drowned in it."[27]

Challenges to the Four Seasons Model

Before turning, lastly, to the values of a seasonal framework for environmental thought and action, we should acknowledge the existence of several challenges for an understanding of seasonality and, specifically, the "four-seasons model," ones that are related to seasonal variations and geographical differences, along with global climate change.

First, some places seem to express or embody but one single season rather than four or more. Judging by outward appearances at least, they lack the nuanced "spices" of seasonality or appear to possess a negligible sense of varied "seasoning." They may give the impression to visitors and outsiders of existing outside of the conventional rhythms of time, enduring as static islands in a surrounding seasonal sea. Southern California, for example, is stereotypically sunny, warm, and without rain—a kind of endless summer, in effect. The Pacific Northwest is, by contrast, all rain much of the time, as those who live there like to remind us—a hybrid perhaps of spring and fall. More generally, deserts often display either very intense heat during the day (an excess of summer) or bone-chilling cold at night (extreme winter), while jungles can also appear devoid of well-defined seasons. Both environments are disorienting and pose challenges to familiar forms of temporality and seasonality, as do the deep ocean, Antarctica (a polar desert), mountain heights, the moon, and other planets, where seasons can vary greatly depending on axial tilt and distance from the sun. (Uranus has forty-two years of summer in one hemisphere followed by forty-two years of winter.)

Of course, a more generous reading and attempt to recognize or re-discover seasonality in such liminal locales might insist that seasonal changes are actually much more refined than we've suggested and that we learn how to understand and attune ourselves to them the longer we reside in these places or, alternatively, when we depart and get to know them through a comparative absence. Here, one might think of the many microclimates or "mini-seasons" that seem to inhabit places like San Francisco, where the weather, temperature, and winds change rapidly within the city itself on a regular, short-lived basis.

In this regard, we should recognize that what we might call the "New England model of the seasons"—with its deep, vibrant, colorful, clear-cut, and sweeping changes in weather patterns, plant and animal ecology, and dramatic alterations of light length and intensity over time—has limitations in its extension and application elsewhere. Not everywhere do we find this theatrical view of the seasons where "each one enters like a prima donna, convinced its performance is the reason the world has people in it," to use the words of Toni Morrison.[28] It may signal that the conceptual container of the seasons is either porous or not always portable to distant places. We can't always or easily move this model too quickly across the nation or around world. When we do, the bucket may spring a theoretical leak.

Further, Michael Kammen has pointed out that in the nineteenth century some American writers and artists promoted the four seasons as a way of supporting cultural nationalism by stressing the seasonal beauty of wild lands as opposed to cultivated fields and ornamental gardens. In contrast to European perspectives, they emphasized bright autumn colors and interpreted winter as a time for spiritual growth. With industrialization and urbanization, these interpretations gave way to sentimental and nostalgic views of seasonal change, frameworks that persisted into the twentieth century with nature writing, folk music, and Norman Rockwell calendars.[29]

Temporal Discontinuities and Disruptions

With the emergence of rapid climate change—"global weirding" as it has been called—and the manifestation of "hyperobjects," which are nonlocal entities massively distributed in both space and time, the seasons appear increasingly more unpredictable, episodic, unreliable, and even potentially foreboding of catastrophic changes than ever before. In the *End of Nature*, environmentalist Bill McKibben, for example, speculates that no child born today will experience a "normal" springtime in his or her life. Spring may arrive surprisingly or disturbingly early, belatedly, or perhaps, at some point, not at all.[30]

"Those who contemplate the beauty of the earth," observed Rachel Carson, "find reserves of strength that will endure as long as life lasts. There is something infinitely healing in the repeated refrains of nature—the assurance that dawn comes after night, and spring after winter."[31] But Carson is remembered for a more haunting phrase and warning about what she famously called "Silent Spring": the possibility that we might terminate a familiar and fecund cyclicality, including the deeper rhythms of time marked and manifested by seasonal processes. This would amount to an end to new beginnings, or the very death of birth itself. Whereas McKibben speaks in almost theological terms about the end of an autonomous "nature"—the death of independent other-than-human processes—what we may need to be more realistically and practically concerned about is the violent disruption and possible closure of reliable seasonal time and periodicity.

With rapid climate change, the migrations of birds and mammals are thrown off; growing seasons are stretched out and attenuated or inexplicably curtailed; new species of plants and animals seem suddenly to appear in unusual locations or, more commonly, simply vanish—and with them the loss of indicator species, canaries in the proverbial coal mine who inform us about the waning and waxing seasons and the places that hold them. These changes may be equivalent to a kind of punctured or ruptured equilibrium, where time is uncannily accelerated, or rent asunder. It is, perhaps, a bit like leaping suddenly from five to fifty miles per hour while driving, or maybe fifty to five hundred miles per hour—not merely a quantitative change but also a qualitative transformation.

We encounter disappearing, harsher, or foreshortened winters and more intense, hotter summers. Anthropogenic climate change can even become a kind of meteorological "terrorism" due to seasonal volatility. Like other more familiar forms of terrorism, we don't know where, when, or how long the unpredictable seasonal changes will last or affect us and other organisms. Is this also perhaps a version of so-called seasonal affective disorder (SAD) writ large for the environing world, an atmospheric or mood-altering process? Dangers emerge quickly and with little warning or opportunity to forestall or address them: the shifting seasons, in particular, are causing hunger in developing countries through erratic rainfall, long periods of heat; and declining rice and maize yields.[32]

In the seventeenth century, the English cleric Jeremy Taylor, who was known as "Shakespeare of Divines," summoned the seasons darkly—"where death reigns in all portions of . . . time"—in relation to our too-soon truncated lives. "The autumn with its fruits provides disorders for us, and the winter's cold turns them into sharp diseases, and the spring brings flowers to strew our hearse, and the summer gives green turf and brambles to bind upon our graves."[33] Thoreau, however, later recommended an enlarged sense of temporal order: "Go and measure to what length the silvery willow catkins have crept out beyond their scales, if you would know what time o' the year it is by Nature's clock."[34]

To the extent to which seasonal rhythms have been disrupted and become more discontinuous and less reliable, we might speak of one last and very end-oriented but non-teleological sense of temporality that could be called "catastrophic time." Such a sense of time is much broader and admittedly graver than the sudden or tragic loss of life for individual humans and other organisms. In deeply troubled eras and epochs, time itself seems to be "out of joint," as Shakespeare's Hamlet famously put it. Aporetic time possesses a nonlinear and even anti-narrative quality. It is often born of great disaster, a Latin-based word that implies being without a star (*astro*) and hence disoriented temporally and spatially.

Extinction events, pandemics, massive earthquakes, wars, asteroids, tsunamis, and now anthropogenic climate change can all unravel the familiar flow of time, portend finality, and evoke an experience of the cataclysmic. Alphonso Lingis speaks of how catastrophic events destroy "the time of work and reason" and appear to annihilate the future while nullifying the past. "With fierce eyes," he writes, "we see lethal tides of summer and winter which exact agony from all living things." But he adds, "the catastrophic time that devastates us can also strangely hold us, and even draw us into it."[35] In other words, the demise of familiar equilibria can offer us something potentially constructive, exhilarating, and even ecstatic in the challenges they provide. It is perhaps these opportunities that give us a degree of hope.

The Values of a Seasonal Framework

Given the tensions within the idea, appearance, and experience of the seasons—ranging from distinct geographical differences (e.g., wet and dry seasons in tropical regions as opposed to the canonical fourfold in temperate zones) to fluctuating rates of biological or climactic change, as well as debates concerning the social mediation or construction of time itself—what, then, is the value of a seasonal framework for environmental theory and practice?

Storied Residence and Restor(y)ation

First, the seasons help to provide us with robust social and ecological narratives in an ecologically challenged world. They suggest ways that our moving bodies—which "bestride time," to invoke a phrase from Merleau-Ponty—are bound to the broader elemental rhythms of the land, the sea, the atmosphere, and the sun as they collectively bring forth, shape, and store energy, light, water, and warmth: all causal agents of seasonal alteration. The environmental world is full of stories that tie us powerfully with specific places, including the ecological wisdom rooted in an experience of the seasons.

Many naturalists, poets, and writers have artfully evoked their encounters with seasonal change in ways that provide what environmental philosopher Holmes Rolston calls "storied residence," while avoiding at the same time grounding their views in a master narrative, whether that be religious, scientific, political, or philosophical. Such stories are usually place-specific, situated forms of knowing and heavily context-bound. Ecological restoration in this sense is indeed coupled with *re-story-ation*. As Gary Paul Nabham puts it, "To restore any place, we must also begin to re-story it." Story, he suggests, is the manner through which we "encode deep-seated values within our culture."[36] Thus, environmentalists should be careful about which stories they are telling or listening to as they fashion narratives that are ecologically accurate, publicly compelling, philosophically insightful, and aesthetically interesting. The seasons provide a pedagogical or heuristic "hook" upon which to introduce others to environmental experiences and ecological practices.

INSIDE-OUT AFFECTS

Secondly, there exists a close connection between the seasons as external occurrences and the seasons as internal stages, feelings, or suffused forces. For Thoreau, they provide a "tone" and "hue" to his thought, becoming "a mood of the mind." As he proclaims: "These regular phenomena of the seasons get at last to be—they were *at first*, of course—simply and plainly phenomena or phases of my life. The seasons and all their changes are in me."[37] Or as Emerson maintains with verve: "There is a sort of climate in every man's speech running from hot noon, when words flow like steam & perfume,—to cold night, when they are frozen."[38]

Such remarks point to the inner, affective dimensions of seasonality, and to the overlapping ties between human temperaments (dispositions), temporality (time), and temperature (weather). They suggest the seasons come and go, materialize and dematerialize as indefinite cloudlike moods, media, or atmospheres; they do not just manifest themselves through objects or distinct places. Here, there are connections between seasonal descriptions and elemental language in terms of phenomenological notions such as "ambience" and "attunement." The seasons are not beneath or beyond us as transcendental principles or Platonic Forms. Rather, they exist and endure like the weather (over short periods), the climate (over longer periods) or atmosphere (a more permanent, if mutable, presence) as a kind of medium "around" or "surrounding" plants, animals, humans, and elemental entities— an un-thought or under-thought quasi-environment. As seasons emerge in a given place, they are, in a certain sense, circumambient, depths without clear surfaces, dimensions replete with color, texture, and tempo—metaphorically, something perhaps vaguely or poetically akin to an aesthetic quintessence or "fifth element," as *aither* (ether) was once imagined to be.

In this respect, the notion of "ambient poetics" is relevant because, as Timothy Morton remarks, ambience "suggests something material and physical, though somewhat intangible, as if space itself had a material aspect," a characterization that could fit an encounter with a rainy spring day in the mountains, a snowy winter evening in the woods, or a misty autumn morning by the sea. Applying equally to music, sculpture, and performance, ambience surrounds "on both sides," as the Latin root *ambo* implies. Ambience displays features that we routinely find in engagements with seasonal events and phenomena: *tone* (the way matter vibrates to generate a mood or feel, as in walking on winter snow), *timbre* (the quality of physical sounds like that, say, of birdsong or ice floes breaking up in spring), the *Aeolian* (arriving from no distinct source as might an autumn wind), and the *medial* (contact created in the middle or midst of something, as for example, bathing in the summer sun or a warm sea).[39]

With regard to affects, we speak similarly of birth, growth, maturation, and death in seasonal language. Someone who is "seasoned" is ripe, mature, or experienced. On her album *Season of Glass*, Yoko Ono remarks: "Spring passes and one remembers one's innocence. Summer passes and one remembers one's exuberance. Autumn passes and one remembers one's reverence. Winter passes and one remembers one's perseverance."[40] The poet John Dryden likewise observes:

> Perceiv'st thou not the process of the year, / How the four seasons in four forms appear, / Resembling human life in ev'ry shape they wear? / *Spring* first, like infancy, shoots out her head, / With milky juice requiring to be fed: . . . Proceeding onward whence the year began, / The *Summer* grows adult, and ripens into man . . . / *Autumn* succeeds, a sober, tepid age, / Not froze with fear, nor boiling into rage; . . . / Last, *Winter* creeps along with tardy pace, / Sour is his front, and furrowed is his face.[41]

In the Korean film *Spring, Summer, Fall, Winter . . . and Spring*, we encounter the seasons as in-dwelling forces linked closely with the more external environment, too. The film presents the story of a monk who lives on a small floating monastery in a beautiful lake and whose life and struggles are expressed through the opening and closing gates of four seasons and the Four Noble Truths of Buddhism.

THE ELEMENTAL

Thirdly, the seasons encourage us to make fruitful connections to the commodious elemental world—the other-than-human sphere of ice, light, fire, water, night, shadow, stone, and clouds—that is more sensuous and embodied than an abstract concept such as "nature" or even a neutral-sounding term like "environment." The seasons evoke and express elemental oppositions of cold and hot as well as wet and dry. In a loose manner, we might reasonably correlate winter with earth, which tends to be cold and dry and more exposed in this first season of the year. We can associate spring with water—which becomes wetter and warmer over time—especially as a seasonal catalyst in melting and flooding. We may link summer with fire, which is hot and dry, and particularly the heat and light of the sun. And we might tether autumn with the distinct qualities in the ambient air, which grows cooler and wetter. In such a way, the qualitative "contraries" that Aristotle identified closely with the four elements of earth, air, fire, and water come full cycle to include the four seasons, too.[42]

Historically, the seasons were also connected to the four humors: phlegm in winter, blood (sanguine) in spring, yellow bile (choleric) in summer, and black bile (melancholic) in fall. There is even an aesthetic case to be made that there exists a form of color coordination that occurs as we progress from winter whites and grays to spring greens before moving on to ocean and sky blues of summer, and arriving finally with autumn reds, browns, and gold—a point that might interest those concerned with fashion and clothing choices. The connection between the seasons and elements—or "the elemental"—is visually evident in the work of the sixteenth-century Mannerist Italian artist Giuseppe Arcimboldo, who painted human portraits composed of plants and animals to show the cycles of the four seasons and the four elements, which are correlated with one another. For his inspiration, Arcimboldo may have looked to Plato's *Timaeus,* a philosophical dialogue in which a demiurge (craftsman-deity) generates the cosmos out of primordial chaos and through the four elemental bodies of earth, air, fire, and water, the "ABCs of everything."[43]

While the elements and the elemental are now receiving some attention within philosophy and ecological thought, the perennial notion of the seasons has largely been neglected, except perhaps within the fields of poetry, mythology, and art. One exception is Luce Irigaray, who has devoted a series of short books to the elements and "elemental passions" and has noted a relationship between the four seasons and four elements. In *Through Vegetal Being,* she and her interlocutor, Michael Marder, speak of the "becoming-other" of the summer in the fall, as well as the winter in the spring. "To live out of season is to ignore the alterations and alternations of planetary time and to exist out of tune with the milestones of vegetal time: germination, growth, blossoming, and fruition," they write.[44]

When such disruptions occur, disorder and arrhythmias arise at the most fundamental level of being itself, which they connect with the air, earth, fire, and water. Parts of the planet become too wet or too dry, too hot or too cold. "Elemental dearth and overabundance," they observe, "are the two extremes between which existence is finally possible."[45]

An Alternative to "Nature"

Fourthly, like the notion of the "elements" and the "elemental," the seasons are a sensual and specific alternative to the more abstract and elusive idea of "nature." "Nature" is arguably an over-determined and often overly broad and empty concept that can be used potentially to justify or rationalize nearly any social position or philosophical interpretation. Hence, we need greater specificity and particularity, and the seasons are one phenomenon—both conceptual and tangible—among others of possible use. Thoreau advises us, "Live each season as it passes; breathe the air, drink the drink, taste the fruit, and resign yourself to the influences of each."[46] Here, the recognition of the influences—or even sensual imperatives—of winter, spring, summer, and fall suggests the value of creative receptivity and openness to seasonal change, continuity, and even surprise or enchantment.

Sustainability and the Seasons

Finally, the intimate connections between the gestures and habits of the human body and what Husserl styled the "basis body" of the Earth can be viewed in terms of processes involving fertility, birth, or burial as well as everyday activities like cooking, walking, making art, and gardening that can become sustainable ecological practices through attention to seasonal expressions, cycles, and transitions. Here, it is possible to view the seasons as a framework analogous to the bioregional perspective, which counsels the need to re-inhabit and live in close alliance with natural and cultural place. In bioregionalism (which conjoins *bios* or life with *region* or place), eco-geo-morpho-regions fit elegantly into one other like Chinese boxes. Within a seasonal outlook, time would not so much be "added" to the container of place as discovered to be part and parcel of it already. Season-centeredness might be seen as a healthy hybrid of the best parts of loco-centrism (place-based) and tempero-centrism (time-based) living.

Gardening is one practice through which the enchantment of the seasons is channeled into the charms of our backyards or dispersed into community plots. Gardening provides a deep environmental education with the elemental world (e.g., earthy compost, rainwater, and sunlight) and offers an implicit or even "accidental" practice of sustainability, one that helps us move away from a linear "cradle-to-grave model" of agribusiness toward a greener, circular model of ecologically friendly agriculture.

Gardening does not rely upon an idea or experience of the wild and wilderness as external nature "out there"—as we might find in the work of Thoreau, John Muir, or Ansel Adams—to be contemplated or appreciated disinterestedly. Rather, gardening actively entails both cooperating and grappling with the complex natural world as a way of practically knowing it. It means dealing with the very real challenges of predators, bugs, soil profiles, too much wind, and too little rain. Seasonal knowledge is extremely important: when and where to plant; the best times to harvest; and how to build fences or repair equipment. It involves an understanding of *kairos* and not just chronological time, and an awareness of the contingencies and challenges connected with growing zones, changing temperatures, and now climate change.

Secondly, and related to the potential of gardens, the seasons can serve as guides to both the appropriate places and times in which to prepare and enjoy many foods and beverages: hot soup, stew, or cider (in the fall); vegetable roots or warm cocoa (in the winter); watermelon or iced tea (in the summer), and lemons, cherries, or artichokes (in the spring). Here, we should note the importance of community supported agriculture (CSAs), farmers markets, and the Slow Food movement, all of which stress eating fresh, local foods in season. These practices imply the merits of not trans-porting food long distances—on average, food journeys 800–1,200 miles to arrive on our plates—even as we acknowledge the tensions and contra-dictions of a globalized world where imports bring us tea from China, fruit from South America, and so on. There are, too, many seasonal cookbooks, sometimes tied to specific geographical regions. And here we even speak of "seasoning" foods to heighten their flavor with spices, herbs, or condiments. Part of the seasoning might be calling forth the seasons themselves, with their particular tones, textures, or tastes.

In addition to gardening and food culture, movement through the landscape by hiking, sauntering, pilgrimages, and even more technologically reliant travel can be guided by seasonal knowledge. There are appropriate winter walks, autumn ambles, summer strolls, and spring explorations on foot. In this regard, knowledge of the seasonal dimensions of medicinal plant gathering and wildlife observation—including animal migrations, hibernations, or breeding seasons—is valuable to ambulatory expeditions of the local environment as well, of course, to sharing stories about such journeys when one arrives home.[47]

Finally, the realms of both art and everyday aesthetics might reasonably evoke or benefit from a season-based perspective that cultivates ties with ecological concerns. Fashion and clothes designers, for example, already rely on a framework of seasonality, though they are often more responsive to the anxieties and planned obsolescence of the marketplace than to creating sustainable wear that is also suited for a particular period of the year. Textures, designs, patterns, and fabrics are linked with shapes, scenes, and colors in winter, spring, summer, and fall. As naturalist Henry Beston noted, "The leaves fall, the wind blows, and the farm country slowly changes from the summer cottons into its winter wools."[48] Similarly, decoration, both interior and exterior, draws inspiration from the encompassing seasons, especially around holiday celebrations such as Halloween, Easter, the Fourth of July, and Christmas, which, in the United States, are celebrated in autumn, spring, summer, and winter, respectively.

Conclusion

"There is," observes Annie Dillard, "a little bit of every season in each season."[49] Indeed, a modicum of both warmth and coldness, along with dryness and wetness, exist in all such periods, which emerge out of, differentiate themselves from, and yet retain features of earlier stages and conditions. Such a spiraling progression suggests the possibility of an evolving but differentiated, if ever fragile, temporal cohesion. As the poet John Keats puts it, the seasons "fill the measure of the year."[50] In short, the seasons, despite ecological and social contingencies, still offer us a sensuous and meaningful way of appreciating and apprehending a place-based world by encouraging us to comprehend deep and shallow temporal rhythms of, and relationships between, our bodies, the earth, and human culture. As T. S. Eliot writes in *Four Quartets*: "Earth feet, loam feet . . . / Keeping time, / Keeping the rhythm in their dancing / As in their living in the living seasons / The time of the seasons."[51]

Notes

1. See Lawrence Buell, *The Environmental Imagination* (Cambridge, MA: Harvard University Press, 1995), chap. 7.

2. Nicholas St. Fleur, "Recognizing Spring Scientifically," *New York Times*, March 25, 2016.

3. Harold Ramis, *Groundhog Day* (Burbank, CA: Columbia Pictures, 1993).

4. Annie Dillard, *Pilgrim at Tinker Creek* (New York: HarperCollins, 1991), 51.

5. R. H. Blyth, in *The World of Zen*, ed. Nancy Wilson Ross (New York: Vintage Books, 1960), 120.

6. See Bashō Matsuoand Shirō Tsujimura, *Basho: The Complete Haiku*, trans. Jane Reichhold (New York: Penguin Books, 2008).

7. Dōgen, *The Essential Dogen: Writings of the Great Zen Master*, ed. Kazuaki Tanahashi and Peter Levitt (Boston: Shambhala, 2013).

8. Ryōkan, quoted in Hajime Nakamura, *Ways of Thinking of Eastern Peoples* (Delhi: Montilal Banarsidass Publishers, 1991), 357.

9. Haruo Shirane, *Japan and the Culture of the Four Seasons* (New York: Columbia University Press, 2012).

10. Jay Griffiths, *A Sideways Look at Time* (New York: Penguin Books, 2004), 19.

11. Griffiths, *A Sideways Look at Time*, 19.

12. Edwin Way Teale, in Bill McKibben, *The End of Nature* (New York: Anchor Books), 103.

13. Gilles Deleuze, *Difference and Repetition*, trans. Paul Patton (New York: Columbia University Press, 1994).

14. Deleuze, *Difference and Repetition*.

15. Gilles Deleuze and Félix Guattari, *A Thousand Plateaus*, trans. Brian Massumi (Minneapolis: University of Minnesota Press, 1987), 261.

16. Jane Bennett, *The Enchantment of Modern Life* (Princeton, NJ: Princeton University Press, 2001).

17. See Luke Fischer's essay in the present volume.

18. Marcus Aurelius, *The Meditations*, trans. G. M. A. Grube (New York: Macmillan, 1963), IV, 23.

19. Ecclesiastes 3:1–2 in *The Oxford Study Bible*, ed. M. Jack Suggs, K. Sakenfeld and J. Mueller (New York: Oxford University Press, 1992).

20. William Shakespeare, *Love's Labour's Lost* in *William Shakespeare: The Complete Works*, ed. Alfred Harbage (Baltimore, MD: Penguin Books, 1969), scene i, 178.

21. Aristotle, *Nicomachean Ethics*, trans. W. D. Ross, 1098a18 in *The Basic Works of Aristotle*, ed. Richard McKeon (New York: Random House, 1941). Translation altered.

22. Charles Dickens, *Great Expectations* (New York: Shine Classics, 2014), 254.

23. Northrop Frye, *Anatomy of Criticism* (Princeton, NJ: Princeton University Press, 1973).

24. Dillard, *Pilgrim at Tinker Creek*, 77.

25. John Sallis, *Force of Imagination* (Bloomington: Indiana University Press, 2000), 192.

26. Martin Heidegger, quoted by Sallis, *Force of Imagination*, 195.

27. Joyce Carol Oates, *Marya: A Life* quoted in Stefan Klein, "Time Out of Mind," *New York Times*, March 17, 2008.

28. Toni Morrison, *Beloved* (New York: Random House, 2004), 134.

29. Michael Kammen, *A Time to Every Purpose: The Four Seasons in American Culture* (Chapel Hill: University of North Carolina Press, 2004).

30. See, for example, Margaret Renki, "The Dark Warning of an Early Spring," *New York Times*, March 11, 2018.

31. Rachel Carson, *The Sense of Wonder* (New York: HarperCollins, 1998), 100.

32. Jonathan Safran Foer, *We Are the Weather* (New York: Farrar, Straus and Giroux, 2019).

33. Jeremy Taylor, "The Rule and Exercises of Holy Dying" in *The Whole Works of the Right Rev. Jeremy Taylor* (London: Longman, Brown, Green, and Longmans, 1847), 268.

34. Henry David Thoreau, *The Journal, 1837–1861*, ed. John R. Stilgoe (New York: New York Review of Books, 2009), March 2, 1859.

35. Alphonso Lingis, *Dangerous Emotions* (Berkeley: University of California Press), 121, 134, and 127.

36. Gary Paul Nabham, *Cultures of Habitat* (Washington, DC: Counterpoint, 1998), 319.

37. Thoreau, *The Journal, 1837–1861*, 469.

38. Ralph Waldo Emerson, *The Journals and Miscellaneous Notebooks of Ralph Waldo Emerson*, Vol. XI, ed. A. W. Plumstead et al. (Cambridge, MA: Harvard University Press, 1975), 52.

39. Timothy Morton, *Ecology Without Nature: Rethinking Environmental Aesthetics* (Cambridge, MA: Harvard University Press, 2007), 33 and chapter 1.

40. Yoko Ono, *Season of Glass* (New York: The Hit Factory), 1981.

41. John Dryden, "Of the Pythagorean Philosophy" in *The Works of John Dryden in Verse and Prose*, Vol. 1, ed. John Mitford (New York: Harper and Brothers, 1847), 320.

42. There are, of course, other ways to correlate the four seasons with the four elements. For a discussion of the elements, see David Macauley, *Elemental Philosophy: Earth, Air, Fire, and Water as Environmental Ideas* (Albany: State University of New York Press, 2010).

43. The "ABCs of everything" is a non-literal translation of the Greek, *"stoicheia tou pontos."* See Plato, *Timaeus*, trans. Francis Cornford (New York: Macmillan Publishing, 1959), 48b.

44. Luce Irigaray and Michael Marder, *Through Vegetal Being: Two Philosophical Perspectives* (New York: Columbia University Press, 2016), 143 and 140.

45. Irigaray and Marder, *Through Vegetal Being*, 140.

46. Thoreau, *The Journal, 1837–1861*, 225.

47. David Macauley, "Home on the Road: Pilgrimage, Place, and Peripatetics" in *Home: Lived Experiences*, ed. John Murungi and Linda Ardito (New York:

Springer Publications, 2021); Macauley, "Elemental Beauty: Walking the Sensuous Surface of the Earth," in *The Elemental Sensuous: Phenomenology and Aesthetics*, ed. John Murungi and Linda Ardito (Newcastle upon Tyne, UK: Cambridge Scholars, 2016); Macauley, "Walking the Urban Environment," in *Transformations of Urban and Suburban Landscapes*, ed. Gary Backhaus and John Murungi (Lanham, MD: Rowman and Littlefield Press, 2002); Macauley, "Walking the Elemental Earth: Phenomenological and Literary Foot Notes," *Annalecta Husserliana*, Vol. 71, March 2001, 15–31.

48. Henry Beston, *Northern Farm: A Glorious Year on a Small Main Farm* (New York: Henry Holt and Co., 1948), 218.

49. Dillard, 76.

50. John Keats, "The Human Seasons" in *John Keats: The Complete Poems*, ed. John Barnard (New York: Penguin Books, 1988), 232.

51. T. S. Eliot, *Four Quartets* (Orlando, FL: Harcourt Books, 1971), 24.

2

The Seasons Embodied

The Story of a Plant

CRAIG HOLDREGE

I live in lower upstate New York between the Hudson River and the Taconic Mountains. It's an area where it is easy to speak of seasons. We often have long and cold winters with ample snow cover. Spring brings climbing temperatures and rapid growth of plants, especially in May. Summers are warm and humid. Fall brings cool nights but often warm days, and, in October, the brilliant colors of the dying foliage of trees.

The larger context for our notion of the classic four seasons is an annual rhythm—the changing length of the day during the year. In the Northern Hemisphere, December 22 is the shortest day of the year and marks the beginning of winter.[1] Day length then increases, the sun climbs higher in the sky, and on March 21, there are twelve hours of day and of night. This is the spring equinox, or the beginning of spring. The days continue to get longer until the longest day is reached at summer solstice, June 22. This is the beginning of summer. Day length decreases, and the fall equinox is reached on September 23. From this time on, nights are longer than days until the shortest day is reached again on December 22.

For any given place, the degree of difference in day and night lengths during the year depends on latitude. The closer you are to the equator, the less there is change in day length during the year. The closer to the poles, the greater the difference between the length of day and night in summer and winter. But for every place that lies on the same latitude, the shift in day length during the year is the same. For example, Beijing, Istanbul,

Naples, New York City, Denver, and Eureka (CA) all lie near 40 degrees north of the equator. For each of these places on a given date, the day lengths are the same. From the perspective of the earth-sun relation they share the same seasons. But in Eureka, on the coast of Northern California, the temperatures in the summer are hardly higher than in the winter, and the area has ample fog that sustains the growth of the giant coastal redwood trees. In contrast, Denver lies in the middle of a continent on a mile-high plateau; its climate is semi-arid with large temperature swings both during individual days and during the year. Other than the course of the sun's path during the year, hardly anything about Eureka and Denver would indicate similarity of seasons. The seasons become differentiated and individualized in places. The physical location, its relation to land and water, topography, winds, altitude, and more help to create the concrete seasons in a given place.

Especially when we look at the rhythms and characteristics of living organisms, our understanding of the seasons becomes richer and many-sided. Where I live, in the northeastern United States, I have ample opportunity for such learning. If, by contrast, I were to study the seasons in the Bonneville Salt Flats of Utah, I would have a powerful and yet stark sense of the seasons that would mainly emerge from the strong contrasts in light intensity and temperatures during the year. There are hardly any living organisms in the large horizontal expanse of salt in the middle of North America, so I would be hard pressed to follow rhythmical phenomena of life that would tell me what the seasons mean for life, or to put it differently, how the seasons become embodied in the life of nature.

In this chapter I'd like to share how my study of a particular plant in relation to the seasons helped my understanding of the plant and also the seasons to grow.[2] Before I do that, however, I need to explain the way I carry out such an inquiry. In my work I am inspired by and learn from Johann Wolfgang von Goethe's approach to studying nature.[3]

Method

My study of the skunk cabbage began with my fascination for this somewhat strange plant. It caught my attention; it was in so many ways different from other plants I knew. I had the desire to get to know it better. In a sense I was asking, "Who are you?" I went out regularly to observe the plant and its development through the course of many years. I read all the scientific literature I could find about skunk cabbage. In this way I entered into a kind of dialogue with the plant. Very quickly I experienced what Goethe notes about the nature of organisms:

> An organic being is externally so many-sided and internally so manifold and inexhaustible that we cannot choose enough points of view to behold it, and we cannot develop enough organs in ourselves in order to investigate it without killing it.[4]

The careful and attentive turn toward the plant—in which my attitude is that of a student learning from a master teacher—shows me the richness and dynamism of nature and, at the same time, makes me aware that I have much to learn from that richness and dynamism. Goethe wrote (in 1807): "If we want to behold nature in a living way, we must follow her example and become as mobile and malleable as nature herself."[5] This inner mobility and malleability is enhanced by the continual return to the phenomena and by holding back the desire to fit what I'm experiencing into preexisting, abstract categories. In other words, the effort is not to explain, but, in Goethe's words, "to portray."[6]

While studying a plant, I take in many "snapshots" of its life since I meet it at different times and within different contexts. But I do not simply hold on to these separate snapshots, since they in no way correspond to the continuity of the life of the plant. I proceed instead by consciously building up in my mind a dynamic and vivid picture of the plant in its development. Goethe calls this activity "exact sensorial imagination."[7] I create a vivid picture of how the plant appears in early spring and then its subsequent growth and transformation during the year. I do this repeatedly and complete the picture as I learn more from the plant. In this way I get closer to its generative life. I increasingly come to recognize its special and unique characteristics. I can also say that it speaks to me more clearly through this process. As Goethe remarks, "We labor in vain to describe a person's character, but when we draw together his actions, his deeds, a picture of his character will emerge."[8] The same is true of any natural phenomenon. By dwelling with it, considering it from many sides, and again and again striving to actively recreate in our minds its multitudinous features, a sense of the unity that informs all its expressions grows.

I do not consider the development of the plant in isolation. I bring it into relation with other plants I know, and with other contexts—in the case of this study, the seasons. By broadening the scope of inquiry, I let one phenomenon begin to illuminate the other.[9] I approach this plant at first with a more or less distinct notion of the seasons. I place its development into the seasonal context that I am familiar with, say, early spring. But as soon as I begin to study the plant in more depth, my conception of spring also grows. The plant reveals something to me about the seasons just as the seasons inform my understanding of the plant.

Early Spring—The Warming, Flowering Bud

I moved to the northeastern United States in the early 1990s. I had never lived there before, having grown up in Colorado and then resided in Switzerland and Germany for fourteen years. Therefore, much was new to me and I was excited to experience yet another part of the world. I learned about a nearby wooded wetland, and it soon became a favorite area to visit at all different times of the year. When you take a walk at the beginning of March through the woods that border the wetland, plants give you little indication that spring is on the way. No buds of trees or shrubs are opening. No herbaceous plants are emerging out of the leaf litter. The little green that you see in the mosses, lichens, and needles of conifers is the green of the minimal life activity that these plants have maintained through the winter. The dominant colors are the many shades of gray and brown in tree trunks, shrub branches, and the leaf litter with its remnants of last year's growth. The quietness of the woods is all the more striking when it is broken by a bird singing a few notes in the morning hours. Often there is still snow on the ground. Although the days are getting longer and the warmth of the sun is intensifying, it is still a wintry landscape.

When you arrive in the wetland you find one plant species that is breaking the dormancy of winter: skunk cabbage (*Symplocarpus foetidus*). It does not matter whether the ground is frozen, whether there is a layer of ice covering parts of the wetland, or whether there are eight inches of snow covering the ground; skunk cabbage is growing. What emerges out of the ground is very unusual. You see maroon- and yellow-colored, twisted, pointed hoods that are about three to six inches high (see Figures 2.1 and 2.2). They are unlike any other plant form that appears later in the year. They often grow in groups, sometimes singly.

From a botanical point of view, this hood is a leaf that is twisted around itself so that it encloses an internal space. There remains a small opening to the outside. This leaf is called a spathe. Surprisingly, the spathe encloses a fleshy stalk that ends in a somewhat spherical head of tightly

Figure 2.1. Craig Holdrege, "Group of Skunk Cabbage spathes as they emerge in March."

Figure 2.2. Craig Holdrege, "Two spathes."

packed, small, and inconspicuous flowers (Figure 2.3). This unique formation is called a spadix. So when skunk cabbage spathes are emerging out of the ground, they are at the same time flowering. It's just that the flower head never grows out of the bud-like enclosure of the spathe—it remains hidden and protected within the spathe. There could hardly be a more powerful image of early spring than this plant with flowers that never emerge out of their protective bud-like sheath.

Cold temperatures generally bring quiescence into plant life, but here is a plant that seems to defy this rule and ushers in spring despite the freezing weather. I got a hint of how it accomplishes this feat when I looked more carefully at skunk cabbage growing out of ice or snow. An ice or snow-free area extends around the spathe (Figure 2.4). I have gone down to the wetland on days where the whole area was covered with snow and dug around only to discover little caverns around skunk cabbage spathes. Is skunk cabbage melting the snow?

If you put your finger down into the opening of a spathe and touch the flowerhead or its stalk, you feel that it is warm. Skunk cabbage heats

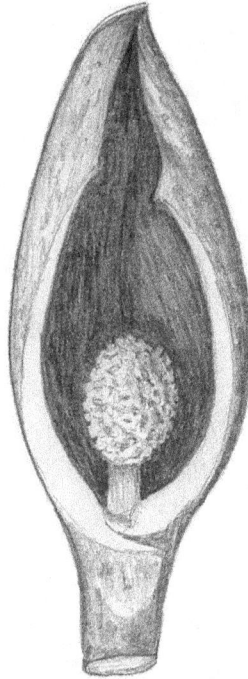

Figure 2.3. Craig Holdrege, "Front part of spathe cut off to show flower head (spadix)."

Figure 2.4. Craig Holdrege, "Skunk cabbage melting the snow."

up when its spathes and spadixes are growing out of the ground. On various occasions I have measured the temperature with a thermometer; I have found the air temperature at ground level to be 30 degrees Fahrenheit, while the flowerhead was 60 degrees Fahrenheit. This is a remarkable and seemingly un-plant-like characteristic. As biologist Roger Knutson found, skunk cabbage can produce warmth over a period of 12–14 days and remains on average 20°C (36°F) above the outside air temperature during this period, no matter if it is day or night.[10]

Skunk cabbage does not produce heat *ex nihilo*. Without the previous summer it could not generate its warmth. It can, in its way, bring forth spring because it thrived during the previous summer. What do I mean? Like other green plants, skunk cabbage has the remarkable ability to build up its substances by being in the light and taking in air, water, and small amounts of minerals out of the soil. This is the process we call photosynthesis. The sugar that is produced in the leaves through this process flows as sap down into the root stalk and roots, and is transformed into starch. This starch is stored in the form of solid granules until the next spring. With its large leaves (that I will describe below) and through the fact that it does not use the products of photosynthesis to create much fiber, skunk cabbage is able to store ample amounts of starch. (If the rootstock is dug out and left to dry over a long period of time, it can be ground into flour.)

When skunk cabbage begins its shift from dormancy to activity in the late winter of the next year, the starch is transformed into fluid sugar sap that in turn, with the help of oxygen, is broken down rapidly and in large amounts. This produces heat. So skunk cabbage interacts with its environment in the spring and early summer, and one result of this interaction is the solid starch. Starch is stored and maintained in the long quiescent phase of the skunk cabbage's life—from September to March in our region. It represents a condition of relative stasis, containment, and withdrawal from active life processes. In this sense, starch as a substance embodies the winter of the plant. Then, in March, activity ensues as starch is broken down, allowing heat generation and also growth. Life begins to flow again and marks the onset of spring.

Movement

Sometimes when I journey down to the wetland in early March, the air is filled with a diffuse, unobtrusive, and mild skunk-like smell. This is the time when skunk cabbage is heating up. If you put your nose to the spathe opening at this time, the skunk-like smell is more intense. This scent emanates from the warming plant and spreads out into the air of the wetland and surrounding forest. So, on the one hand, the flowering of skunk cabbage remains hidden and contained—unlike the showy flowers that other plants bring forth later in spring and summer—in large buds near the ground. On the other hand, its pungent scent moves into the environment on the wings of the self-produced, warmed air that escapes from the spathe, and then intermingles and travels with the ambient air.

We do not see the air movements, but what we cannot see we can imagine. Each skunk cabbage spathe is a little center of warmth generation. The warm air expands and moves up and out of the spathe into the ambient air. Cooler air will in turn be drawn into the spathe, get warmed, and spiral out of the spathe again. So to gain a real sense of what skunk cabbage is doing, we need to imagine countless little vortices of moving air that skunk cabbage creates through its generation of warmth. It brings air movement into the larger environment. And this both highlights and co-creates a main feature of spring: the shift out of quiescence and dormancy into activity, movement, and growth.

During the time of heat production, skunk cabbage flowers release their pollen onto the surface of the flowers. If you rub your finger on the flowerhead, it gets covered with sulfur-yellow pollen. The wafting scent, the warm enclosure of the spathe, and the pollen attract the first insects and spiders that become active in early spring. Spiders, nestled in the warm interior of the spathe, sometimes make webs across the opening. Flies and bees visit the flowers, where they gather and feed on pollen. So in coming to life in early spring, skunk cabbage not only engenders movement in its own growth, in the warming process, and in the circulating air, but also in the lives of animals.

After the period of heat production, and as the days grow longer, the skunk cabbage begins to unfold its leaves. Spear-like, large, bright-green buds grow out of the subterranean root stock to which the spathe and spadix are also connected. In May the leaves emerge from these buds and unfold rapidly in flowing, out-spiraling movements (Figure 2.5). The leaves form

Figure 2.5. Craig Holdrege, "Skunk cabbage development."

a large rosette, and each leaf has a long stalk and a large, elongated, heart-shaped leaf blade. The entire leaf can be up to a yard long and is much bigger than those of any other plant in the area. By the end of May the wetland is flooded with the bright green of skunk cabbage leaves.

By consciously following the rapid unfolding that results in such large, spreading leaves, you see spring as a process, but you also witness the process as embodied in a wetland and in a plant that is at home there. Skunk cabbage takes in large amounts of water from the ever-wet soil. Where the soil over time becomes too dry, skunk cabbage ceases to thrive. The water that skunk cabbage draws out of the wetland becomes a main structural feature of the leaves. The leaves have hardly any fiber, and the stalks have a spongy consistency. (When crushed, the leaves release a pungent, somewhat skunk-like odor from which the plant derives its name.)

The skunk cabbage's flowering process moves air into the surroundings through its heat production. In its leafing phase it also brings about water movement: water from the soil is taken up by the roots, moves into the leaves, and, through evaporation, dissipates into the air.

Withdrawing and Preparing

Skunk cabbage's leafing phase occurs over a relatively short period of time—from May through June. Already in July they are decomposing, and in August there may just be a remnant of a leaf here or there. In keeping with their watery nature, the leaves leave almost no organic matter behind when they decompose. It is more like a process of dissolving than breaking apart. So the height of summer, in terms of day length and increasing daily temperatures, is fall for skunk cabbage—a time of receding. But it is also the time of fruiting.

While the leaves are decomposing, the fruits are developing. The spathe that enclosed the flowerhead wilts while the leaves unfold. Then the flowerhead swells and turns a deep wine-red. In a dark woodland wetland, it appears almost black. Within this growing sphere (see Figure 2.6), the berry-like fruits develop, each containing one seed. The sphere can grow to two or more inches in diameter and, telling of its wetland nature, the fruit head hugs the moist and cool ground. When by August the leaves have decomposed, the head of fruits falls apart, and the individual fruits lie on the ground where they may be eaten (for example, by wild turkeys), decompose, or germinate (either in the fall or the next spring).

Figure 2.6. Craig Holdrege, "Fruit heads surrounded by decaying leaf stalks."

If the seeds germinate, they form small plants in the following year that have only a few small leaves. Skunk cabbage is a perennial, so each year it recedes into below-ground rootstock. Each consecutive year the plant gets larger, and at some point it will form spathes, flowers, and fruits. No one knows the age of the oldest skunk cabbage plant, but in any case one plant can live for decades.

When the fruits of a mature plant have fallen apart in August, we can no longer see any part of the skunk cabbage above the ground. But this is only a temporary state, since buds often begin to emerge from the rootstock and peek out of the soil as one- to two-inch long green spears. (Not all skunk cabbage plants extend their buds aboveground.) They stay like this throughout the fall and winter. These buds contain the rosette of tightly enfolded leaves and sometimes the spathe that will grow out in the following year. So in late summer and early fall we see that skunk cabbage is ready for the next spring. It begins its winter early, just as it moves out of winter early the next year.

Another fascinating aspect of skunk cabbage is that it does not only form buds for the coming year. While a mature plant is in the leafing process, buds at the base of the leaves develop. The ones destined to unfold in the coming year grow significantly. However, other buds begin to develop, grow only little, and stay buds for two to four or even more years before they grow out. This is remarkable. Most plants only form buds for the coming year. Skunk cabbage is continually forming new buds—centers of potential—that remain in their germinal state for years. Skunk cabbage flowers in a bud, and while it is expanding out into the environment in its leaves it is also forming and growing many buds below the soil surface. It is as if skunk cabbage is preparing and holding within itself a sketch of many springs to come. If there is a plant that embodies budding life, it is skunk cabbage.

Conclusion

The seasons are not "things" in the way that a rock is a thing to which one can point. They are rhythmical and relational phenomena. An eternal spring would be no spring. Spring arises out of winter and becomes summer. Spring is what it is through its movement and relations.

Due to the relational nature of the seasons, there is not a moment in time—except in relation to the equinox—at which we can say: winter has stopped, and spring has just begun. Where I live, winter is coldest during late January and February. The ground is frozen solid and often blanketed with snow. The daily temperature may not rise above 32 degrees Fahrenheit. From this perspective, spring seems far away. In the beginning of February, as the days are becoming longer, we begin to hear birds singing in the morning—it is by no means the full chorus of April and May, but it is a beginning. The birds are giving us an intimation of spring in deep winter. In this sense, the seasons interweave. Spring is gestating in winter just as winter makes itself known already in fall.

When I am walking in the wetland with someone, I can show them a skunk cabbage. I cannot in the same way show them spring. However, I can reveal spring to them through the skunk cabbage. I do this when I begin to consider skunk cabbage in its developmental dynamics through the year. I take it seriously as a temporal, transforming being. Then spring lights up through skunk cabbage. Earlier I used the expression that skunk cabbage "ushers in" spring. Skunk cabbage begins its activity in early spring and brings about not only physiological movement and growth, but also—through warmth, air, and water—movement into the surrounding environment. In this sense, we can say that skunk cabbage is in its activity an embodiment of spring, or that spring brings forth itself through skunk cabbage. The wetland is "early springing" in skunk cabbage.

I get to know the seasons in new ways when I attend to rhythmical phenomena of life that are always embedded in the large cosmic rhythm of the annual changing relation of the earth to the sun. The character and interweaving of the seasons show themselves in different ways depending upon my focus. Were I to study other plants—or animals—I would discover multitudinous experiences of spring and the other seasons. What do fireflies tell me about midsummer, and what do crickets or milkweed pods tell me about late summer? What do flaming sugar maple leaves tell me about fall, and what do snow fleas during a warm spell tell me about winter? Each of these pursuits would reveal new features of these creatures, the seasons, and their mutual relations. As Merleau-Ponty writes,

> This perspectival character of my knowledge is not conceived as an accident [or] imperfection. . . . Perspective does not appear to me to be a subjective deformation of things but, on the contrary to be one of their properties, perhaps their essential property. It is precisely because of it that the perceived possesses in itself a hidden and inexhaustible richness.[11]

The more I attend to, the richer my meeting with the world becomes. The world shows me ever new perspectives. Skunk cabbage provides one such powerful perspective that has much to reveal. To consider it within the seasons leads to a deepening experience of the world's "hidden and inexhaustible richness."

Notes

1. The exact calendar date of the solstices and equinoxes varies from year to year.

2. Craig Holdrege, "Skunk Cabbage (*Symplocarpus foetidus*)," *In Context* 4 (2000): 12–18. Available online: http://natureinstitute.org/pub/ic/ic4/skunkcabbage.pdf.

3. See the following books and article: Henri Bortoft, *The Wholeness of Nature* (Great Barrington, MA: Lindisfarne Books, 1996); Johann Wolfgang von Goethe, *The Scientific Studies*, trans. and ed. Douglas Miller (Princeton, NJ: Princeton University Press, 1995); Craig Holdrege, "Doing Goethean Science," *Janus Head*, 8.1 (2005): 27–52.

4. Johann Wolfgang von Goethe and Friedrich Schiller, *Der Briefwechsel zwischen Schiller und Goethe*, vol. 1, ed. Emil Staiger (Frankfurt: Insel Verlag, 1977), 39. This translation is by Craig Holdrege; the words were written in 1794.

5. Johann Wolfgang von Goethe, *Naturwissenschaftliche Schriften I*, Hamburger Ausgabe, vol. 1 (Munich: Verlag C. H. Beck, 2002), 56. This passage translated by Craig Holdrege.

6. Goethe, *The Scientific Studies*, 57.

7. Goethe, *The Scientific Studies*, 46.

8. Goethe, *The Scientific Studies*, 158.

9. Craig Holdrege, "Phenomenon illuminates phenomenon," *In Context* 26 (2011): 14–18. Available online: http://natureinstitute.org/pub/ic/ic26/phenomeno-nilluminatesphenomenon.pdf

10. R. M. Knutson, "Heat Production and Temperature Regulation in Eastern Skunk Cabbage," *Science* 186 (1974): 746–747.

11. Maurice Merleau-Ponty, *The Essential Writings of Merleau-Ponty*, ed. Alden Fisher (New York: Harcourt, Brace & World, 1969), 138–139.

Phenomenology and Poetics

3

A Poetic Phenomenology of the Seasons

LUKE FISCHER

Müsset im Naturbetrachten
Immer eins wie alles achten.
Nichts ist drinnen, nichts ist draußen:
Denn was innen das ist außen.

[In observing nature you must
Always attend to one and all.
Nothing is inside, nothing outside:
For what is within that is without.]

—Johann Wolfgang von Goethe[1]

Introduction

The aim of this essay is to sketch a poetic phenomenology of the four seasons that are discerned in certain temperate regions. More specifically, I aim to give a non-reductive account of how the human experience of the seasons is deeply connected to natural seasonal phenomena and to indicate ways in which we can deepen our understanding of, and participation in, the seasons. This poetic phenomenology will be developed through drawing on key concepts from the French phenomenologist Maurice Merleau-Ponty, the poet and scientist Johann Wolfgang von Goethe, as well as on poetic writings that thematize the seasons (including my own). While I grew up in

Sydney, Australia, my approach here is largely informed by my experience of
the seasons in Europe (especially Germany) and the United States (especially
Philadelphia), where I lived respectively for several years.[2]

Much of my research has focused on the intersection between philosophy and poetry, and I share the view with major phenomenologists (Martin
Heidegger, for instance) and poets in the Romantic tradition (Novalis and
Samuel Taylor Coleridge, among others) that poetry can reveal significant
insights into the nature of the world. Previously I have argued that philosophy
itself must become more poetic, and that a dialogue between philosophy
and poetry is crucial to the future of thinking. In particular, the way in
which poetry can assist in the overcoming of the problem of dualism has
been a key theme of this earlier research.[3] The present essay demonstrates
the significance of a poetic way of thinking, feeling, and perceiving for an
understanding of the seasons.

The seasons have been a perennial theme for poetry, the arts, mythology,
and religion, but they have been almost completely neglected by philosophy.[4]
There are many reasons why this might be the case; only a few of which
will be touched on here.

First, the seasons are phenomena of natural time. Although temporality
has been a central concern of modern philosophy, the philosophical consideration of time has been primarily limited to the internal time-consciousness
of the subject. Both Immanuel Kant and Edmund Husserl are exemplary
in this respect. From the point of view of a subjective consideration of
time, the seasons could not become a proper theme because they would
be regarded solely as examples of internal time-consciousness. The seasons
would not be manifestations of nature, rather they would be an example
of the subjective constitution of natural appearances.

Second, we are affectively stirred by the seasons. We speak, for instance,
of the loneliness of winter, the joy of spring, the fullness of summer, etc.
The seasons have an affective or atmospheric dimension (and more generally
speaking, one of the reasons why weather is a favorite topic of conversations
is due to its intimate connection to our moods). Prior to the revaluation of
dispositions and moods in the phenomenology of Max Scheler and Martin
Heidegger, affects were primarily relegated to a merely subjective status. From
the common point of view, only thoughts and concepts (in cooperation
with observation through the senses) are capable of truly grasping reality.
If the search for truth is constitutive of philosophy, and affectively-charged
phenomena such as the seasons are understood as merely subjective, then
they remain philosophically irrelevant. In contrast, Scheler considered feel-

ings to be as intersubjective as thoughts, and Heidegger, already in *Being and Time*, discussed the equiprimordiality of disposition and understanding (*Befindlichkeit und Verstehen*).[5] According to Heidegger, moods are world-disclosive; they are co-attunements of self (or *Dasein*, to be precise) and world; in other words, they bear an essential relationship to truth (understood as unconcealment). More recently, Gernot Böhme (drawing on the "new phenomenology" of Hermann Schmitz) has advocated a "quasi-objective" conception of atmospheres that is also beneficial for overcoming a merely subjective view of affects.[6] Böhme describes *atmospheres* as basic affects that we sense or feel ("*spüren*") along with our sense perceptions in the narrower sense, and as a "shared reality" "between subject and object."[7] Both the Heideggerian conception of dispositions and the Böhmean understanding of atmospheres have been directly applied to seasonal experience. Following Böhme's approach, one can speak, for instance, of the atmosphere of a misty autumnal morning or the atmosphere of a still, clear winter day (and poetry is a key source for Böhme's discussion of seasonal atmospheres). Paola-Ludovika Coriando has drawn on Heidegger's statements about seasons and applied his general conception of moods as disclosive attunements in her interpretation of the seasonal poems Friedrich Hölderlin wrote in the last phase of his life.[8] In this context, she regards the moods of the seasons as ways in which nature reveals itself in the human psyche or *Gemüt*. This experience of specific seasonal moods—autumnal decay, winter concealment, the erupting joy of spring, the maturing calm of summer—is made possible by a fundamental mood (*Grundstimmung*) of harmony (*Einklang*) between nature and the human psyche.[9] While Böhme's and Coriando's approaches differ, they are related insofar as they regard seasonal affects as a form of participation in seasonal phenomena and natural time. Here I will not discuss their views in detail, but these phenomenological approaches to moods and atmospheres inform my treatment of the seasons.

Third, while the period of European Romanticism and German idealism was rich in endeavors to articulate an ultimate unity between mind and nature (e.g., the philosophy of nature and Goethean science), subsequently the task of understanding the natural world was increasingly left to the (mostly reductive) natural sciences. The natural sciences assumed responsibility for our knowledge of nature while the humanities focused on cultural phenomena. Philosophy primarily understood itself as belonging to the humanities, and for this reason neglected nature, including the phenomena of the seasons. Only in recent years has there been a resurgence of philosophical interest in the natural world, in areas such as environmental philosophy and environmental ethics (as well as the history and philosophy of science), in response to the ecological crisis.

Poets, in contrast to philosophers, have always fostered a deep interest in the seasons as both natural phenomena and affective attunements. This is not surprising, as the musical language of poetry is suited not only to refer to moods but also to evoke them; its concrete imagery can portray natural phenomena in a more vivid manner than the general concepts of philosophy. Relatedly, the lyrical sensibility that underlies much poetry fuses feeling, perception, and thought in a way that facilitates a deep attunement to the seasons. While the goal of this essay is to sketch a poetic phenomenology of the seasons, it should be said that it also aims to approach the seasons with a certain systematicity. I seek an appropriate synthesis of the more intuitive approach of the poet and the systematic disposition of the philosopher, to elucidate a poetic order of things or, to be more precise, a poetic structuration of time. A few key concepts will facilitate this *poetic thinking* of the seasons: Merleau-Ponty's notion of "sensible ideas," a phenomenological understanding of moods and atmospheres, and Goethe's concepts of expansion and contraction as well as "intensification" or *Steigerung*. These concepts will both grant cohesion to the discussion of various poetic writings on the seasons and serve to reveal the overall dynamic structure of the seasons.

Key Concepts

Throughout his philosophical writings Merleau-Ponty sought to reinterpret the relationship between the sensible and the intelligible, the visible and the invisible. Rather than the dualism that pervades much modern thought and that found its most definitive articulation in Descartes, Merleau-Ponty, in his phenomenology of perceptual experience, his turn to visual artists such as Cézanne, and his lectures on nature sought to articulate a more intimate relationship between the sensible and the ideal. In his late unfinished work *The Visible and the Invisible,* Merleau-Ponty coins an especially helpful expression for a kind of perception in which the ideal and the real are closely entwined: "sensible ideas."[10] This expression intentionally unites two terms, ideas and sense perceptions, that have often been regarded as opposed. Merleau-Ponty formulates the notion of "sensible ideas" in relation to Proust and states: "No one has gone further than Proust in fixing the relations between the visible and the invisible, in describing an idea that is not the contrary of the sensible, that is its lining and its depth."[11]

Music is an exemplary manifestation of a sensible idea for Merleau-Ponty, but he also applies the notion to the other arts and ultimately to the entire perceptual world. In order to understand a piece of music I do not abstract myself from its sensible or audible appearance, I attend to the performance itself. The meaning of any musical work, moreover, is not separate from its sensible embodiment but rather manifest in and through its sensible form. The music is ultimately a sensible-intelligible unity with a distinctive integrity, which means that the sensible and the intelligible cannot be divided. The musical idea is not an abstract concept or generalization; it is the distinctive sense of the work in its fullness of appearing. In notes for his 1957–58 lecture course on nature Merleau-Ponty states,

> At the moment when the melody begins, the last note is there, in its own manner. In a melody, a reciprocal influence between the first and last note takes place, and we have to say that the first note is possible only because of the last, and vice versa. . . . Just as we cannot say that the last note is the end of the melody and that the first is the effect of it, neither can we distinguish the meaning apart from the meaning where it is expressed. As Proust says, melody is a Platonic idea that we cannot see separately. It is impossible to distinguish the means and the end, the essence and the existence in it.[12]

Merleau-Ponty does not use the expression "sensible idea" in his earlier works (including his magnum opus, *The Phenomenology of Perception*), but this notion is thoroughly in keeping with his earlier writings. Concepts with artistic connotations, such as the concept of "style," also play a crucial role in his earlier understanding of perception. The following passage from the *Phenomenology of Perception* can assist in articulating further features of "sensible ideas" (even though this terminology is not used). Merleau-Ponty describes the sense of the city of Paris as follows:

> Paris for me is not an object of many facets, a collection of perceptions, nor is it the law governing all these perceptions. Just as a person gives evidence of the same emotional essence in his gestures with his hands, in his way of walking and in the sound of his voice, each express perception occurring in my journey through Paris—the cafés, people's faces, the poplars along the quays, the bends of the Seine—stands out against the

city's whole being, and merely confirms that there is a certain style or a certain significance which Paris possesses. . . . There is present a latent significance diffused throughout . . . the city.[13]

In light of this formulation one could call Paris a sensible idea.[14] How is this idea of Paris revealed and perceived? It is manifest in an analogous manner to the way in which a person's character is revealed through their behavior and physiognomy. In the city's various perceptible manifestations—"the cafés, people's faces, the poplars along the quays, the bends of the Seine"—a latent significance, the essence of Paris, comes to expression. I sense the idea of Paris as an immanent meaning that is manifest in all the aspects of the city, just as the meaning of a musical work is sensed as an integrity in the relationship of the sounding notes to one another. One of the main conjectures of the present essay is that it is illuminating to view seasons as sensible ideas, and that conceiving them in this way can assist in overcoming common oppositions between the inner and the outer, the sensible and the intelligible, to which we can also add the opposition between the natural and the human. Moreover, much poetry on the seasons could be described as evocations of seasons as sensible ideas, as the unconcealing of "a latent significance diffused" throughout seasonal phenomena.

Although, as far as I know, Goethe exercised no direct influence on Merleau-Ponty's thought, there are significant connections between their views.[15] In recent times, Goethe's approach to science has, with a good deal of justification, been explicated as a phenomenology of nature.[16] Goethe also strove, in his whole approach to nature, to overcome the opposition between the sensible and the intelligible, and his methodology has been characterized in ways that imply a reconciliation of common oppositions. Schiller, for instance, regarded Goethe's approach as a "rational empiricism" and Goethe himself refers to a "higher empiricism" that seeks to reconcile the real and the ideal.[17] Moreover, I think that it is totally apt to use the expression "sensible idea" in relation to Goethe's science. In his scientific works on optics, plant and animal morphology, and other areas, Goethe always sought to discover and reveal the immanent intelligibility of the world; the goal of his science is to see the unity of the sensible and the intelligible rather than to seek hidden causes behind the phenomena.[18] In discussions of his methodology Goethe offers examples and analogies that are very close to Merleau-Ponty's views. For instance, in the 1810 preface to his *Theory of Colors* (*Farbenlehre*), Goethe gives the following analogy for how we should understand light and color:

strictly speaking, it is useless to attempt to express the nature
of a thing abstractedly. Effects we can perceive, and a complete
history of those effects would, in fact, sufficiently define the
nature of the thing itself. We should try in vain to describe a
man's character, but let his acts be collected and an idea of the
character will be presented to us.[19]

In other words, the way to the nature of something is through its manifestations, and further, we could say that the "thing itself" *is* a sensible idea.
If there is a difference between Goethe's and Merleau-Ponty's views in this
respect, then it could be said that Goethe, especially the later Goethe, was
more of an idealist (in the sense of "objective idealism" and not "subjective
idealism")[20] than Merleau-Ponty.[21] This very slight difference of emphasis
could be characterized by saying that in Goethe one can speak of "sensible
ideas" and in Merleau-Ponty of "*sensible* ideas."

Central concepts from Goethe's morphological writings, namely the
polarity of expansion and contraction, and "intensification," will serve to
deepen and differentiate our understanding of seasons as sensible ideas, in
that they will explicate a dynamic structure in the cycle of the seasons and
enable the discernment of *difference* in unity.[22] These concepts are particularly
important to Goethe's understanding of plant metamorphosis. While our
approach to the seasons will extend beyond this domain, my claim is that
if these concepts are employed in a broad and plastic way they can illumine
seasonal phenomena and our human experience of them.

Goethe understands the unfolding of the plant as a series of stages of
contraction and expansion.[23] Beginning with the seed, where the idea of the
plant is most concealed, one can speak of three stages of contraction and
expansion. The development of the cotyledons and stem leaves is the first
expansion, and the first contraction begins toward the calyx. The second
expansion is in the development of the petals, while the second contraction
occurs in the division of sexes into stamens and pistil. This second stage
is like a repetition of the earlier stage of contraction and expansion in a
higher and more concentrated way; it is an intensification in comparison to
the first stage (see below). Following pollination the third stage of expansion and contraction occurs in the development of the fruit and the seed.
Goethe regards all stages and parts of the plant as a metamorphosis of a
single protean organ, which he calls "the leaf."[24] In this sense, the petals,
for instance, can be regarded as more refined "stem leaves" that are arranged
differently around the stem. They are a higher expression or an intensification

of the same principle that is manifest in the stem leaves. For the purposes of clarification it should be mentioned that there is no literal transformation of one part into another part; rather, when one compares the forms of the different parts of a plant one can see them as morphologically related in the aforementioned ways.

The notions of "sensible ideas," "contraction and expansion," "intensification" and "seasonal moods" will each play a key role in the subsequent description of the seasons. The notion of "sensible ideas" is significant in that it allows one to perceive a meaningful integrity across various seasonal phenomena. The four seasons will be presented as sensible ideas, akin to different movements of a symphony. The concept of intensification is significant in that it allows for difference in unity. Various seasonal phenomena are not an amorphous unity but rather a differentiated unity or polyphony. While the concept of intensification will be applied a little more loosely than Goethe applies it in his descriptions of plant morphology, this concept allows one to see a meaningful continuity between, for instance, warmth as a force of expansion in relation to material states (for instance, in turning liquid into gas) and the expanding of plant life. In addition, I interpret the seasonal moods experienced by human beings as a kind of interiorized intensification of natural seasonal phenomena. This allows one to see a deep continuity between the human and the natural, without resorting to either a reductive or an amorphous kind of monism. Finally, the polarity of contraction and expansion, when applied in a plastic and poetic way to the seasons, facilitates a perception of the overall dynamic structure and a relatedness of different seasonal expressions. Summer and winter will be treated as poles of expansion and contraction respectively, and autumn and spring as intermediate yet distinctive phases between these poles. While not all the phenomena belonging to a specific season might be captured by this application of the ideas of contraction and expansion, this polarity facilitates insight into the characteristic gestures of each season.

An Idealized Sketch of the Four Temperate Seasons

With which season shall we begin? While spring might seem like the best place to begin, I will start with winter. Just as a piece of music begins in silence, it makes sense to begin with winter, and the essence of spring can be better perceived when seen in contrast to winter. Winter can be regarded as the pole of contraction in my treatment. In the case of plants, this is literally true. Deciduous trees reveal only their empty branches and their buds, which Goethe understood as a contracted state. Annual plants are contracted into seeds that lie dormant underneath the snow or the earth (along with the seeds from a wide variety of plants). In the seed, the plant is in its least visible or manifest condition. More generally speaking, plant life is less active in winter than in the months when the days are longer and warmer. Persephone is hidden under the earth. The cold is also a force of contraction for matter. The majority of fluids, gases, and materials contract with the influence of cold. Although water is most dense at 4°C (39°F), when the temperature is slightly colder, water freezes, assumes determinate forms, and its molecules form hexagonal crystals (the reason for its lower density). This increasing structuration is also evident in the difference between a raindrop and a snowflake. Animal life appears similarly contracted. There are few ducks in the river, and their instinctive desires appear concealed or frozen. Few animals are heard or seen. Human beings also seem wrapped up and concealed like the surrounding environment. We spend much time indoors, concealed in houses like the trees withdrawn into their buds, and when we go outside we are wrapped in layers of clothing. Generally we are also less active. There are fewer daylight hours. In winter the outlines of all things seem clear and distinct—not only the trees and the ice but also the boundaries of our own bodies. The cold air against our skin gives us a clear experience of our own distinct bodily presence and warmth in contrast with our surroundings. Herman Melville, in *Moby Dick* (chapter 11), brilliantly characterizes this contrast in Ishmael's narration about being wrapped in a blanket in the cold and having "nothing but the blanket between you and your snugness and the cold of the outer air . . . there you lie like the one warm spark in the heart of an arctic crystal."[25] This experience of the cold is also connected to an experience of wakefulness. The freshness of the cold rouses us. Winter has its characteristic mood. It is the time of loneliness, solitude, and reflection. In the poem "Labyrinth" from my collection *A Personal History of Vision,* the image of being wrapped in layers of clothing is extended to the psyche and contrasted with a more exterior—or one-dimensional—summery mood: "Winter arrives / and wraps extra layers / around our souls."[26] In winter we turn inward, rediscover our inner dimensions. The life of the outer world is quiet, and interiority becomes more significant. The long nights that hide the world in darkness are also conducive to this withdrawal from the outer world. As David Macauley writes in the "Interstice: Night" in his book *Elemental Philosophy: Earth, Air, Fire, and Water as Environmental Ideas,* "The passage from evening to night is the time for philosophy, when, as Hegel noticed, the Owl of Minerva takes flight. Introspection blossoms; mental acuity is sharpened; the senses are heightened and abandon their defenses; meditation is made possible . . ."[27] Winter is a time for introversion, and might this introversion not be regarded as a kind of contraction at the psychological level? Might we not regard introversion as an intensification of the same principle that comes to expression in other winter phenomena, i.e., as the appearance of winter within the human psyche?

There is a widespread tendency to regard interiority and moods as merely subjective, in opposition to the objective external world. This is one reason why seasonal poems are commonly interpreted subjectivistically; they are seen as expressions of a poet's sentiments about nature, rather than as revealing a dimension of the season itself. In contrast (as mentioned above), Coriando explicates Hölderlin's seasonal poems as attunements of the human psyche to the natural world, and Böhme's phenomenological aesthetics reveals the seasons as environmental atmospheres that can be "sensed" ("gespürt") by the embodied subject and evoked in poetry.[28] The notion of seasons as sensible ideas—along with our other key concepts—can build on these phenomenological approaches through specifying a continuity between various "outer" seasonal phenomena and distinctive moods; in the case of winter there is a shared gesture of contraction.

With regard to the correlation between interiority and exteriority in the case of winter we can turn to the first lines of Wallace Stevens's poem, "The Snow Man": "One must have a mind of winter / To regard the frost and the boughs / Of the pine-trees covered with snow . . ."[29] The first word here, "One," not only implies the third person neuter but also suggests the notion of unity; our interior state in winter can be attuned to the season, can be one with the season. In a certain sense this state belongs to the winter; it is a "mind *of winter.*" The poem "In Late Winter" that appears in my collection *Paths of Flight* explores in detail the internal mood of winter.

In Late Winter

For months I've been a neo-Platonist
inhabiting the crystal palace of my mind,
a palace not unlike an Escher lithograph.
Each morning I rise early and climb the spiral staircase

while descending in reflection through the glassy floor
until I reach my study in the loft. I spend the day
seated at my desk beside a pentagonal window
and under the quiet glow of a lamp

etch patterns in silver plates.
From time to time I look over my shoulder
and see a man seated at his desk
beside a pentagonal window;

he looks over his shoulder until we both
turn away. I work until I've finished etching
a dodecahedron inside a snowflake
then climb the spiral staircase through the glassy floor

and nap on my printed bed. On rising
I descend back into my study
take snow-white sheets from a drawer
and fold them into origami storks

which I release into the crystal night. Departing
they return through the opposite window
and glide into my hands which unfold them—
my hands etched in a pentagonal plate of silver.

This morning I rise at dawn
and descending the spiral staircase
notice my image is blurred, the floor melting:
A falling snowflake about to dissolve in a stream.[30]

The poem contains many layers and multivalent images. Here I will
only draw attention to a few of the most pertinent features. The title is "In
Late Winter," and the preposition "In" has a threefold significance: spatial,
temporal, and psychological. The poem thematizes the time, and by implication, the place, of late winter as well as the *in*terior mood of this time.
One is in winter in all three senses: temporally, spatially, and spiritually.
The first line states that the "I" of the poem has been a neo-Platonist for

months. This suggests that the person is concerned with the interior and supersensible world. His psyche is turned inward. This person dwells in a crystal palace of the mind. A crystal is a transparent stone, and it is fitting that we often refer to clear and definite thoughts as *transparent* or as *crystal clear*. A mathematical or philosophical proof can be transparent, which means that the truth is clear to the eye of the mind. The crystal palace of the mind described in the poem suggests an interior space of mental clarity. This interior palace also bears a relation to the mystical tradition. In the Gospel of John, for instance, one finds the passage: "In my Father's house are many mansions . . ."[31] The sixteenth-century mystic, Teresa of Ávila, also speaks of "the interior castle" in her book by that name. In the poem, the crystal walls of the palace serve to develop a mirror-motif, which is reminiscent of the lithographs by M. C. Escher. There are many reflections in the poem, and upward movement, for instance, thereby appears as downward movement and vice versa. This mirroring enables a certain complexity in the text and evokes the inner precision of a winter mood as well as an intensified self-consciousness. The human figure etches a pattern on a silver plate—a calm and exact activity, which resembles the quality of a snowflake. The figure pauses and notices another person, who appears like a mirror image. The second stanza describes him working beside a pentagonal window. The fourth stanza makes clear that he is etching a dodecahedron inside a snowflake. These indications suggest that the crystal palace is also in the shape of a dodecahedron, a figure constituted by twelve pentagons. A dodecahedron is one of the "Platonic solids" and thus further elaborates the reference to Platonism early in the poem. In the *Timaeus* Plato relates the dodecahedron to the shape of the universe or cosmos (*Timaeus* 55c). In the context of the poem, the dodecahedron-motif evokes the interior cosmos of the winter mood. These observations serve to indicate a few key aspects of the poem. In the final line it becomes clear that the entire palace is also contained and reflected in a snowflake. This suggests a correspondence between the large and the small, the inner and the outer. The moment is described when the falling snowflake touches a stream and dissolves. This is the dissolving of the winter mood and the beginning of the more relaxed and fluid mood of spring.

The transition to a new season often announces itself in a particular phenomenon. One notices that the birdcalls are louder than usual in the morning, or that the light suddenly seems to have a more yellowish glow, or that the snowdrops are sprouting, or an unfamiliar warmth is felt in the air. Are these phenomena not like the first notes of a new movement in a symphony? Are they not the inception of the sensible idea and mood of spring? In a poem that concentrates on Apollo and poetry, "Früher Apollo [Early Apollo]" Rainer Maria Rilke describes a morning light that already seems to anticipate the whole of the spring, "As sometimes through the branches still void / of foliage a morning looks which already / is wholly in spring . . . [Wie manches Mal durch das noch unbelaubte / Gezweig ein Morgen durchsieht der schon ganz / im Frühling ist]."[32] Similarly, Pablo Neruda in his poem "Spring [La Primavera]" describes a bird trill with metaphors of water and light: "And between water and light that unroll the air / now the spring is inaugurated . . . [Y entre agua y luz el aire desarrollan / ya está la primavera inaugurada]."[33]

Although every being has its own relationship to natural time and every region is distinctive,[34] the diverse phenomena of the seasons are not a disconnected plurality but a choir or polyphony. The frozen river melts in response to the force of warmth. Although ice is actually less dense than the fluid state of water (when it freezes, as noted above, the water molecules form hexagonal crystals), warmth is generally an expansive force; this is clear, for instance, in its general role in altering the states of matter. With regard to ice, the warmth makes it melt, and the water thereby becomes softer and more mobile, even though it is not less dense. The previously inactive vegetation expands out of the seeds and the buds. With the fresh green and the unfolding of new blossoms, the colors of our surroundings become more varied and diverse. We naturally open our senses more. We notice the bees, butterflies, and other insects moving among the plants (moreover, there are clear resemblances, for instance, between butterfly metamorphosis and plant metamorphosis, and close connections in that caterpillars feed on leaves and butterflies feed on nectar from flowers; a key difference is that the entire organism of the butterfly undergoes transformation, whereas a plant maintains its earlier stages). As the ice melts in the river the ducks also grow frisky, as though the warmth were also thawing their desires, making them flow again. Many more animals are seen and heard. They grow more active, begin mating; we notice the birds and squirrels chasing each other. Not dissimilar to the animals, human desires can also be stirred in the spring. Even poets who have taken an unfavorable look at this traditionally most cherished of seasons associate spring with desire. Thus, T. S. Eliot's *The Wasteland* begins with the words (which allude to lines from Chaucer's *The Canterbury Tales*)[35]: "April is the cruellest month, breeding / Lilacs out of the dead land, mixing / Memory and desire, stirring / Dull roots with spring rain."[36]

The warmth against our skins makes our surroundings seem friendlier; the opposition between our natural body warmth and the environing air becomes less distinct. Similar to the manner in which the new colors draw our gaze outward, the aroma of blossoms invites us to partake in the surroundings. We leave interior spaces, both literally and affectively. As the days grow longer and warmer, more people are seen outdoors, in the streets and parks. Our senses turn outwards, and we are surprised by the commotion in nature. We strip off layers and wear more colorful clothes. In my poem titled "Snowdrops in West Philadelphia" (which has as its main focus a time just prior to spring), a connection is drawn between human appearances and the flowers of spring in the simile, "men and women shed clothes / like petals."[37]

Often we can experience a tension between the reserved mood of winter, to which we have become accustomed, and the eruption of spring (this in itself shows that moods are not solely subjective responses to a moodless environment; this kind of discrepancy between a personal affective state and an environmental atmosphere is also used by Böhme as evidence for his "quasi-objective" view of atmospheres).[38] One can feel overwhelmed by the "excess" of spring. My poem "Dealing with Early Spring" thematizes this tension; it contrasts a child who is already attuned to the spring with an adult speaker who still clings to a winter mood:

> . . . A clear
> plastic ball hovers a moment before
> it falls, while the boy who launched it,
> anticipating, already raises his arms.
> I keep my hands tight in my pockets
> like a boat clinging to its anchor.[39]

The boy is playing ball and is thus in a light mood that is attuned to the spring. His hands are lifted upward in an open gesture in order to catch the ball; this gesture is akin to the rising and expanding of leaves. In contrast, the adult speaker keeps his hands tight in his pockets; he clings to the security of the winter mood that contrasts with the activity and plasticity of spring. In a poem belonging to a relatively unknown sequence of poems with the fictive title, *From the Posthumous Writings of Count C. W.: A Poetry Cycle* (*Aus dem Nachlaß des Grafen C. W.: Ein Gedichtkreis*), Rilke thematizes this tension in the transition from winter into spring.[40] The poem begins by describing how a speaker watches a butterfly and suggests that the butterfly could form a bridge between human experience and the natural world. However, in the second stanza the speaker expresses a sense of feeling unworthy to participate in the gift of spring. Finally, in the third verse, the speaker lets himself merge into the spring, stating "but now you [the butterfly] have drawn the thread of my gaze / into the weave of April . . . [Doch nun hast du meines Blickes Faden / eingezogen ins Aprilgeweb]."[41] Spring is here a tapestry into which the flight of a butterfly threads the speaker's gaze. Rumi also conveys spring as a time when we become aware of the connectedness of our life with a larger life. He states (in Coleman Barks's version): "Spring, and everything outside is growing . . . Around the lip of the cup we share, these words, / *My Life Is Not Mine*."[42] The self and the outer world are joined in spring in a manner that contrasts with the solitude of winter.

In spring we are gradually taken out of ourselves, into the warmth, the light, into the increasing activity of surrounding nature. A process of extroversion begins. The outward turning of the psyche in spring, this extroversion, can be understood as a human equivalent of natural expansion, as an intensification that takes place in the human interior. Although it again thematizes early spring, I would like to consider a beautiful passage from Goethe's *Faust* that directly links the expanding of natural phenomena in spring with the moods and behavior of human beings. On a relatively warm Easter morning, Faust is walking with Wagner and describes the landscape and human beings as follows:

> . . . the Sun is hostile to whiteness
> and seeks to enliven with color the forms
> that everywhere strive to develop;
> yet the countryside still has no flowers,
> and so he takes smartly dressed people instead.
> Turn around, now we're up here,
> and look back down at the city!
> Out from the depths of its gloomy gate
> a teeming mass of color is surging—
> everyone's eager to get into the sun.
> They celebrate the resurrection of their Lord,
> for they themselves are risen;
> from wretched houses and dreary rooms,
> from the bonds of their crafts and professions,
> from the pressing weight of roof and gable,

from the narrow, cramping streets,
from their churches' night-like solemnity—
they all have been brought forth into the light. . . .

[. . . die Sonne duldet kein Weißes:
Überall regt sich Bildung und Streben,
Alles will sie mit Farben beleben;
Doch an Blumen fehlts im Revier,
Sie nimmt geputzte Menschen dafür.
Kehre dich um, von diesen Höhen
Nach der Stadt zurück zu sehen!
Aus dem hohlen, finstren Tor
Dringt ein buntes Gewimmel hervor.
Jeder sonnt sich heute so gern.
Sie feiern die Auferstehung des Herrn,
Denn sie sind selber auferstanden,
Aus niedriger Häuser dumpfen Gemächern,
Aus Handwerks- und Gewerbes-banden,
Aus dem Druck von Giebeln und Dächern,
Aus der Straßen quetschender Enge,
Aus der Kirchen ehrwürdiger Nacht
Sind sie alle ans Licht gebracht. . . .][43]

In the manner in which the sun will only later call forth colorful flowers, on this splendid Easter morning it draws colorfully clothed people outside from interior spaces. The way in which Goethe describes this scene directly corresponds to his understanding of the unfolding and expansion of plants from their hidden seeds. Although the behavior of human beings is the foregrounded theme in this passage, the scene can at the same time be understood as an image for the turn of the soul from within to without, from introversion to extroversion.

The distinctive seasons of spring and fall have a more intermediate character, while winter and summer can be regarded as two poles—the poles of contraction and expansion respectively. (These poles could also be compared to those of breathing—those of inhalation and exhalation respectively.[44]) Summer is the height of expansion. While one of Adam Zagajewski's summer poems ultimately deals with the shadow side of life, its title, "Summer's Fullness," along with descriptions such as the "purple butterflies, red admirals, and swallowtails" that are "heavy with beauty," suggest the feeling of plenitude associated with summer.[45] In his poem "Calendulas" the Australian poet Peter Boyle writes, "In summer I am a woman with five children . . ."[46] Rilke characterizes this aspect of summer in his well-known poem, "Herbsttag" or "Autumn Day." In the first line we find the statement: "the summer was very great [der Sommer war sehr groß]," encapsulating the idea of summer's expansiveness.[47] The English poet, critic, and translator Michael Hamburger also intimates a connection between summer and expansion in his poem "At Home," which begins with the lines, "Early June. In a heatwave London is loosened. / Over fences, brick walls grown lighter / Wandering tendrils play . . ."[48]

The air is hot. Especially in humid climates we almost feel as if we are swimming through the air rather than walking. A sense of boundary between our own body warmth and the warmth of our surroundings almost completely dissolves. We feel merged with the surroundings. Many of the plants and trees have already blossomed; while they had little foliage in early spring they are now replete with foliage. The fruits hanging from branches, especially large fruits, appear like symbols of the plenitude of summer in its height of expansion. In contrast to the chill wakeful clarity of winter, summer is the time of dreaming, the time in which boundaries dissolve and merge. We certainly cannot imagine Shakespeare writing "A Mid-*Winter* Night's Dream" with the same events taking place. In an article on Gernot Böhme's ecological conception of atmospheres, Kate Rigby discusses the sleepiness of summer in relation to the poem "Midsummer Noon" by the nineteenth-century Australian poet, Charles Harpur: "In keeping with the tradition of European pastoral poetry, the atmosphere attributed to this midsummer noon induces a pleasantly drowsy disposition, in which the self seems on the verge of melting into its surroundings."[49] In Harpur's poem summer herself is described as sleeping: "Tired Summer, in her forest bower / Turning with the noontide hour, Heaves a slumberous breath, ere she / Once more slumbers peacefully."[50] While as Rigby importantly points out,[51] the importation of the European four seasons (a part of the process of colonization) does not fit with regionally specific seasonal patterns in Australia and Indigenous understandings of them, there are some points of overlap between seasonal experiences in different parts of the world.[52] For example, even on a sunny day in July in Sydney (at times warmer than the temperature in London at the same time of year) when wattle trees are flowering, I have sensed an atmosphere of quietude, a wintry mood, but of a much more subtle kind than that experienced in a snowy landscape.

In this presentation of the seasons I have primarily focused on the polarity of contraction and expansion. A few other related polarities that have not yet been explicitly discussed include life and death, upward and downward movement, levity and gravity. The earliest meaning of the word *spring* refers to the rising of water from the ground (the issue of a stream), and the word is apt in conveying the upward sprouting and growing of plants in spring. The American term for autumn, *fall,* fittingly conveys the falling or downward movement of the leaves of deciduous trees. These polarities also have a strong connection to the polarities of sun and earth. When a given hemisphere is, in the course of the earth's orbit, tilted toward the sun, the days grow warmer and longer (though there is some delay in the warming and cooling of the atmosphere, known as "seasonal lag," such that the longest day or summer solstice, for instance, is not the warmest day of the year). When the sun, relatively speaking, shines more obliquely on a given hemisphere, the days become cooler and darker for longer periods. These polarities also relate to the polarity of gravity and levity. Growing plants are drawn in the direction of the sun, whereas the dying leaves fall toward the earth. Poetically speaking, growth could be regarded as the sun-like overcoming of earthly gravity. When one walks under tall trees in spring, it is possible to sense a certain levity, which contrasts with the autumnal return to the earth. It should be evident how these recurrent movements earthward and skyward are closely related to contraction and expansion. Even in Australia, where the majority of trees are evergreen, I have a sensed the autumnal mood of a return to the earth (though it is also important to reiterate the inadequacies and problems associated with the traditional European model of the four seasons in Australia).[53] My poem "Early Autumn Morning" suggests a feeling of intimacy with the surroundings, which is neither the expansiveness of summer nor the solitude of winter. The poem describes the "images" of things as "returning to their places" in contrast to the "liquid oblivion of summer" (a reference to the summer pastime in Sydney of swimming in the sea) and suggests an awareness of the surroundings that fuses the interiority of reflection with a perception of the outer world, an awareness that finds a distinctive depth in things.[54] While this mellow mood is not quite the same as that described in the well-known English poem by Keats, "To Autumn," there are some points of connection between these different experiences of autumn.[55] In the poem "The Human Seasons," which characterizes the stages of human life with the metaphor of the four seasons, Keats at the same time reveals the genuine quality of seasonal moods, referring to autumn as follows: "quiet coves / His soul has in its Autumn, when his wings / He furleth close . . ."[56]

Autumn or fall as should now be clear is the transition into a more contracted state. In response to the cool, the leaves of trees begin to decay and fall, annual plants slowly wither and die. In the falling of leaves to the earth and the contracted state of living forms, we find the opposite gesture to the expansion and vertical tendency toward the sun that are characteristic of spring and summer. Once all the leaves have fallen only the contracted buds remain. We feel the cool against our skin and have the sense that we are beginning to detach from our surroundings and return to a more distinct awareness of ourselves. Autumn is the beginning of a more interior time, a contracted or introverted time, but one that is still more expansive than the winter. This can be felt as a time of increasing solitude. In "Autumn Day [Herbsttag]" Rilke says: "Whoever is alone now will remain so for a long time, / will stay awake, read, write long letters / and restlessly wander the avenues / back and forth, when the leaves blow [Wer jetzt kein Haus hat baut sich keines mehr. / Wer jetzt allein ist wird es lange bleiben, / wird wachen, lesen, lange Briefe schreiben / und wird in den Alleen hin und her / unruhig wandern, wenn die Blätter treiben]."[57] Autumn is the gradual return to a more interior state; in an unpublished autumn poem I have written that "the earth remembers / it has a soul."

Conclusion

The appearance of seasons varies greatly in different regions and is inextricable from the specific contexts of climate, ecology, topography, and local plant and animal life. It should also be mentioned that climate change is upsetting seasonal patterns.[58] Here I have sought to offer a typical or idealized picture of the differentiated experience of the four seasons in certain temperate regions. Obviously, this particular picture is limited and only touches on a few seasonal phenomena. However, this typifying presentation should not be taken as a static stereotype but rather as a "sensible idea" that can be creatively adapted and applied. My proposition is that the notions of "sensible ideas," the polarity of "contraction and expansion," "intensification" (or a related notion that enables a perception of a non-reductive continuity in nature), and "seasonal moods," if they are seized in a plastic and poetic manner, could benefit an understanding and perception of the seasons in specific regions. Moreover, this approach can foster a deeper awareness of our participation in natural time. Every being has a special relationship to the seasons. The arrival of swifts in central Europe announces the coming summer, and their departure to Africa signals that the summer is almost over. Similarly, the yellow appearance of buttercups in garden beds in the northeastern United States signifies the beginning of spring. Every being is a riddle and has its distinctive connection to the seasons. This means that every being that we observe can open up a new perspective and diversify our understanding. However, the plurality is not a mere multiplicity, rather it is a choir or symphony, a fugal unfolding of many voices.[59] This plurality manifests a sensible idea, an idea in which our seasonal moods also take part (as much as the mood of a piece of music belongs to the music) and of which they are an expression. It is apt to bring this essay full circle and to end with the words from Goethe's poem "Epirrhema" quoted in the epigraph: "In observing nature you must / Always attend to one and all. / Nothing is inside, nothing outside: / For what is within that is without. . . ."[60]

Notes

1. Johann Wolfgang von Goethe, *Sämtliche Werke nach Epochen seines Schaffens: Zur Naturwissenschaft überhaupt, besonders zur Morphologie*, vol. 12, ed. Karl Richter et al. (Munich: Carl Hanser Verlag, 1989), 92.

2. While there is some overlap between the experience of the seasons in Sydney and in these places in the Northern Hemisphere, there are significant differences, such that the European model of the four seasons is highly problematic in Sydney and other regions of Australia. The "winters" in Sydney are mild, most of the flora is evergreen, there are plants that flower at every time of year, the differences between seasons are generally more subtle, Aboriginal cultures divide the year differently, etc. See Deborah Bird Rose, "Rhythms, Patterns, Connectivities: Indigenous Concepts of Seasons and Change, Victoria River District, NT," in *A Change in the Weather: Climate and Culture in Australia*, ed. T. Griffiths and L. Robin, 32–41 (Canberra: National Museum of Australia, 2005); Deborah Bird Rose, "Arts of Flow: Poetics of 'Fit' in Aboriginal Australia," *Dialectical Anthropology* 38, no. 4 (2014): 431–445. See also the essays by John Charles Ryan, Rod Giblett, and Tom Bristow in the present volume.

3. See, for example, Luke Fischer, *The Poet as Phenomenologist: Rilke and the "New Poems"* (New York: Bloomsbury, 2015).

4. See the Introduction to the present volume.

5. Max Scheler, *Wesen und Formen der Sympathie*, ed. Manfred S. Frings (Bern: Francke Verlag, 1973). Martin Heidegger, *Sein und Zeit, Gesamtausgabe*, vol. 2, ed. F. W. von Herrmann (Frankfurt am Main: Vittorio Klostermann, 1977), 130ff.

6. Gernot Böhme, *Anmutungen: Über das Atmosphärische* (Ostfildern vor Stuttgart: Edition Tertium Arcaden, 1998), 8ff.

7. Böhme, *Anmutungen*, 7ff.

8. Paola-Ludovika Coriando,. 2002. *Affektenlehre und Phänomenologie der Stimmungen: Wege einer Ontologie und Ethik des Emotionalen.* Frankfurt am Main: Vittorio Klostermann, 2002), 187ff. See also Coriando's essay in the present volume.

9. Coriando, *Affektenlehre und Phänomenologie der Stimmungen,* 205.

10. Maurice Merleau-Ponty, *The Visible and the Invisible,* ed. Claude Lefort, trans. Alphonso Lingis (Evanston, IL: Northwestern University Press, 1968), 151.

11. Merleau-Ponty, *The Visible and the Invisible,* 149.

12. Maurice Merleau-Ponty, *Nature: Course Notes from the Collège de France,* trans. Robert Vallier (Evanston, IL: Northwestern University Press, 2003), 174.

13. Maurice Merleau-Ponty, *Phenomenology of Perception,* trans. Colin Smith (London: Routledge Classics, 2002), 327–328.

14. It is perhaps worthwhile to state that the purpose of this essay is not to give an accurate or orthodox account of Merleau-Ponty's notion of "sensible ideas"; the purpose is to apply this notion in a creative and illuminating way to the seasons.

15. There are, however, indirect influences by way of the work of the zoologist Jakob von Uexküll, who drew on Goethe and was an important source for Merleau-Ponty's philosophical reflections on nature. Merleau-Ponty was also influenced by Schelling, whose views of nature shared much in common with, and were influenced by, Goethe. See Dalia Nassar, *The Romantic Absolute: Being and Knowing in Early German Romantic Philosophy, 1795–1804* (Chicago: The University of Chicago Press, 2013) and Frederick Amrine, "The Music of the Organism: Uexküll, Merleau-Ponty, Zuckerkandl, and Deleuze as Goethean Ecologists in Search of a New Paradigm." *Goethe Yearbook* 21 (2015): 45–72.

16. See, for example, Gernot Böhme and Gregor Schiemann, eds., *Phänomenologie der Natur* (Frankfurt am Main: Suhrkamp, 1997); David Seamon and Arthur Zajonc, eds., *Goethe's Way of Science: A Phenomenology of Nature* (Albany: State University of New York Press, 1998); Henri Bortoft, *The Wholeness of Nature: Goethe's Way Toward a Conscious Participation in Nature* (Great Barrington, MA: Lindisfarne Books, 1996); Iris Hennigfeld, "Goethe's Phenomenological Way of Thinking and the Urphänomen," *Goethe Yearbook* 22 (2015): 143–168. On Goethe's significance for environmental thought and ecocriticism, see Luke Fischer and Dalia Nassar, "Introduction: Goethe and Environmentalism," special section of the *Goethe Yearbook* 22 (2015): 3–22.

17. Goethe, *Sämtliche Werke nach Epochen seines Schaffens: Briefwechsel zwischen Schiller und Goethe in den Jahren 1794 bis 1805,* vol. 8.1, ed. Karl Richter et al. (Munich: Carl Hanser Verlag, 1990), 492, 499. Goethe, *Sämtliche Werke nach Epochen seines Schaffens: Wilhelm Meisters Wanderjahre: Maximen und Reflexionen,* vol. 17, ed. Karl Richter et al. (Munich: Carl Hanser Verlag, 1991), 792. Goethe, *Sprüche in Prosa: Sämtliche Maximen und Reflexionen,* ed. Harald Ficke (Frankfurt am Main: Insel Verlag, 2005), 223–224.

18. Goethe's most pithy formulation of this view is in his maxim that includes the advice that one should "seek nothing behind the phenomena, they themselves

are the teaching [or theory] [Man suche nur nichts hinter den Phänomenen, sie selbst sind die Lehre]" (*Sämtliche Werke*, vol. 17, 824).

19. Goethe, *Theory of Colours*, trans. Charles Lock Eastlake (Cambridge, MA: The M.I.T. Press, 1970), xvii.

20. I mention this distinction because beyond philosophical circles that are familiar with German idealism, it is still not uncommon to encounter the misconception that all forms of idealism imply a kind of subjectivism, such as that attributed to Berkeley or Fichte. For an overview of various kinds of idealism, see Frederick Beiser, *German Idealism: The Struggle against Subjectivism, 1781–1801* (Cambridge, MA: Harvard University Press, 2002). For an excellent account of Goethe's place within German idealism, see Eckart Förster, *The Twenty-Five Years of Philosophy: A Systematic Reconstruction*, trans. Brady Bowman (Cambridge, MA: Harvard University Press, 2012).

21. Schiller, and other philosophical contemporaries, influenced Goethe to develop his thought in a more idealist direction, but an idealism that emphasized the importance of an empirical methodology and objectivity. Goethe's view of sensible ideas at the commencement of his friendship with Schiller was still relatively naïve according to his own recollection in "Fortunate Encounter." Goethe, *Sämtliche Werke*, vol. 12, 12:88–89. See Luke Fischer, "Goethe contra Hegel: The Question of the End of Art," *Goethe Yearbook* 18 (2011), 130.

22. Elsewhere I have explicated similar continuities by taking Goethe's understanding of plant metamorphosis as an exemplary model. On the continuity between nature and art, for example, see Fischer, "Goethe contra Hegel": 127–157.

23. Goethe, *Sämtliche Werke*, vol. 12, 29–68.

24. Goethe, *Sämtliche Werke*, vol. 12, 67.

25. Herman Melville, *Moby-Dick, or The Whale* (Evanston, IL: Northwestern University Press, 1988), 54.

26. Luke Fischer, *A Personal History of Vision* (Crawley: University of Western Australia Publishing, 2017), 82.

27. David Macauley, *Elemental Philosophy: Earth, Air, Fire, and Water as Environmental Ideas* (Albany: State University of New York Press, 2010), 285.

28. Coriando, *Affektenlehre und Phänomenologie der Stimmungen*, 187ff. Gernot Böhme, *Aisthetik: Vorlesungen über Ästhetik als allgemeine Wahrnehmungslehre* (Munich: Wilhelm Fink Verlag. 2001), 48ff. See also Coriando's essay in the present volume. In that ancient and medieval humoral theory identified deep correspondences between affective predispositions (humors or temperaments), the elements, and the seasons, it is also relevant in this respect. See the Introduction to the present volume.

29. Wallace Stevens, *The Palm at the End of the Mind: Selected Poems and a Play* (New York: Vintage Books, 1990), 54.

30. Luke Fischer, *Paths of Flight* (North Fitzroy, VIC: Black Pepper, 2013), 3.

31. *The Bible: Authorized King James Version* (Oxford: Oxford University Press, 2008), John 14:2, 136.

32. Rilke, Rainer Maria, *Werke: Kommentierte Ausgabe in vier Bänden: Gedichte 1895 bis 1910*, vol. 1, ed. Manfred Engel et al. (Frankfurt am Main: Insel Verlag, 1996), 449 (unless indicated otherwise, all translations from the German in this essay are my own).

33. Pablo Neruda, *Full Woman, Fleshly Apple, Hot Moon: Selected Poems of Pablo Neruda*, trans. Stephen Mitchell (New York: HarperCollins, 1998), 241.

34. See, for example, Craig Holdrege's essay in the present volume on the unique seasonal expressions of one plant species, *Symplocarpus foetidus* (commonly known as skunk cabbage).

35. See the discussion of Chaucer's *Canterbury Tales* in the Introduction to the present volume.

36. T. S. Eliot, *The Complete Poems and Plays* (London: Faber & Faber, 1969), 61.

37. Fischer, *Paths of Flight*, 4.

38. Böhme, *Aisthetik*, 48–49.

39. Fischer, *Paths of Flight*, 5.

40. Rilke, *Werke: Kommentierte Ausgabe in vier Bänden: Gedichte 1910 bis 1926*, vol. 2., ed. Manfred Engel et al. (Frankfurt am Main: Insel Verlag, 1996) 178–179.

41. Rilke, *Werke*, vol. 2, 179.

42. Rumi, *The Essential Rumi*, trans. Coleman Barks (London: Penguin Books, 1995), 41.

43. Goethe, *Faust 1 & 2*, trans. Stuart Atkins (Princeton, NJ: Princeton University Press, 1994), 26.

44. The philosopher and Goethe scholar Rudolf Steiner draws a strong analogy between the breathing process and the cycle of the seasons in his lecture series titled, *The Cycle of the Year as Breathing Process of the Earth* [*Der Jahreskreislauf als Atmungsvorgang der Erde und die vier grossen Festeszeiten*], trans. Barbara E. Betteridge and Frances E. Dawson (Great Barrington, MA: Steiner Books, 1988). Steiner devoted a number of lecture series (subsequently published) to the theme of the seasons and the earth as a living being. These accounts have also influenced my own approach to the seasons.

45. Adam Zagajewski, *Selected Poems*, trans. Clare Cavanagh et al. (London: Faber & Faber, 2004), 144.

46. Peter Boyle, *Towns in the Great Desert: New & Selected Poems* (Glebe, NSW: Puncher & Wattmann, 2013), 30.

47. Rilke, *Werke*, vol. 1, 281.

48. Michael Hamburger, *Collected Poems: 1941–1994* (London: Anvil Press Poetry, 1995), 319.

49. Kate Rigby, "Gernot Böhme's Ecological Aesthetics of Atmosphere," in *Ecocritical Theory: New European Approaches*, ed. Axel Goodbody and Kate Rigby, 139–152. Charlottesville: University of Virginia Press, 2011), 148.

50. Quoted in Rigby, "Gernot Böhme's Ecological Aesthetics of Atmosphere," 148.

51. Rigby, "Gernot Böhme's Ecological Aesthetics of Atmosphere," 149. See also the essays by Rod Giblett and John Charles Ryan in the present volume.

52. In the interest of cross-cultural and cross-regional understanding, I think it is important to keep in view the great diversity and variation across regions and cultures as well as the unity of the earth.

53. See Note 2.

54. Fischer, *Paths of Flight*, 64.

55. However, there are many differences. Most of "autumn" in Sydney, just to mention a difference in climate, is similar in temperature to summer in England.

56. John Keats, *Complete Poems and Selected Letters of John Keats* (New York: Random House, 2001), 305.

57. Rilke, *Werke*, vol. 1, 281.

58. An increased awareness of our participation in the seasons, along the lines that I have suggested in this essay, would also contribute to a heightened sense of the meaning and consequences of the destruction of these patterns. In his essay in the present volume (and elsewhere) Rod Giblett argues that a thematization of the seasons can facilitate a better understanding of climate change and proposes "seasonal dislocation" and "seasonal disruption" as better designations than "climate change." See also the Introduction.

59. The formulation of a "fugal unfolding" is indebted to John Charles Ryan's related expression of a "fugue-like progression" in his essay in the present volume. Coriando's essay also suggests a similar notion in her employment of several words that are cognate with the German *Fuge*.

60. Goethe, *Sämtliche Werke*, vol. 12, 92.

4

Hölderlin, Heidegger, and Seasonal Time

PAOLA-LUDOVIKA CORIANDO

(Translated by Luke Fischer)

The Possibility of a Phenomenology of the Seasons

THE SEASONS AS A HISTORICALLY DETERMINED PHENOMENON OF HUMAN EXISTENCE AND A-THEORETICAL THINKING

No less than other living beings, we humans are exposed to the cyclical transformations of nature. The rhythms of nature that we call seasons are not merely a phenomenon that unfolds outside of us, rather they belong to the fundamental experiences of human existence. Since time immemorial, the course and return of the seasons have also been attributed symbolic meanings that discern in the seasons a correspondence to the phases of life in the cycle of birth and death.

For contemporary Westernized city-dwellers, the rhythm of the seasons has, however, largely lost its original valency. To be sure, we dress differently in winter than in summer; we look forward to the first warm days of spring; and we bemoan the too-cold summer or the early incursion of winter. Nevertheless, many of the meanings that the course of the seasons held in the lives of earlier generations are gone for us today.

Whether the progress of the sciences and the—allegedly or actually—"improved living conditions" in our Western world can compensate for this ontological loss [*Wesensverlust*],[1] is more than questionable. From a philosophical viewpoint, this progressive distancing from nature and her[2] rhythms is not, however, especially strange. Western philosophy, in its long history, has barely thematized the phenomenon of the seasons—a fact that should not be regarded as a mere omission, but rather as an essential consequence of its historical development. If we look back on this history, then we discover the reasons for the neglect of this elementary phenomenon of existence. Moreover, we also discover the fundamental decisions that directed our particular technological development and, as a consequence, led to an increasing estrangement of humanity from nature and her rhythms.

Classical Western philosophy has conceived itself since Plato and Aristotle—and in an intensified manner since the early-modern rationalist turn—as *theoria*, as rational-objectifying contemplation of fundamental and universally valid structures. The primacy of this "theoretical attitude" had the consequence that the basic phenomena of *everyday life* were largely excluded from the thematic scope of philosophy. The priority of the theoretical attitude had the further consequence that the *historical transformation* [*geschichtliche Wandel*] of our relations to the world and to nature was either dismissed as a merely accidental phenomenon or—as has mostly been the case—interpreted in terms of a linear conception of progress. Neither the phenomenon of the seasons as such nor its historical transformation have ever found admittance into the horizon of classical philosophy.

Within the modern Western interpretative paradigm, the human being is distinguished as the entity that possesses rationality, and, as such, is entitled to reign over other living beings and over the whole of nature. The progressive technological manipulation of nature is an essential consequence of the fact that humanity, distinguished by the possession of understanding and reason, conceives itself as an *absolute exception* among living beings. While the enormous advances in the sciences have brought about indisputably positive developments, we should not be deceived about their other side. Out of life-fostering possibilities there increasingly developed a limitless drive to realize evermore far-reaching manipulations, which today raise substantial ethical as well as ontological questions.

As a result of the end of the great metaphysical—as well as the post-Kantian-idealist—systems, a rupture in the modern self-understanding of humanity became apparent. It is a rupture that—for example, in Nietzsche and Kierkegaard—provided the basis for an orientation toward the (historical) phenomenon of human existence. It was not until Heidegger, however, that the overcoming of the classical—and above all, the modern—conception of the human being as subject and *res cogitans* was fundamentally and systematically elaborated. In the concepts of *Da-sein*[3] and *existence* [*Existenz*], a fundamentally new determination of the essence [*Wesen*] of humanity and being is evinced, which facilitates a transformation in the self-understanding of philosophy.[4] In conjunction with the overcoming of the centrality of reason and understanding [*Vernunft und Verstand*]—more specifically, their re-grounding in the original dimension of *Dasein* and the disclosedness of being in general—Heidegger, already in his early lectures, connects the project of philosophy as a pre-theoretical or a-theoretical "primal-science" [*"Urwissenschaft"*] of factual life with the project of philosophy conceived and carried out as a hermeneutic-phenomenological ontology.[5] In this new program "everyday" human life and, along with it, foundational existential experiences such as the alternation and return of the seasons acquire the dignity of an *ontologically questionable* phenomenon.

Beyond these fundamental conditions, it is above all Heidegger's understanding of *temporality* that assumes an eminent significance for the disclosure of this phenomenon. The elaboration of a hermeneutics of facticity into a fundamental ontology of Da-sein in *Being and Time* entails,[6] as is well known, that the essence of time is no longer sought in the objective time of "present" [*"vorhandenen"*] nature—nor in the time of consciousness in its various iterations, for example, in Kant, Husserl, or life-philosophies—but rather in the *temporal-ecstasies of Da-sein* and their corresponding *temporality of being*.[7] If Da-sein is conceived as an originally "temporalizing"—rather than as a merely "temporally immanent"—being, then an immensely significant path comes into view for a hermeneutic-phenomenological approach to the seasons. The course and alternation of the seasons no longer, so to speak, confront a timeless, "substantial" soul as mere "accidents," but rather themselves belong to the essential fabric of existence and to the ecstatic temporality of Da-sein.

Moreover, the *onto-historical* [seinsgeschichtlichen] *course of the question of being* opens up a further horizon that enables a philosophical disclosure of our contemporary engagement with nature—an "engagement" [*"Umgang"*] that must be situated within the essencing [*Wesung*] of being as "machination."[8]

THE SEASONS AND MACHINATION AS THE FUNDAMENTAL FEATURE OF BEING

In Heidegger's thinking of the history of being, time is no longer conceived merely as the executed temporality of Dasein that in each case belongs to me [*"jemeinig"*], but rather as the *historical time* (as the time-play-space) of the event-of-appropriation [*Ereignis*].[9] "Our" time reveals itself as the epoch of the transition from the "first" metaphysical beginning to the "other" beginning. It is a time of "need," a need that shows itself in the lack of a supporting ground, the need of an "abyss" [*"Ab-grundes"*] which calls for the "founding" of a transformed relation between humanity and being—a transformed Da-sein.

In our epoch, according to Heidegger, the consequences of the modern-metaphysical conception of the human being as subject with its corresponding determination of being as universal objectivity [*Gegenständlich-keit*] have intensified immeasurably. Beings are now only encountered as "manipulable" objects [*"Machbares"*], which urge the realization of ever new possibilities. Everything, including human beings, is disclosed and projected within the horizon and the fundamental mood [*Grundstimmung*] of technological manipulation, of programmable alteration and "improvement." The fundamental feature and the fundamental mood of machination are not solely "manufactured" [*"gemacht"*] by humans and cannot be overcome by humans alone. For machination is the event-of-appropriation itself,[10] the event-of-appropriation in its fundamental structure as appropriating projection [*Zuwurf*] of being and appropriative project [*Entwurf*] of Da-sein—the event-of-appropriation in its epochal-historical essencing as "expropriation" (as the self-withholding event-of-appropriation).[11]

The supremacy of "machination" also shapes, without a doubt, the predominating engagement with nature and her times or seasons. In the post-industrial world, the seasons tend to be neutralized. There is a striving for the greatest possible independence of humans from nature and thereby—whether consciously or not—for a uniformity of life, in which everything is simultaneously accessible and utilizable. The universal availability [*Vorhandenheit*] and usability of raw materials and natural products appears as the leading goal. The fact that climate change and severe weather plunge us increasingly into incomprehension and elicit clumsy attempts at a planetarily operated damage control is a sign that we are far from overcoming machination as the fundamental feature of being. Individuals can, to be sure, with good will resist the progressive destruction of the earth, rediscover lost values of life, and endeavor to foster a transformed relationship to nature—and yet this attempt on the part of individuals remains historically isolated; it is not able to become "historically-founding."

What proposed solutions does the thinking of the history of being offer? Certainly no immediate ones. As long as—in Heidegger's language—no transformed "truth" of being shows itself and is historically grounded,[12] there is only the possibility of the *preparation* of a transformation, which the human being cannot forcefully effect through his own power, but can indeed fore-think and fore-know [*vor-denken und vor-erfahren*]. Above all in his conversation with poetry, Heidegger sought and found "hints" [*"Winke"*], which in the midst of machination help to prepare a free space for this transformation. In particular, Hölderlin accompanied and inspired the development of Heidegger's thinking of the history of being and his later conception of the fourfold. For Heidegger, Hölderlin is the "most futural" poet because he experiences our epoch as the age of the "flight of the gods" and fore-poetizes [*vordichtet*] a possible new return.[13] Hölderlin thereby *poetically* opens up the time-play-space [*Zeit-spiel-raum*] of transition, which also pertains to Heidegger's contemplative *thinking*. Hölderlin is, moreover, the poet who sings the co-belongingness of human beings and nature—and, more specifically, the poet who in the nearly forty years of his mysterious "derangement" [*"Umnachtung"*] almost exclusively poetized the course and return of the seasons.

The Simplicity of the Year: Hölderlin, Heidegger, and the World as Fourfold

On the Conversation between Thinking and Poetizing

In Western cultural history, poetry and philosophy proceed, for the most part, in parallel with one another and, despite occasional points of contact, remain strictly distinguished. Philosophy concerns itself with the rationally disclosable structures of reality, whereas poetry emphasizes the particular and transfigures it in the poetic image. Philosophy strives for the emotionally neutral objectivity of knowledge, while poetry depends on subjective feelings and is unconcerned with truth and knowledge. That the course and return of the seasons has always been a theme of poetry, but not of philosophy, is—from a traditional philosophical standpoint—almost a matter of self-evidence.

By contrast, in the onto-historical horizon of Da-sein, thinking and poetizing abide in an essential nearness to one another, which enables a fundamental conversation. It is this essential relation that Heidegger has in mind in his articulation of the "subtle [*zarten*] but lucid difference."[14] The a-theoretical and hermeneutic-phenomenological way of thinking—which essentially inhabits a fundamental mood—and poetizing—freed from the status of a mere "cultural manifestation"—are coequal in that they are conceived as original, truth-disclosing sources of relations between humanity and the world, and between humanity and being. Their difference is not sharp, rather it is subtle. It is nevertheless a lucid difference because thinking and poetizing respectively convey the *same* phenomena *differently* in language. Heidegger adheres even in his late thinking to the—no longer metaphysically determined—distinction between the poetic image and the noetic concept [*dichterischem Bild und denkerischem Begriff*]: a distinction that would require its own elucidation (not to be carried out here), but that will become immediately apparent as soon as we consider Hölderlin's poems and Heidegger's thinking of the fourfold.

The Seasons in Hölderlin's "Latest" Poems

The co-belongingness [*Zusammengehörigkeit*] of "humanity" and "nature" is already poetized in Hölderlin's great hymns and elegies from the years 1799–1805. In "As on a Holiday . . ." [*"Wie wenn am Feiertage . . ."*] Hölderlin poetizes the essence of nature as the realm of the holy, which embraces and "in-spirits" [*"be-geistert"*] all oppositions.[15] "Omnipresent" [*"allgegenwärtige"*] nature allows the encounter between humans and gods. Yet in the time of the "flight of the gods" this co-belongingness is shaped by the fundamental mood of *holy mourning* for the withdrawal of the divine.[16] Nature reveals itself as the place of a *denied harmony* between humans and the divine: "the heart's love" laments *with* the "native waters" [*"heimatlichen Wassern"*].[17] This gathering in mourning is a determinate historical-epochal manner of "harmony" [*"Einklangs"*], of companionship and affiliation between humanity and nature. Nevertheless, this harmony is determined by an internal disunity—by, as it were, an internal discordance [*"Ver-stimmung"*]. The gods remain distant.

In contrast, the so-called "latest" poems, which we can also designate as seasonal poems, speak of a "complete" [*"vollkommenen"*] harmony, of a fulfilled companionship [*Mitgehen*] of humans with nature and her times.[18] The basic experience of these poems is the circularity of nature in the alternation and return of the seasons: their self-announcements, their transition and vanishing, their colors and moods, which appear to abide in perfected concord with human life. Out of the forty-seven texts stemming from the period from 1806 until 1843, twenty-two are titled with the name of a season. Other titles designate friendship, love, birth, and death, humanity, life, the good, contentment, the zeitgeist, prospect, and Greece.

The seasonal poems stem from the time of Hölderlin's "derangement." In many quarters these texts have, therefore, been interpreted as a sign of Hölderlin's mental illness. In this connection, the simplicity and monotony of the themes, the stereotypes and uniformity of the figurative structure, the repeatedly extolled and evoked harmony, appear as the poet's therapeutic attempt to counter the progressive dissolution of his mental vigor. In truth, however, an original experience of nature and her times is concealed in these poems, which cannot be entirely traced back to psychological factors. Irrespective of their psychological-biographical situatedness, these texts are among the deepest poetic disclosures of the co-belongingness of humanity and nature.[19]

As is already the case in the hymns and elegies, in the latest poems humanity and nature are not opposed as two separate realms, rather they dispositionally [*Stimmungsmäßig*] belong to one another. But in these, it is in the seasons that this co-belongingness is attested. The temporality of nature and the temporality of humanity correspond to one another and are originally safeguarded in the poetic image. This sense is rendered in lines of one of the spring poems:

> The adornment of nature appears to the heart,
> As if arisen are lyric and songs.[20]

> Die Zierde der Natur erscheint sich dem Gemüte,
> Als wie entstanden sind Gesang und Lieder.

Here the "adornment of nature" and the "heart" [*"Gemüt"*] name the relational whole of the correspondence between humanity and nature. The "self-appearing" [*"Sich-erscheinen"*] of nature is her essence, the *"nasci"* of nature—*physis*, which manifests in the irrepressible emergence of spring as well as in the darkness of autumnal decay, in the bright fullness of summer and in the self-enclosure of wintery nature. The adornment of nature is, depending on the specific time, that which emerges and self-encloses, and in its "current" appearance always carries the whole of the yearly cycle with it. That which at any time "most purely appears"—the current time of year—is latent with the other seasons and yet appears in its resplendence as the *ekfanestaton*, as the prevailing of the beautiful. Hölderlin also names the adornment of nature, "the gleaming" [*"das Glänzen"*] and the "splendor" [*"Pracht"*]:

The gleaming of nature is higher appearance,
When the day ends with many joys,
It is the year that culminates in splendor . . .[21]

Das Glänzen der Natur ist höheres Erscheinen,
Wo sich der Tag mit vielen Freuden endet,
Es ist das Jahr, das sich mit Pracht vollendet . . .

The gleaming of nature is her gathering and her respective dispersing in the seasons. In that she shows herself differently in her respective "times," nature at the same time "complements" ["ergänzt"] her current appearance. She keeps the plurality gathered and joined in an underlying simplicity, such that we are always already temporally extended and joined into the whole of the yearly cycle.

That nature complements the image of times,
That she abides, they quickly glide by,
Is out of perfection, the heaven's height
Then gleams on humans, as blossoms garland trees.[22]

Daß die Natur ergänzt das Bild der Zeiten,
Daß die verweilt, sie schnell vorübergleiten,
Ist aus Vollkommenheit, des Himmels Höhe glänzet
Den Menschen dann, wie Bäume Blüt' umkränzet.

The circulation of the seasons reveals the constantly regenerative essence of nature, which holds within it beginning and end. The alternation of seasons is "out of perfection"—the alternation is unneedy, the "holiness" of the yearly cycle in its original temporality. In a late text Heidegger elucidates these lines as follows:

The plurality of images in the plurality of seasons is pervaded by the simplicity of the year. The gleaming of nature lets the course of the seasons appear. The gleaming of nature is not a condition, rather it is a happening. In the course [Gang] of the seasons the year completes itself. But this course does not consist in the mere succession of times. Rather, in each season there appears an anticipative and anterior reference to the other seasons, in that they interchange. The gleaming of nature is an appearance, in which the whole of the year always already shines through and thus always precedes the particular times.[23]

Each current appearance of nature gifts the "heart"—"as if arisen are lyric and songs." Lyric and songs here name the poetic submission [Sichfügen] to the rhythm of nature, the poetic not merely in the sense of poesy, but rather in the far more encompassing meaning of the lines: "full of merit, yet poetically / the human being dwells on this earth,"[24] which consider the human being as an originally poetic being.

Hölderlin calls the realm of the co-belonging of humanity—as a poetically dwelling being—and nature, the image:

> The whole meaning of the lucid image lives
> As an image surrounded by golden splendor.[25]

> Der ganze Sinn des hellen Bildes lebet
> Als wie ein Bild, das goldne Pracht umschwebet.

The poetic image—the images in poetry, but beforehand, the poetic existence of the human as human—"complements" or "completes" ["er-gänzt"] each current time of year, as it lets the whole of the yearly cycle be co-present in it. In winter, the human being "knows" of the forthcoming new beginning; in spring the splendor of summer is preparing itself, but also—more distantly and hidden—the autumnal end and the winterly calm that allows a new beginning to grow within it. In that each season lets the whole temporality of the yearly cycle be co-present, it appears as brighter and "holier" in its current being [Wesen]. The "image" is the harmony experienced in poetic existence, the harmony of the temporality of humanity and the temporality of nature. In related contexts, Hölderlin also speaks of the "innerness of the world":

> Often the innerness of the world seems clouded over,
> The human mind full of doubts, morose,
> Splendid nature brightens up the days,
> And distant is doubt's dark question.[26]

> Oft scheint die Innerheit der Welt umwölkt verschlossen,
> Des Menschen Sinn von Zweifeln voll, verdrossen,
> Die prächtige Natur erheitert seine Tage,
> Und ferne steht des Zweifels dunkle Frage.

The innerness of the world is, as it were, the source of the co-belonging of humanity and nature. It is the "unsayable" center, with regard to which the "monotony" of the simple saying is "transparent." The innerness of the world is the heart of the completed year of nature, of the ever-returning cycle, which in the plurality or multiplicity [*Vielfalt*] of times unfolds [*auseinanderfaltet*] and yet remains folded [*eingefaltet*] within the simplicity [*Einfalt*] of the origin. The simplicity of the origin is itself unsayable—just as in life we can never experience the simultaneity of the seasons, although we carry within us the knowledge of the cycle and return. The simplicity of the origin cannot be brought to immediate expression. Therefore, saying itself becomes a cycle or circle. Just as nature shows herself (in the manifold of the current season) and simultaneously (as a whole and simple origin) hides herself, so saying circles around the simplicity of the origin and nevertheless remains a step behind. "However simple the images are, they are so holy that one often genuinely fears to describe them."[27]

In the "simple saying" the poetic essence of the human being expressly yields [*fügt sich*] to the temporality of appearance, ex-tends [*ent-grenzt*] itself to this temporality and thereby incorporates it. Poetic existence—and with a particular emphasis the poet himself—expressly and originally submits itself to the yearly cycle and its times by letting the whole of the yearly cycle—the end in the beginning and the beginning in the end—work and grow within it. Here Hölderlin explicitly maintains an understanding of temporality that strongly calls to mind Heidegger's conception of the ecstatic temporality of Dasein and also recalls Augustine's concept of *distention animi* [extension of the soul].[28]

Hölderlin says of time:

> The sagas, which withdraw from the earth,
> Of the spirit, which was and returns,
> They turn to humanity, and much we learn
> From time, which hurriedly consumes itself.[29]

> Die Sagen, die der Erde sich entfernen,
> Vom Geiste, der gewesen ist und wiederkehret,
> Sie kehren zu der Menschheit sich, und vieles lernen
> Wir aus der Zeit, die eilends sich verzehret.

The spirit is, like the heart [*Gemüt*], an original companion of nature. One of the winter poems contemplates this as follows:

When the year is changed, and the shimmer
Of splendid nature is gone, the gleam of the season
Blossoms no longer, and more quickly
The days hurry by, which slowly also linger.

The spirit of life is varied in the times
Of living nature, various days spread
Out the gleaming, and to humans ever new being
Fittingly appears, exquisite and distinguished.[30]

Wenn sich das Jahr geändert, und der Schimmer
Der prächtigen Natur vorüber, blühet nimmer
Der Glanz der Jahreszeit, und schneller eilen
Die Tage dann vorbei, die langsam auch verweilen.

Der Geist des Lebens ist verschieden in den Zeiten
Der lebenden Natur, verschiedne Tage breiten
Das Glänzen aus, und immerneues Wesen
Erscheint den Menschen recht, vorzüglich und erlesen.

The "spirit of life" is not understanding [*Verstand*] and reason, not the *ratio*
of the *animal rationale*. It is the "poetic dwelling" of the human being, which
is not divided from "living nature," but rather transforms together with her,
accompanies her times, and—above all—does not insist on understanding
itself as an absolute exception, as separated by a chasm from nature and
other living beings. As a part of living nature, the human being learns "from
time," learns to know "time itself" in its appearance as the cycle of nature,
learns to know "true life":

Higher Humanity

The inward sense is given to humans,
That they, with recognition, choose the preferable,
It is deemed as a goal, it is true life
In which the years of life more spiritually count.[31]

Den Menschen ist der Sinn ins Innere gegeben,
Daß sie als anerkannt das Beßre wählen,
Es gilt als Ziel, es ist das wahre Leben
Von dem sich geistiger des Lebens Jahre zählen.

In the complementarity of poetic existence, the human being learns to abide originally in the appearance of nature, learns to submit [*Sichfügen*] to the yearly cycle, which contains in itself beginning and end and allows emergence "always in accord with the time." The human being learns *ex-tended remembrance* [ent-grenzte Gedächtnis]. This is the knowledge—the life-bearing presentiment [*Ahnung*]—that in the dehiscent beginning the end prepares itself and in the end another, new beginning. The beginning and end of the yearly cycle as well as the various seasons are not in this regard a "symbol" or even a "metaphor" for the beginning and end of human life and the various stations of life. Temporality of nature and temporality of humanity are in a certain sense the same, because humanity and nature are one in their co-belonging. That which we have here called "extended remembrance," suggests a certain similarity to Heidegger's thinking of "running-ahead into death."[32] However, death in this context is, for Hölderlin, not merely the end, not only the self-closure of the cycle; it is also, at the same time, the openness to the new beginning—a "shrine of the nothing"—which *essentially* contains in itself the *indication* [*Hinweis*] of a new life.[33]

If the human being has learned this original disposition, has learned to experience the essence of the human as a poetic essence, then:

The year appears with its times
As a splendor where festivities spread out.[34]

Das Jahr erscheint mit seinen Zeiten
Wie eine Pracht, wo Feste sich verbreiten.

Hölderlin's seasonal poems speak of a harmony and of learning this harmony. They not only "describe" but also contain an "ethical" demand. It is the demand authentically to take up one's own being. How can the human being become what he is? Not through reflection, not through theoretical elevation, not by way of dissociating and distinguishing himself from nature, not through the labor of action and industry ("Full of merit . . ."). The human being corresponds to his own ("poetic") essence by learning the "simple" *submission to the emergence and self-enclosing of nature.* This "poetic ethos" is Hölderlin's counter-project to that which Heidegger calls "machination." Nature and her times teach us the way toward healing. In *this* sense these texts by Hölderlin are "therapeutic," because they fore-poetize healing—a transformed self-understanding of the human being. They are therapeutic in the same sense in which Heidegger's thinking of the fourfold is therapeutic. They make present that which is *not*—not any longer, not yet—and nonetheless "is" more than the epochal sickness from which we suffer. In remembering and fore-poetizing, the present is transformed. The knowledge of the coming spring allows us to weather the winter and suffuses it with life. The poet who in "Half of Life" had poetized this lament for the summer gone by:

> Alas, where, when it's winter,
> Can I take the flowers, and where
> The sunshine,
> And shadows of the earth?
> The walls stand
> Speechless and cold, in the wind
> The weather vanes clatter.[35]

> Weh mir, wo nehm ich, wenn
> Es Winter ist, die Blumen, und wo
> Den Sonnenschein,
> Und Schatten der Erde?
> Die Mauern stehn
> Sprachlos und kalt, im Winde
> Klirren die Fahnen.

now appears to have penetrated this knowledge more deeply than ever before. The splendor of the year "presences" as *meaningfulness,* because its current time can be poetically complemented with the simplicity from which it originates. In the darkness the poet knows of the corresponding brightness. In the darkness the brightness is admittedly present in *another*—concealed—way than as the brightness itself. Nevertheless, it *is*. In this rediscovered harmony, the cycle of the year itself becomes a holy site, which is able to offer a space for "the gods."

THE SEASONS AND THE WORLD AS FOURFOLD

In his late work Heidegger thinks the world as the "fourfold," as the gathering of the four regions of worldly significance: the "earth," the "sky," "mortals," and "divinities" (designations that already in their wording strongly evoke the conversation with Hölderlin).[36] In his writings from the 1950s—above all, "Building Dwelling Thinking" and "The Thing"—Heidegger phenomenologically describes a world suffused with significance, a world in which the "meaning," the ground, no longer withdraws itself, but rather is present in things, in the life of human beings. It is a world in which nature and her times are not altered and manipulated, in which the human being does not relate "machinatingly" to nature and himself, but rather in a way that leaves open and conserves. In the world as fourfold, the essence of enframing [*Ge-stells*] is overcome.[37] It is the world of "another-beginning," which, as it were, conveys the thinking that corresponds to the world that Hölderlin sings in his latest poems. Admittedly, Heidegger also responds in these texts to our epoch in its characteristics of machination and abandonment-of-being [*Seinsverlassenheit*]. Even so, the fourfold-writings *phenomenologically describe* a world, which in the manner of a formal-indication can be designated as the world of the "other beginning." Although they might appear on a hasty reading as such, these descriptions are not "nostalgic" evocations of times past. They are rather a fore-thinking into the fulfilled event [*Ereignis*] of the co-belongingness of humanity and nature.

What is the valency of this saying? It is a saying that—like Hölderlin's poetizing—does not limit its "description" to the "is-condition," but rather phenomenologically complements it and, so to speak, transposes the "it is" into its "futural essencing" ["*zukünftige Wesung*"]. Just as in his latest poems Hölderlin poetizes a poetic ethos that is not presently available [*vorhanden*], but rather must be learned, so Heidegger thinks in the fourfold a futural being of the human and, as it were, anticipates this being. The thinking of the fourfold does not speak of a distant vision, but rather gives the world that it describes a possibility of and, right to, existence. In the midst of enframing, the fourfold "presences" as the forethought co-belonging of humanity and nature. This saying too is a "therapeutic" saying. It no longer speaks to the now, but rather to a possible future, and thus holds it before us as a summons to healing. A healing, which, in Heidegger as in Hölderlin, proceeds primarily and originally by way of a transformed relation to nature and her times.

Prospect: The Seasons— and a Transformed Understanding of Metaphysics

If we now glance back on the apparent texture of Heidegger's thinking and Hölderlin's poetizing, then the following shows itself. Hölderlin and, along with him, Heidegger understand our epoch as a time of "ontological loss"—of enframing, abandonment-of-being, machination (Heidegger) and the "flight of the gods" (Hölderlin). In our epoch, our being with nature and her times has been displaced, such that we "machinatingly" counterpose the laws of nature to ourselves. Suffering in this situation is a first indication of a possible transformation. Both the poet and the thinker move beyond a mere diagnosis by disclosing a way toward "healing." The "therapeutic" actualization of a transformed, fulfilled realization [*Wesensvollzug*] of the human being is essentially defined by the task of *learning* an "authentic" relation to nature and her times. What needs to be learned is a transformed, dispositional participation [*Sicheinlassen*] in nature and her laws. What needs to be learned is the "complemented time" [*"er-gänzte Zeit"*] of the (life)cycle of beginning and end, of birth and death.

In Heidegger, the ontological loss—including the dissociation from nature and her rhythms—is explicitly brought into connection with the development and the consequences of Western metaphysics. This should not, however, be misunderstood as a mere critique of metaphysics as such, but rather demands an "original retrieval" [*"ursprüngliche Wiederholung"*] of metaphysics. Just as metaphysics cannot, for instance, be regarded as a monolithic mass of "life-negating" impulses (Nietzsche), it would also be disastrous to reduce—and thus fundamentally misunderstand Heidegger—the basic experiences of metaphysics to their common "machinating" feature. Admittedly, metaphysics has repeatedly sought to uncover meaning in a rational—and this also means "calculating"—manner. Nevertheless, a *concealed heart* lies in the basic experiences of metaphysics, whose "original retrieval" can itself be a way toward "healing."

Metaphysics is carried by a fundamental mood of *trust* in the meaningful order of the universe. The *insufficiently* experienced "end" of metaphysics as it, for example, works on in so-called post-modernity, has robbed us of this trust and of the "complementing presentiment" [*"ergänzenden Ahnung"*]. We have lost a sense for the "earth," for the circularity of nature and also, therewith, for the divine. We—Western planetary humanity—are blindly and linearly projected toward death, whose machinatingly driven repression becomes increasingly burdensome to us. The yearly cycle that was firmly integrated with life gave human beings an experiential *indication* that death is perhaps not the absolute end—and metaphysics knew how to *interpret* this indication, even as it had to fall to the temptation to make of the dispositionally disclosed indication a (putatively) rational understanding and thus to "calculate." Just as the dimension of the pre-intellectual, dispositional access to the world remained remote to metaphysical reflection, so too did the pre-theoretical, basic experience of the seasons. Nevertheless, in the "fundamental mood of metaphysics"—a fundamental mood, which *as* a fundamental mood, of course, had to remain hidden to metaphysics itself—a "deeper" ground worked subliminally and *behind* the evident project of a purely rational disclosure of reality. It is the dispositionally experienced presage [*Vorgriff*] of a continuous nexus of beings and of a sustaining "meaningfulness," which is actually more primordial [*ursprünglicher*] than religious (Christian) experience and dispositionally founds such experience. "Waiting for spring" is a, if not *the*, basic experience of metaphysics.

Perhaps a new appropriation of metaphysics is thinkable, an appropriation that originally discloses the significance of *this* basic experience—a, so to speak, *de-theorized* and *de-intellectualized* "metaphysics," which knows of the "poetic" valency of its basic experience and abandons any claim to a final rational explanation. However, this new appropriation of metaphysics would have to overcome radically—in its very foundations—its own *self-understanding* as the "first theoretical science." Freed of the drive for *certitudo* and its strained proofs, a thus-transformed "metaphysics" could yet learn to receive from nature signs of trust and hope and thus correspond "more originally" to its own basic experience.

Is such a de-theorized metaphysics thinkable, which overcomes Western intellectualism and thus also our (literally) measure-less anthropocentrism—an anthropocentrism that is founded on the *ratio*, which presses on in the destruction of our earth? Is there perhaps—as paradoxical as this may appear!—in the "speechless" being of animals and their enigmatic companionship with nature an indication for a transformed human "dwelling" on the earth? Can the "difference" from other living beings assigned to us as humans be appropriated in a way other than the elevation of the *ratio*? Contemplation of the basic experience of the seasons could help to prepare an answer to these questions.

Notes

1. Translator's note: Coriando frequently uses (as does the late Heidegger) the German word *Wesen* as well as cognates of, and compounds including, this word. In its simultaneous connotations of "essence" and "being," it is not translatable into English. I have variously chosen "essence," "being," "ontological," etc., depending on the context.

2. Translator's note: "Nature" is a feminine noun (*die Natur*) in German. Given that there is a historical precedence for treating nature as feminine (as "she"

rather than "it") in English, I have chosen to use a feminine gender in this translation. Nevertheless, I would like to underscore that this choice deviates from English convention, in contrast to Coriando's use of the feminine, which follows standard German convention.

3. Translator's note: I have followed the convention of retaining the German *Dasein*—Heidegger's term for "human existence" (in common German it simply means "existence"). A compound of "da" (here/there) and "Sein," *Dasein* can also be construed as "being-there." Coriando often emphasizes this by hyphenating the word as *Da-sein*.

4. On the overcoming of subjectivity in Heidegger's fundamental ontology, see F.-W. v. Herrmann, *Subjekt und Dasein: Interpretationen zu "Sein und Zeit"* [second, expanded edition] (Frankfurt a. M.: Klostermann, 1985).

5. See, for example, Martin Heidegger, *Ontologie (Hermeneutik der Faktizität)* [*Ontologie: The Hermeneutics of Facticity*], *Gesamtausgabe* [henceforth *GA*], vol. 63, ed. Käte Bröcker-Oltmanns (Frankfurt a. M.: Klostermann, 1982).

6. Martin Heidegger, *Sein und Zeit* [*Being and Time*] (Tübingen: Verlag Max Niemeyer, 16th edition, 1986).

7. See Martin Heidegger, *Die Grundprobleme der Phänomenologie* [*The Basic Problems of Phenomenology*], *GA* 24, ed. F.-W. v. Herrmann (1975).

8. See Martin Heidegger, *Beiträge zur Philosophie (vom Ereignis)* [*Contributions to Philosophy*], *GA* 65, F.-W. v. Herrmann (1989). See also F.-W. v. Herrmann, *Wege ins Ereignis: Zu Heideggers "Beiträgen zur Philosophie"* (Frankfurt a. M.: Klostermann, 1994).

9. Translator's note: *Ereignis* is a key term in Heidegger's later thought. It refers to the disclosure of being as a historically determinative event and the way in which being and interpretation (or thinking) always mutually correspond to one another. Heidegger's distinctive employment of this word draws on its normal sense of "event" as well as its etymological connection to words that convey the sense of "making one's own" (*eigen* means "own") and "appropriating" (*aneignen* is "to appropriate"). In short, *Ereignis* refers to the co-appropriating event of being and thinking or the way in which being and thinking reciprocally come into relation to one another.

10. Translator's note: Heidegger uses the word "machination" (*Machenschaft*) in describing what can be indicated in less technical terms as the technological world-interpretation that characterizes modernity. Coriando and Heidegger employ various German words that are related to *machen* ("to make," "to do," etc.), including *Machenschaft*, to explicate this character of modernity.

11. Translator's note: For Heidegger, any unconcealment of being always involves, at the same time, a self-concealing of being. In the technological world-disclosure, this self-concealing character becomes especially determinative. This is what Heidegger and Coriando are pointing to in speaking of "expropriation" and "self-withholding." A rough and preliminary indication of what Heidegger is getting

at (for readers unfamiliar with Heidegger) could be expressed as follows: a key characteristic of the technological world-interpretation is its tendency to conceal the fact that it is a world-interpretation.

12. Translator's note: "Truth" is here meant in the Heideggerian sense of a revelation or unconcealment of being, rather than as the correctness of a proposition or the correspondence between a statement and reality.

13. Martin Heidegger, *Beiträge zur Philosophie*, 401.

14. Martin Heidegger, "Das Wesen der Sprache," in *Unterwegs zur Sprache* [*On the Way to Language*] (Pfullingen: Günther Neske, 1979), 196. See also F.-W. v. Herrmann, *Die zarte, aber helle Differenz: Heidegger und Stefan George* (Frankfurt a. M.: Klostermann, 1999).

15. Friedrich Hölderlin, *Sämtliche Gedichte*, ed. Detlev Lüders (Wiesbaden: Sammlung Aula, 1989), 300ff. All subsequent citations of Hölderlin's poetry reference this edition. On Heidegger's interpretation of "Wie wenn am Feiertage . . . ," see Paola-Ludovika Coriando, "Sprachen des Heiligen: Heidegger und Hölderlin," in *Heidegger und die christliche Tradition: Annäherung an ein schwieriges Thema*, ed. Norbert Fischer and Friedrich-Wilhelm v. Herrmann (Hamburg: Felix Meiner Verlag, 2007), 207–218.

16. Translator's note: For readers unfamiliar with Hölderlin's or Heidegger's thought: "the flight of the gods" here refers to modernity as a historical period that is characterized by an absence of the divine. For both Hölderlin and Heidegger, ancient Greece—a time in which "the gods" played a crucial role in human life and nature—represents a focal point of contrast to the modern period. A good entry point into Hölderlin's view of modernity in contrast to ancient Greece is his celebrated poem "Bread and Wine" ("Brod und Wein").

17. Friedrich Hölderlin, "Germanien," 317.

18. Friedrich Hölderlin, *Sämtliche Gedichte*, 406ff.

19. For a detailed analysis of Hölderlin's latest poems see Paola-Ludovika Coriando, *Affektenlehre und Phänomenologie der Stimmungen: Wege einer Ontologie und Ethik des Emotionalen* (Frankfurt a. M.: Klostermann, 2002), 187ff.

20. "Der Frühling [Spring]," 427.

21. "Der Herbst [Autumn]," 423.

22. "Die Aussicht [Prospect]," 429.

23. Martin Heidegger, *Zu Hölderlin/Griechenlandreisen*, GA 75, ed. Curd Ochwadt (Frankfurt a. M.: Klostermann, 2000), 207. Heidegger writes of this poem in the same text: "The poem originated a year before Hölderlin's death, which brought the long time of his night of derangement [*Umnachtung*] to an end. A mysterious night, whose darkness grants such saying. As Hölderlin already at the high point of his poetizing calls the night, 'the stranger among humans,' 'the wondrous,' which awakens wonder, openness to the extraordinary in the ordinary [p. 205]."

24. "In lieblicher Bläue . . . [In lovely blue]," 462f.

25. "Der Herbst," 424.

26. "Aussicht," 419.

27. "In lieblicher Bläue . . . ," 462.

28. See Aurelius Augustinus, *Confessiones*, Book XI. See also F.-W. v. Herrmann, *Augustinus und die phänomenologische Frage nach der Zeit* (Frankfurt a. M.: Klostermann, 1992).

29. "Der Herbst," 417.

30. "Der Winter," 425f.

31. "Höhere Menschheit," 420.

32. Translator's note: In *Being and Time* Heidegger discusses "running-ahead into death" in the context of Dasein's futural orientation toward its own death.

33. Martin Heidegger, "Das Ding," in *Vorträge und Aufsätze* (Pfullingen: Neske, 1990), 171.

34. "Der Frühling," 419.

35. "Hälfte des Lebens," 300.

36. See Martin Heidegger, "Bauen Wohnen Denken," in *Vorträge und Aufsätze*, 179–156 as well as "Das Ding," in *Vorträge und Aufsätze*, 157–175. On the relationship of the four regions of worldly significance to Hölderlin's poetry see F.-W. v. Herrmann, *Die zarte, aber helle Differenz*, 259ff.

37. Translator's note: "Enframing" [*Gestell*] is a key word in Heidegger's thinking of the technological world-interpretation of modernity. See Heidegger, "The Question Concerning Technology," in *Basic Writings*, ed. David Farrell Krell (London: Routledge, 1978), 311–341.

5

Toward a Phen(omen)ology of the Seasons

The Emergence of the Indigenous Weather Knowledge Project

JOHN CHARLES RYAN

Introduction: Revising the Australian Seasons

In an *Australian Geographic* article, Tim Entwistle, director of conservation at Kew Gardens and former director of the Sydney Botanic Gardens Trust, proposes a five-season model for Australia. Entwistle's schema includes a weightier four-month summer (December–March), a slenderer two-month autumn (April–May), and a compressed two-month winter (June–July). Revising the antipodean seasons, he divides spring into a two-month "sprinter" (August–September) and two-month "sprummer" (October–November). Entwistle's revisionist five-season thinking emphasizes the Australian summer, comprising one-third of the calendar year in his schema. Additionally, spring (as the neologism "sprinter") begins in August—one month earlier than its four-season counterpart—to correspond to the flowering of native plants in many parts of the country. Critical of the European temporal grid, Entwistle regards seasons as "cultural constructs reminding us that there are cyclic changes in the environment."[1] The argument behind his revisionist proposal is that the usual constructs—spring, summer, autumn, winter—are unsatisfactory Down Under.

In Entwistle's view, the Australian seasons require reconsideration, leading to new modes of seasonal awareness. On the surface, five seasons more sensibly accommodate the natural cycles of the Australian landscape. His ecologically inspired calendar, in part, adjusts its demarcations to the chief flowering time of Australian native flora as a whole. While I recognize that Entwistle's five-season tender is praiseworthy, any template for generalizing the Australian seasons inevitably becomes ensnared in the mode of cultural construction that it seeks to overcome. In its reconfiguring yet compartmentalizing of the cyclical progression of time, Entwistle's model reproduces the ineluctable weaknesses of a single seasonal paradigm for a land mass as vast as Australia. The cultural construction of the seasons—exemplified by the Gregorian or Christian calendar now used by nearly all Western countries[2]—implies a monologic rendering of seasonality, dislocated from the ecological nuances of bioregions.

Whether four or five in number, an Australian seasonal standard needs to be continually counterbalanced by local knowledge of the seasons, encapsulated within Indigenous ecological calendars. While an incomplete formulation of Australian seasonal plurality, the five-season model's opening to regional land-based calendars offers a promising way forward and a means for deeper understanding of the seasons. Broad-based models of seasonality—including Entwistle's—can be enhanced through sustained dialogue with the embodied knowledge encoded within Indigenous calendars. In response to Entwistle, hence, a dialogic perspective on the seasons considers multiple places, scales, temporalities, ecologies, bodies, and cultural traditions. In contrast to the five-part proposal, the Indigenous Weather Knowledge Project (IWKP) counterbalances any single, fixed system of seasonality. The project aims to consolidate the seasonal knowledge of Aboriginal Australian cultures in consultation with their Elders.[3] One of the practical outcomes of the IWKP is the digital documentation of Indigenous calendars on the project's website.[4] The IWKP, hence, provides a platform for educating the public through open-access information about land-based or endemic seasons.

My intention in this chapter is to trace the backstory to Entwistle's call to reformulate the Australian seasons. In sketching the context broadly, I begin with the origin of the Gregorian construct, alluding to its importation to Australia as part of the processes of colonization since the eighteenth century. Here, I argue that the singular model of the four seasons displaced—and potentially still displaces where traditional knowledge networks are threatened—the heterogeneous modes of season-reckoning in Australia. I then go on to consider the twin notions of endemic seasonality and Indigenous calendars through historical reflection on the six-season Nyoongar calendar.[5] The Nyoongar are the Aboriginal people of the southwest corner of Western Australia.[6] After the case study of the Nyoongar calendar and its phenomenological aspects, I proceed to a brief analysis of the IWKP.

Throughout my longitudinal discussion of the Australian seasons—from long-standing Indigenous traditions to the Gregorian import and to contemporary modes of Australian season-telling, represented by the IWKP—I propose and develop the portmanteau "phen(omen)ology" in relation to the seasons. I argue that the IWKP is best conceived of as a digital *phenological* template that gives actual human *phenomenological* exploration of the seasons a reference point for contemporary Australians interested in getting to know the endemic seasonalities of their places. Both phenology and phenomenology are essential to the process of grasping endemic seasonality in Australia and to learning to live with the seasons more consciously.

Seasons of Things: A Phenomenology of Dwelling With/in

Before addressing the backstory to Entwistle's five-season call, I outline a philosophical position on the seasons through the phen(omen)ology neologism. I ask: How should we rethink the four-season Australian grid in a manner that is sensitive to Australian places and cultures? How can individuals learn about the seasonal specificities of where they live in connection to national standards of seasonality—whether four or five? And, how can settler culture in Australia—enmeshed in four-season awareness—begin to appreciate and, even, "dwell" *with* and *in* the endemic seasonalities of regions, as evident in Aboriginal biocultural systems? As suggested in the previous section, the incorporation of land-based seasonal knowledge into Australian culture through Indigenous calendars can be optimally approached through the interplay of phenomenology and phenology. The former takes shape as an individual experiences the seasons through sight, hearing, touch, taste, and olfaction: as physical sensations registering in the sensorium. The latter refers to cognitive awareness of the progression of ecological events in time linked to plants, animals, the wind, constellations, and other biotic and abiotic phenomena. To begin with, phenomenological engagement centralizes immediate physical knowledge of the endemic seasons of a place: seeing, tasting, feeling, touching, and smelling the seasons, in their tangible manifestations, as they unfold. In adumbrating a phenomenology, Martin Heidegger's notions of dwelling[7] and "the thing,"[8] in conjunction with Maurice Merleau-Ponty's embodied phenomenology,[9] present productive frameworks. Recent theoretical developments in phenomenological geography[10] and phenomenological approaches to literary and cultural studies through the concept of "embodied temporality"[11] also provide generative positions.

Here, it is crucial to recognize that Indigenous ecological calendars, such as those of the Nyoongar and Yawuru of Western Australia, are lived calendars. The sensory cues of ecological calendars are intrinsically connected to intimate seasonal knowledge. When navigated phenomenologically in the environment, these cues—for example, the ripening of the cocky apple and its sensory materializations through pungent smells, sweet tastes, and pleasing images—signal the changing of the seasons integrated to human bodily experiences. Thus, for Australian settler society, a return to endemic seasonality entails corporeal participation in places of dwelling. This phenomenological call is heightened by the fact that ecological indicators of seasonal onset and transition vary annually according to manifold factors—such as rainfall—made even more irregular by the seasonal disruption associated with climate change.[12] To state the need differently, in order to appreciate endemic calendars, one must recognize their indications physically; a phenomenology of the seasons integrates bodily, multisensorial, and cultural-natural perspectives.

A phenomenology of the seasons attends to the "things" of nature (animals, plants, rain, wind) which, in their sensuous being, announce the seasons and their passage. Heidegger's "dwelling" is a key concept developed in his essay "Building Dwelling Thinking."[13] Through human place-dwelling, the presencing of the seasons comes forth and registers sensorially. For Heidegger, dwelling is the necessary quality of being. In examining the notion of dwelling in relation to Heidegger's articulation of "the thing,"[14] a philosophy of the seasons situates the vital things of nature—in their particular modes of being as sensorially manifested—before the fixed, mathematical, and political logos of the Gregorian model. Heidegger argues that *to dwell* means "to remain, to stay in a place."[15] *To dwell* implies the verb "to be" and "the way in which you are and I am, the manner in which we humans *are* on the earth [italics in original]."[16] To this effect, Heidegger links etymologically the Old English and High German word *bauen*—for building—to "dwelling" and, more compellingly, to "be" such that "I am" signifies intrinsically "I dwell." More apposite to the vitality of seasonal being in place, *bauen* connotes "to cherish and protect, to preserve and care for, specifically to till the soil, to cultivate the vine."[17]

As integrated being, dwelling consists of the fourfold oneness of earth, sky, divinities, and mortals; each implies the other so that, for example, thinking of earth entails thinking of sky and divinities. For Heidegger, "earth" refers to "blossoming and fruiting," whereas "sky" connotes "the course of the changing moon . . . the year's seasons and their changes . . . the clemency and inclemency of the weather."[18] To dwell phenomenologically in the seasons is to leave "to the seasons their blessing and their inclemency"[19]—to apprehend the seasons without exerting predetermination, control, or constraint; to allow the seasons to "presence," in their originary places to the human sensorium in the act of season-telling. Dwelling, moreover, is "always a staying with things."[20] Heidegger foregrounds the exigency of dwelling. Writing in the early twentieth century, he asserted that humanity "*must ever learn to dwell* [italics in original]."[21] In developing a "phenomenology of landscape," Christopher Tilley observes that, for Heidegger, "spaces open up by virtue of the *dwelling* of humanity or the *staying with things* that cannot be separated: the earth, the sky and the constellations, the divinities, birth and death [italics in original]."[22] Additionally, Tilley identifies the "total social fact of dwelling, serving to link place, praxis, cosmology and nurture."[23] The primacy of Heideggerian dwelling, in Tilley's analysis, involves the human body as the plenum of apprehension within the landscape and, by extension, within the seasons. Dwelling *with* and *in* the seasons is a habitus of being that reflects the integration of ontology, cosmology, plants, animals, insects, and consciousness.

But what does Heidegger mean by "things"—a word which, in common speak, tends to denote the inanimate stuff or commoditized objects of the world rather than the living beings calling forth the seasons in their sensuous nature? In the essay "The Thing," Heidegger differentiates between objects and things. An object is "that which stands before, over against, opposite us"[24] as the objectified "standing reserve" of technological enframement or *Ge-stell*.[25] In comparison to the instrumentally derived value of objects, a thing "stands forth"[26] agentically in its own right, manifesting the fourfold oneness of earth, sky, divinities, and mortals. "Thing" refers to the presencing of an essential nature of living and non-living entities.[27] As the gathering of oneness, the thing entails the process of bringing forth Heidegger's notion of fourfold unity: "The thing stays—gathers and unites—the fourfold."[28] While they can be dead matter, things can also be animate, in Heidegger's view as "things, each thinging from time to time in its own way."[29] Rethinking the Australian seasons, accordingly, means to dwell with things through the seasons in the places that circumscribe each, for instance, the cocky apples and the wild yams in Yawuru country north of Broome, Western Australia, or the banksia and red gums in Nyoongar country near Perth. The "thinging" of seasonal things is their sensory manifestation—their

ripening, effusions, stridulations—at particular times of year. The human
body, as such, is a sensing agent of the seasons activated in conjunction
with cognitive knowledge, such as that recorded by the IWKP, including,
for example, flowering, fruiting, nesting, and molting times.

The concept of the human body as a sensory plenum, while weak in
Heidegger's account of the presencing of things, is more clearly emphasized
in Merleau-Ponty's work, particularly *Phenomenology of Perception*. Part One,
"The Body," outlines Merleau-Ponty's corporeal phenomenology—a complex
position drawing from psychology, which I will only describe briefly here in
order to suggest a complementary conceptual perspective to "the thing."[30] In
comparable terms to Heidegger, Merleau-Ponty avers that "sense experience
is that vital communication with the world which makes it present as a
familiar setting of our life."[31] Sense experience is crucial to the presencing
of things. Moreover, embodiment—living in one's senses and knowing/
navigating the world sensuously through one's body—is a condition of "the
temporal structure of being in the world."[32] Time is integral to the twin
conditions of embodiment and being. Importantly, Merleau-Ponty's account
of phenomenology attends to human sensation. As part of the plenum of
apprehension, kinesthetic sensations arise from the movements of one's body
in space.[33] On the whole, Merleau-Ponty's concern is for the incarnate subject; his phenomenology counters the objectification—that is, the dissection,
commoditization, minimalization—of the living body.[34] Instead, the human
body, rather than an object in the world, is the principal means through
which we interchange with others and our environments.[35]

Extending Heidegger and Merleau-Ponty, recent work in phenomenological geography and embodied cultural studies provides an additional
conceptual cornerstone for developing a phenomenology of the seasons.
Barbara Bender outlines a perspective on geographical research "where the
time duration is measured in terms of human embodied experience of place
and movement, of memory and expectation."[36] Bender implies that, in lieu
of fixed points of reference for season-keeping, the human body acts as an
ever-open sensorium, marking the seasons somatically in their fugue-like
progression. I have previously termed this "embodied temporality" or the
"sense for time and seasons engendered through multisensorial interactions
with place."[37] Australian ethnobotanist Philip Clarke's work on Aboriginal
"calendar plants" describes seasonal things as those that provide—often
simultaneously—a time-keeping measure and a source of physical sustenance.[38] Similarly, Tilley argues that human embodiment—entailing sensory
openness to the things of the seasons—is essential to a phenomenology of

place: "A phenomenologist's experience of landscape is one that takes place through the medium of his or her sensing and sensed carnal body"[39]—a Merleau-Pontian perspective indeed. Extending Tilley's framework, a phenomenological approach to the seasons implies a "dialogic relationship between person and landscape," which stresses the materiality of landscapes as "real and physical rather than simply cognised or imagined."[40] In Heideggerian terms, the materiality of earth is the "blossoming and fruiting"—the ecological processes which underlie the presencing of things. For Tilley, a number of attributes and dispositions define phenomenological being in landscape, including "perception (seeing, hearing, touching), bodily actions and movements, and intentionality, emotion, and awareness residing in systems of belief and decision-making, remembrance and evaluation."[41] I suggest that all of these modes of experience and cognition are integral to a phenomenology of the seasons.

Seasons of Our Inheritance:
The Appearance of the Gregorian Model

Turning from phenomenology, this section outlines the emergence of the twelve-month, four-season Gregorian calendar—also known as the Christian or Western calendar—from the Julian calendar of the ancient Romans. Why should Entwistle go through the trouble of redefining the Australian seasons? What's wrong with the four-season score—the venerable subject of much European and North American cultural reverie—in Australia? I follow Entwistle's proposal to the origin of the four seasons to argue that phenomenological, place-based awareness is not an integral aspect of the Western calendar that most of us use on a daily basis. In fact, the global transition to the Gregorian calendar took until the early 1900s to reach completion. In 1582, the transition was instigated when the Gregorian calendar ("new style," *N.S.*), replaced the Julian calendar ("old style," *O.S.*).[42] This erasure of an "extra" ten days—yielded over time by the Julian system—corrected cumulative calendrical "shifts since Caesar."[43] The Gregorian calendar is now the international civil calendar and derives from the sixteenth century European desire to normalize Catholic and Protestant ceremonial dates.[44] In the Julian and Gregorian schemes, the four seasons—each approximately three months in duration—correspond to two equinoxes and two solstices per annum. Whereas land-based calendars must be experienced phenomenologically to be appreciated and often have fewer or greater than four seasons, the Gregorian model principally stems from structural, religious, political, and, later, colonial prerogatives.

The current use of the Gregorian calendar and associated four seasons in Australia can be traced to the British adoption of the calendar in 1752. Mathematically mediated, the Gregorian seasons are structured around solstices and equinoxes. Winter solstice is the shortest day, while summer solstice is the longest; the two equinoxes occur when night and day are of equal length. The Gregorian calendar—the underlying template for the four Western seasons—constitutes a grid-like temporal imposition on the seasonally diverse places of the Australian landmass. The institutionalization of the calendar is an aspect of the colonization of time—which belies the mismatch, at the core of Entwistle's call, between the diverse climates of Australian regions and the four-season overlay.

The Gregorian calendar and its Julian precedent are structural devices for reckoning time. Anthony Aveni discerns between structural and ecological time in order to identify different modes of season-reckoning, as well as the colonizing intersection of Western and Indigenous calendrical systems.[45] Aveni defines ecological time as "temporal knowledge . . . determined by the individual as a participant in organized society" encompassing "events in the natural world that portend change."[46] Cyclical and integrative of culture and nature, eco-time foregrounds occurrences in the natural world: "The time marker—whether flood, worm, or stars—is recognized to have a seasonal cyclic rhythm independent of human action."[47] Whereas eco-time relates "the response of human behavior to the cycles of nature,"[48] structural time prioritizes the rituals and behaviors that regulate societies. In other words, structural time is based on socially significant reference points—for example, rituals and ceremonies. According to Aveni, Indigenous calendars tend to integrate ecological and structural time-keeping, leading to nuanced modes of season-reckoning that are subjective, perceptual, fluid, and likely variable from year to year.

The meaning and function of a calendar are linked to predictability and temporal control. Agnes Kirsopp Michels defines a calendar as "a device for measuring time, by which [people] can plan for the future and keep a record of the past."[49] Comparably, L. E. Doggett defines a calendar as "a system of organizing units of time for the purpose of reckoning time over extended periods . . . some calendars are codified in written laws [i.e., the Gregorian]; others are transmitted by oral tradition [i.e., the traditional Nyoongar system]."[50] Aveni states that the underlying premise of a calendrical system is that a "temporal order" already exists in the natural world.[51] A calendar merely identifies, exposes, and codifies this order. By establishing a structure for capturing and controlling the order, an institutionalized calendar avoids the problem of variation in seasonal durations in places such as Australia, which has a diverse geography. The problem of variation, according to structural thinking, is intrinsic to the subjective reckoning of seasons, as evident in many Indigenous calendar systems.[52] In differentiating between structural time and ecological time, Aveni emphasizes that the seasons overlap in reality; their edges are not hard and fast and do not strike firmly at certain calendrical nodes. This overlapping denotes "a sense of instability to the event sequences that make up the cycle of nature's behavior."[53] Such instability in nature, however, for Michels, renders the (Northern Hemisphere) seasons an unsound basis of "only relative value" for a calendar: "although the seasons proceed in a regular sequence from year to year, they may vary considerably in length owing to variations in the weather."[54] Moreover, to compound the difficulty of seasonal standardization and the need for a uniform system not derived from ecology, the "seasons also vary locally"[55]—which is certainly the case in Australia.

Four-season thinking is evident in the writings of the English Saint Bede (also known as the Venerable Bede, ca. 672–735). He connects the four seasons to the temperate conditions of the Northern Hemisphere and also to the four humors of the human body. For Bede, the seasons firstly derive from the English climate as the proper markers of the temporal order:

> The seasons [*tempora*] take their name from this temperateness; or else they are rightly called *tempora* because they turn one into the other, being tempered one to another by some qualitative likeness. For winter is cold and wet, inasmuch as the Sun is quite far off; spring, when [the Sun] comes back above the Earth, is wet and warm; summer, when it waxes very hot, is warm and dry; autumn, when it falls to the lower regions, dry and cold.[56]

Bede then characterizes the human body as a "microcosm" and "a smaller universe" in which the four humors—blood, black bile, red bile, phlegmatic humors—correspond to the four seasons.[57] Hence, certain humors manifest during certain seasons. The four qualities of hot, cold, wet, and dry—coupling to produce the conditions of the seasons—constitute the human humors as well. Bede associates qualities and humors with the seasons. While Bede's thinking is an embodied seasonal philosophy, it reiterates the quarterly division of the year implied in the ancient Roman term *tempora annu* or "times of year."[58] Bede's humoral philosophy speaks of the genesis of the four-season model in northern hemispherical climates and bodies.

In 46 BCE, Julius Caesar replaced the ten-month Roman lunar calendar with a twelve-month system.[59] Caesar's schema, which became known as the Julian calendar, averaged 365.25 days per year.[60] As the ancient precedent for the modern calendar, it comprised twelve months, although they were denoted by somewhat different names (e.g., *Sextilis* rather than August). The main disadvantage of the Julian calendar—addressed by the Gregorian reform—was calendrical drift: the tropical year measured approximately 365.24219 mean solar days.[61] Pointing to the discrepancy between Gregorian and Julian calendars, Ernest Fredregill terms the Julian calendar "slow."[62] In calculating slightly more days in the calendar year than the tropical year, the Julian system caused annual events to fall earlier in the calendar year at a rate of one day per 128 years.[63] To its discredit, the average Julian annum comprised slightly too many days. Of temporal and religious concern, the actual vernal equinox began occurring before its calendar date March 21, and astronomical new moons were reckoned earlier and earlier.[64] Of particular concern for the medieval Church, calendrical drift caused Easter to fall on undesirable days.[65]

In February 1582, Pope Gregory XIII introduced the Gregorian calendar, instigating the Julian reformation by a bull known as *Inter Gravissimas*.[66] In consultation with the astronomer Ignazio Danti (1536–86), Gregory became certain that the equinoxes were falling on incorrect days as a result of Julian drift.[67] By 1582, the accumulated error of the Julian drift tallied more than ten days. In an edict issued eight months before the calendar reform would be instituted, Pope Gregory XIII corrected the ten-day error, mandating that October 15, 1582, revert to October 4, 1582. This reformation eliminated about ten days of Julian drift that had accumulated over 1,600 years since the institution of Caesar's calendar.[68] Through this mandate, Gregory advanced the recommendations of the Council of Trent (1545–63); although it was on the agenda of the Council, calendar reform was not sufficiently carried out until the papal decree.[69]

Physician and astronomer Aluise Baldassar Lilio (1510–76) designed the Gregorian calendar for Pope Gregory.[70] To correct the Julian drift, Lilio recommended that the first year of each century skip the leap year, except for years that could be divided evenly by 400 (1600 and 2000, for instance).[71] The Gregorian reform mandated that the leap year occur every four years, but not during these particular years. It also included standards for calculating Easter based on a revised table of new and full moons,[72] and assigned the beginning of spring to March 21.[73] Considering the calendar's relevance now, David Ewing Duncan calls the Gregorian scheme "the world's calendar: a code for measuring time that today all but the most isolated peoples use as the global standard for measuring time."[74] In comparable terms, E. G. Richards comments that, following its introduction to Britain in 1752, "the Gregorian calendar was later taken to the four corners of the globe on the back of the British Empire. It is now all but universally used."[75] In comparison to the Julian, the Gregorian system preserves three days every 400 years, allowing the activities of Western cultures to align almost uniformly with the solar year until 4000 CE.

In *The Oxford Companion to the Year*, Bonnie Blackburn and Leofranc Holford-Strevens observe that the "adjustment was necessary because the Julian year, consisting of 365 days, with a 366th day added every fourth year, has an average length of 365 days 6 hours, which is some 11 minutes 12 seconds too long, causing Julian dates to fall progressively further behind the sun."[76] The Gregorian schema, however, was not instantly adopted by all Western countries. It took approximately 300 years to become the calendrical norm and was met with social, political, and religious resistance.[77] In England, the reform sparked controversy, as the opposition's oft-cited motto attests: "Give us back our eleven days." A British Act of Parliament in 1752 introduced the Gregorian calendar or the "new style."[78] Britain's decision came 170 years after the rest of Europe, making it one of the last European countries to do so. The Act (24 Geo. II, ch. 23) was passed "for regulating the commencement of the year, and for correcting the calendar now in use."[79] Presented to Parliament by Lord Chesterfield, it became law on May 22, 1751.[80] Accordingly, twelve days were "eliminated" when September 14, 1752, reverted to September 2, 1752[81].

After its legalization in Britain, the Gregorian calendar was distributed to the colonies, including North America and, later, Australia. The standardization of season-reckoning in Australia culminated in the Meteorology Act of August 1906 and, subsequently, the creation of the Bureau of Meteorology in 1908.[82] In 2017, the autumn equinox in Australia was March 20; the winter solstice, June 21; the spring equinox, September 23; and the summer solstice, December 22.[83] Rather than following the solstices and equinoxes in determining the start dates for seasons, however, Australia uses the international meteorological definition for the Southern Hemisphere. This mandates three-month "meteorological" or "calendrical" (rather than astronomical) seasons beginning the first of each month: September 1 (spring), December 1 (summer), March 1 (autumn), and June 1 (winter). The Australian convention makes the highly statistical process of record-keeping—as regulated by the Australian Bureau of Meteorology—more convenient and consistent.

Entwistle's initiative to rework the Australian seasons responds to the imperialist history of the Gregorian calendar and reflects his awareness of the Indigenous calendars and endemic seasons of Australia that preceded colonization. His critique of the four seasons Down Under, nevertheless, is not new. In the mid-1990s, Steve Symonds, a spokesperson for the Weather Bureau of New South Wales, commented bluntly that:

> We [settler society] are cultural imperialists and we have just said what we want the weather to be. We came out here and said that there are four seasons in Europe so four seasons there should be here. Why should there be four seasons in Australia just because there are four seasons in London?[84]

The Gregorian calendar—applied to the immense landmass and cultural diversity of Australia—reinscribes the processes of colonization and indefinitely reinvokes a history of religious conflict and ecological repression. The Western calendar disregards the ground of places and the materiality of things entangled with temporal awareness. In his analysis of Indigenous calendrical systems, the anthropologist Alfred Gell avers that "the intertwining of calendars and power . . . extends to the processes of colonial subjugation."[85] The importation of the four seasons to Australia—originating in the Julian drift, the Gregorian reform, and the dissemination of the calendar through British empire—posed the possibility of erasing the endemic seasons of Aboriginal cultures. As the next section will highlight through a case study of the Nyoongar of the southwest region of Western Australia (WA), however, vibrant traditions of endemic seasonality endure, notwithstanding the impact of the colonial regime. Indigenous seasonal traditions are necessary counter-phenomena to any broadly applied, national seasonal paradigm—whether four or five.

Seasons of the Southwest: The Endemic Calendar of the Nyoongar

Traditions of endemic seasonality—along with the cultural integrity underlying them—should not be overshadowed by national standards—

revisionist or Gregorian. Like the Western calendar, seasonal calendars or "indigenous ecological calendars" are cultural constructs—"timetables that divide the year into seasons and describe expected conditions and resource availability."[86] Yet, a land-based seasonal calendar, unlike the Western calendar, is intrinsically connected to the ground—the ecology and culture of a place, and the corporeal things of nature that herald the seasons.[87] In contrast to the Western four-season regime, Indigenous calendars, as Tim Entwistle suggests in *Australian Geographic*, more accurately reflect regional Australian climates than the globalized four-season schema formulated in Europe. Australian Indigenous calendars offer the vital complement to Entwistle's revised calendar. Aboriginal cultures have unique place-based systems of season-keeping, recognizing, for example, two, four, six, seven, and nine seasons.[88] The risk of Entwistle's proposal is that a new model, with its relatively minor reorientation toward native flora, will stand in for the Gregorian scheme—the complex nuances of each Indigenous calendar again rendered one-dimensional by the imposition of a "fixed system of reference" over the whole country.[89]

Derived from European political, religious, and climatic circumstances, the Gregorian calendar is an apparatus of colonization that has been leveraged in Australia and "staunchly retained" since the 1800s.[90] In contrast, the endemic calendars of Australian Aboriginal people offer portals to ecological time—foregrounding events in the natural world—and structural time, relating the seasons to events of social significance, including ceremonies and festivals. The Nyoongar calendar of the Southwest Australian region is a living system of timekeeping that is predicated on phenomenological interaction with the environment. Here, the presencing of the things of nature—wind, temperature, fire, flora, fauna—signifies the seasons.

In supporting these assertions, I begin with historical interpretations of the six Nyoongar seasons, recorded by Western Australian settlers and colonists, then shift to contemporary explanations of the traditional seasons by Nyoongar Elders and teachers. In proposing "embodied temporality" in my previous reading of the Nyoongar seasons, I examined historical sources, including the diaries of Albany-based doctor and settler Scott Nind (1831), lawyer and farmer George Fletcher Moore (1884), and early twentieth-century ethnographer and journalist Daisy Bates.[91] Extending this historical research, I introduce in this section additional material from George Fletcher Moore's diaries, as well as extracts from the published journals of the Benedictine monk Dom Rosendo Salvado and colonial Western Australian newspaper articles referencing the Nyoongar seasons.

In Aboriginal Australia, according to Clarke, totemic associations, burning regimes, celestial movements, animal behaviors, wind patterns, temperature shifts, flowering phases, and rainfall levels together announce the arrival of seasons.[92] Instead of the mathematical measurement of time intrinsic to the Gregorian system, Aboriginal season-reckoning involves the corporeal apprehension of environmental changes in order to mark the movement of the seasons.[93] Unlike the Western calendar, Australian "bush calendars" have between two and nine divisions, and the duration of each season varies annually.[94] Prior to European settlement, Nyoongar people gathered plant foods and hunted animals according to a six-season calendar, with whole camps moving into areas when particular foods became harvestable.[95] In Albany, oral histories describe the local Nyoongar tradition of moving with the seasons from the coast in the summer to the inland in the winter.[96] Nyoongar seasonal awareness "comprises organized artisanal knowledge gained through observation and adjustment over timeframes of thousands of years, often strongly linked with an ontology such as that shaped by the 'Dreaming.' "[97]

Examining historical sources, including the writings of Bates, Nind, and Moore, Neville Green provides a summary of the six Nyoongar seasons and their differing orthographies in Perth and Albany, Western Australia.[98] In Perth, about two-hundred-and-fifty miles northwest of Albany, *Birok* is comparable to early summer (the first summer) and comprises December and January; in Albany, the season is known as *Meerningal*. *Burnoru* is the Nyoongar late summer (the second summer) and comprises February and March; in Albany, known as *Maungernan*. *Geran* includes the autumn months of April and May; known as *Beruc* to Albany Nyoongar people. *Maggoro* includes the winter months of June and July; known as *Meertilluc* in Albany. *Jilba* refers to the spring months of August and September; *Pourner* in Albany. Finally, *Kambarang* encompasses the spring months of October and November; denoted as *Mokkar* in Albany. The six seasons are made palpable through the presencing of diverse natural things—"roots, birds, eggs, edible grubs, lizards,"[99] registered by human percipients through their sensory faculties.

The Benedictine monk, Dom Rosendo Salvado (1814–1900), who established the New Norcia monastery on the banks of the Moore River north of Perth, commented that "it seems that some natives divide the year into six different seasons; but many others divide it into four, which they call *cielba* [*jilba*], *mocur*, *ponar*, *piroc*, that is, autumn, winter, spring, and summer. The months are distinguished from one another by the moon, but they are not given individual names, or divided into weeks. Again, the days are not distinguished except by the position of the moon."[100] Curiously, Salvado only references four of six Albany seasons, *Jilba* (*cielba*), *Mokkar* (*mocur*), *Pourner* (*ponar*), and *Birok* (*piroc*), notwithstanding the existing account of colonial doctor Isaac Scott Nind (1797–1868), published in 1831. Nind notes that "the greatest assemblages [of Albany area Nyoongar people] are in the autumn (*pourner*), when fish are to be procured in the greatest abundance."[101] He observed six seasons "beginning with June and July, or Winter: *Mawkur, Meerningal, Maungernan, Beruc, Meertilluc,* and *Pourer* [italics added]."[102] Salvado's emphasis on the four Nyoongar seasons might reflect an intractable four-season logos that simply could not rationalize in-between states of temporality for, as he says, "it *seems* that some natives divide the year into six different seasons [italics added]."[103] Salvado moreover noted that Nyoongars reckoned weeks and days according to the moon, but that these smaller divisions of time were not as important in their temporal order as the six seasons.

In contrast to the Nyoongar bush calendar, the Gregorian calendar pivots on the precise calculation of time in determining the four seasons and the exact placement of Christian holy days. In his discussion of Aboriginal temporality, Mike Donaldson describes a non-Western sense of time as "enveloping. Both cyclical and circular, it accorded with the need for seasonal movement, the aggregation and disaggregation of groups."[104] "Nyoongar time," for Donaldson, reflects "close ties with the land . . . which blurred the distinctions between work and leisure."[105] Based on this temporal sense, Nyoongar seasons reflect natural events connected to the procurement of food and movements of communities—bridging ecological and structural time. Salvado observed, "it is worth noting that the Australian natives . . . use the title 'grass season' of the period in which the new grass is born and the buds open, that is, the months corresponding to April–May of the Northern Hemisphere (our months, however, being autumn for them)."[106] In the Perth-area Nyoongar calendar, the months of October and November (equivalent to April and May in the Northern Hemisphere) correspond to *Geran,* signified by the presencing of grass buds and associated flora and fauna. The budding of grass is an important ecological phenomenon in the annual cycle of the *kwongan* sand plain ecosystem fringing Salvado's New Norcia settlement to the west. Salvado's statements suggest that *Geran* is a shifting denominator—a mutable category of time—predicated on a heterogeneity of biotic, abiotic, astronomical, and cultural factors, rather than predetermined temporal markers.

As "embodied temporality"—a term encompassing ecological and structural time—the seasons governed traditional Nyoongar movements, activities, and customs.[107] An article in an 1833 edition of *The Perth Gazette* noted that a reconciliatory meeting between warring settlers and Nyoongars "could not be effected at present, as the tribes were so much dispursed [*sic*], and not until the *yellow* season (the bloom of the Banksia,) in December, January, and February. At this time the country is generally fired [italics in original]."[108] The three months listed in the article correspond to *Birok* and *Burnoru,* when different species of banksia bloom, including the bull banksia (*mangite* or *Banksia grandis*)—the flowers producing an abundance of nectar, steeped in water or sucked directly by Aboriginal peoples. During the yellow season, the Christmas tree (*Nuytsia floribunda*), known as *mudja*—the Nyoongar word for "fire"—also blossomed.[109] Further in the color symbology of the seasons, it was during *Birok* and *Burnoru* that Nyoongars set fires to encourage grazing animals and the regrowth of food plants.[110] However, banksia nectar—as a sensuous thing announcing the seasons—was also important during other times of year. Writing in October 1833, George Fletcher Moore reported that "this is the season now for young parrots. I am told that the natives suck the honey out of their bills which the mother has just fed them with from the Banksia flowers."[111] During the season of *Kambarang*, Nyoongars hunted young birds and eggs.[112] In an entry from March 1834, Moore additionally observed that Nyoongars "pull the blossoms of the red gum tree (now in flower), steep them in water, and drink the water, which acquires a taste like sugar and water by this process."[113] Between *Burnoru* and *Makaru*, the red gum tree (*marri* or *Corymbia calophylla*) flowers throughout the Southwest region.

As suggested by the term "the yellow season," some contemporary explanations of the Nyoongar seasons point to color typologies with phenomenological bearing on temporal perception. These typologies, however, are not always consistent between sources. *Our Place Newsletter* notes that colors are used to teach seasonal knowledge and to help Nyoongar people identify "the correct time of year" for certain activities.[114] *Birok* is associated with the color red or *mirda*, symbolizing heat, fire, and the sun. *Burnoru* is signified by the color orange or *yoornt mirda*, representing the profusion of fish and lack of rain characteristic of this season. *Geran*'s color is green, or *nodjam*, correlating to the return of cooler weather and the light green appearance of eucalypt trees. *Maggoro* is blue, or *wooyan*, with dark blue, specifically signifying the onset of rain and cold temperatures. *Jilba* is associated with the color pink, or *mirda mokiny*, with pink or purple indicating the proliferation of wildflowers in the region during this season. Finally, *Kambarang* (not *Birok* and *Burnoru*, as indicated above) is linked to the color yellow, or *yoornt*, symbolizing the arrival of hot weather and other "yellow" events that complete the yearly cycle.[115]

As a contemporary teacher of Nyoongar seasonal knowledge, Len Collard, a Traditional Owner of the Whadjuck or Perth metropolitan area Nyoongar, comments that "we utilize six seasons of the year for food and sustenance, and never damage or kill our resources unnecessarily. The land is our mother and our nurturer and our guiding light."[116] Collard connects the six Nyoongar seasons to meteorological conditions (ecological time), such as wind directions and temperatures, but also to the procurement of food, maintenance of cultural knowledge, and performance of ceremonies (structural time):

> The Nyoongar seasons are *Bunuru* with hot easterly and north winds . . . *Djeran* becomes cooler with wind from the southwest . . . *Makuru*, cold and wet with westerly gales . . . *Djilba*, becoming warmer . . . *Kambarang*, rain decreasing . . . *Birak*, hot and dry with easterly winds during the day and south-west sea breezes in the afternoon . . . There were between thirty and forty distinct roots, nuts, and vegetables eaten by Nyoongar, which are gathered nearly all-year round . . . There was hardly any shortage of food throughout the six-season cycle with *katitjin* or knowledge given to the Nyoongar by the *Waagal* [Creation Serpent] to manage our land according to the seasons.[117]

Hence, for Collard, the Nyoongar seasons derive uniquely from the meteorological, botanical, and cultural contexts of the Southwest Australian region. Such variables factoring into the Nyoongar bush calendar coalesce to signify the onset of each of the seasons. Crucially, however, the physical openness of humans to the sensuous nuances of experience is the mode through which the things of the Southwest—red gums, banksias, the wind, roots, nuts, vegetables, nectar, birds—present themselves. This phenomenological mode of acquiring seasonal knowledge shifts, not only from season to season, but from region to region. Thus, a phenomenology of the seasons engages people and the things of nature in their milieux of dwelling, leading to place-based embodied temporality.

Seasons of Our Dwelling:
The Indigenous Weather Knowledge Project (IWKP)

In December 2012, Edith Cowan University and the Bureau of Meteorology launched the Nyoongar weather calendar as part of the Indigenous Weather Knowledge Project's continuing effort to preserve and promote Aboriginal Australian seasonal knowledge.[118] The online calendar lists the six Nyoongar seasons as *Birak, Bunuru, Djeran, Makuru, Djilba,* and *Kambarang*.[119] (See http://www.bom.gov.au/iwk/). As an educational and heritage-based platform, the IWKP website emphasizes that human perception is fundamental to understanding the endemic Southwest seasons: "the Nyoongar seasons can be long or short and are indicated by what is happening and changing around us rather than by dates on a calendar."[120] For example, *Birak* (December–January), the first summer or the season of the young, is marked by the easing of rain, the onset of warm weather, sea breezes from the southwest, easterly winds, fledgling birds, reptiles shedding their skin, and baby frogs. *Bunuru* (February–March), the second summer or season of adolescence, is signified by high heat and little rain, hot easterly winds, the white flowers of jarrah, marri, and ghost gums, and the bright red cones of female zamia (*Macrozamia riedlei*). *Djeran* (April–May), the ant season or season of adulthood, features the breaking of hot weather, cooler nights, light breezes from the southeast or southwest, flying ants, the red flowers of *Corymbia ficifolia* and *Beaufortia aestiva*, and the flowering of other banksias. During *Djeran*, Nyoongars traditionally consumed zamia nuts that were, earlier in the year, stored underground or in water to hasten the food crop's detoxification. Shelters known as *mia-mias* were repaired in preparation for the coming cold season.

In addition to the Nyoongar calendar, the IWKP outlines the endemic seasonal knowledge of thirteen other Aboriginal cultures, including Brambuk, D'harawal, Walabunnba, Yanyuwa, Jawoyn, Miriwoong, Wardaman, and Yawuru. For example, the Yawuru calendar of Broome, Western Australia, uses ecological indicators, such as the ripening of the cocky apple and the availability of wild yams, to indicate *Man-gala* or the wet season.[121] The Walabunnba people, living approximately 300 kilometers north of Alice Springs in central Australia, recognize two seasons: *Wantangka* (the hot weather) and *Yurluurrp* (the cold weather). During *Wantangka*, the sweet bush plum is eaten when the fruit turns dark, and special "hot weather" ceremonies are performed during the season.

The IWKP website is the outcome of a collaboration between Indigenous Australian communities, the Aboriginal and Torres Strait Islander Commission (ATSIC), the Bureau of Meteorology, and Monash University's Centre for Australian Indigenous Studies (CAIS) and School of Geography and Environmental Science. The Southwest Aboriginal Land and Sea Council granted permission to the IWKP to display culturally sensitive Nyoongar seasonal information. The IWKP, moreover, is integral to the Bureau of Meteorology's *Reconciliation Action Plan 2012–2015*. One of the plan's objectives is "to liaise with community elders to expand traditional knowledge of weather and climate through seasonal calendar information."[122] Indeed, as one of the original promulgators of the Western seasons in Australia, the Bureau of Meteorology concedes that "the four seasons we've adopted are not entirely appropriate for all regions of Australia." The Bureau praises "natural calendars" or "bush calendars" for reckoning the "natural seasons" according to ecological phenomena, such as "fruits, blossoms, insects, animals, as well as the temperature and whether it was a wet time of year."[123]

In foregrounding ecocultural (environmental and cultural) waymarks that declaim the passage of time, such as the ripening of the bush plum, the IWKP offers a phenological tool for appreciating the Aboriginal Australian seasons. The word *phenology* stems from the Latin *phaeno* and the Greek *phaino*. The words *phenology* and *phenomenon* share a common etymological root in the Greek: *phainein* for "to show,"[124] from which the words *phantasm* and *phenotype* come. Introduced in an 1853 article by Belgian botanist Charles Morren (1807–1858) and advanced in the 1880s by the Austrian botanist Karl Fritsch (1864–1934), *phenology* can be defined as "the study of periodic biological events in the animal and plant world as influenced by the environment, especially temperature changes driven by the environment."[125] For Morren, *phenology* meant "to show, to appear: the science of phenomena that appear successively on the globe."[126] The first published English definition of phenology, following the term's adoption by the Council of the Meteorological Society in 1875, read "the observation of the first flowering and fruiting of plants, the foliation and defoliation of trees, the arrival, nesting, and departure of birds, and such like."[127] Further along, a 1972 American committee on phenology employed the following definition: "the study of the timing of recurring biological events."[128]

As developed by the Bureau of Meteorology, the IWKP intersects with scientific knowledge of weather and the seasons while highlighting the seasonal heterogeneity of Australia. As an online resource containing a growing collection of phenological information about endemic seasons, the IWKP provides catalog-like indications of the first occurrences of ecocultural events in the respective regions of the Indigenous societies featured. However, immediate experience through the senses—of the endemic things of Australian places, including bush plums, zamia nuts, and wild yams—proves indispensable in comprehending the seasons in their sensuousness. The phenomena that indicate seasonal passage—archived by the IWKP in consultation with Elders—are integral to the habitus of people in place. In a scientific sense, a phenology functions, in part, as a compendium of events. In contrast, a phenology of the Australian seasons integrates biotic, abiotic, cultural, cosmological, ceremonial, ontological, and corporeal aspects—all essential to Aboriginal temporal systems. Fostered through a phenomenological grounding, embodied knowledge of the seasons complements the largely cognitive, visual, and events-based ordering of temporality. For example, although the bush plum flowers in summer, if I have never seen, tasted, or smelled its fruit, my knowledge of the endemic seasons of where I live will be limited. I must engage with the things of the seasons through which such events manifest. Hence, endemic seasonality—whether *Man-gala* of the Yawuru calendar or *Djeran* of the Nyoongar calendar—is embodied temporality, or the recognition of time's passing through corporeal interchange with one's place. The IWKP presents a groundwork for phenomenological exploration of the seasons. The information preserved and promoted by the IWKP, nonetheless, is not a substitute for immediate, real-time encounter with seasonal things—but is instead a cognitive prompt for such encounters.

Although an incomplete digital platform, the IWKP offers an accessible means for engaging with the Australian seasons. In analyzing the IWKP in these terms, I have distinguished between a phenology of the seasons—as cognitive recognition of temporal events—and a phenomenology of the seasons—as embodied interaction with the seasonal things that announce such events. In my view, a phenomenology complements a phenology of the seasons, as encapsulated by the IWKP. Returning to Entwistle's proposal, even the more considered kinds of seasonal paradigms risk imposing a managerialist grid on the plural landscapes—bioregions, places, locales—that constitute Australia as a diverse ecocultural whole. In the five-season scheme, for instance, the temporal denomination of "spring" entwines with the flowering of native plant species. Although botanically inflected, this privileging of flora backgrounds related events in the annual cycles of plants—as well as the cultural, sensorial, spiritual, ethnozoological, astronomical, and climatic considerations that collectively signify the seasons.[129] Ecological and structural time lived out in place syncretically become embodied temporality. Flowering phases reflect only one aspect of an endemic (land-based or Indigenous) calendar as an integrated system. Through the fusion of phenomenological (experiential, sensory, place-based, actual) and phenological (cognitive, visual, enumerative, digital) approaches, the endemic seasons of Australia can be appreciated in their depth and extent.

Conclusion: Living with Seasonal Diversity in Australia

As suggested by Entwistle's call, Australia has an uneasy relationship to the four seasons of the Western calendar and the Northern Hemisphere. The rethinking of the Australian seasons entails the recognition of a multiplicity of seasons, calendars, cultures, and places. National models—whether the Gregorian four seasons or Entwistle's proposal for five seasons—can co-exist dynamically with robust traditions of endemic seasonality, exemplified by the Nyoongar six seasons and the Indigenous Weather Knowledge Project. As Clarke comments, "while increasing globalization prevents European Australians from rejecting the European-derived calendar in favour of a plethora of regional calendars, the future investigation of indigenous seasonal knowledge and behaviour offers to help develop more relevant approaches to landscape management."[130] As this chapter has suggested, the "future investigation" of Indigenous calendars would benefit from experiential, sensory, and place-based approaches.

A dialogic perspective on the seasons is both phenomenological and phenological—cognitive and bodily—constituting the idea of a "phen(omen)ology." Attending to the seasonal things of place that declaim the passage of time, a phen(omen)ology offers a reflexive perspective on the seasons that blurs the distinction between intellection and embodiment. A phen(omen)ology, moreover, recognizes that actual seasonal boundaries vary year to year, and from place to place, according to a spectrum of ecocultural factors. As Heidegger acknowledged, "a boundary is not that at which something stops but, as the Greeks recognized, the boundary is that from which something *begins its presencing* [italics in original]."[131] Learning to be in the presence of seasonal things requires foreknowledge of when things happen coupled to unmediated sensory witnessing of their emergence.

Notes

1. Quoted in Katie Duncan, "Sprinting into Sprummer," *Australian Geographic* 102 (2011): 19.

2. Anthony Aveni, *Empires of Time: Calendars, Clocks, and Cultures* (London: I. B. Tauris, 1990), 116–117.

3. Australian Bureau of Meteorology, "Indigenous Weather Knowledge," 2012, accessed September 1, 2018, www.bom.gov.au/iwk/.

4. Australian Bureau of Meteorology, "Indigenous Weather Knowledge," accessed December 23, 2020, http://www.bom.gov.au/iwk/.

5. Daisy Bates, *The Native Tribes of Western Australia*, ed. Isobel White (Canberra, Australia: National Library of Australia, 1985); Peter Bindon and Trevor Walley, "Hunters and Gatherers," *Landscope* 8.1 (1992): 28–35; George Fletcher Moore, *Diary of Ten Years Eventful Life of an Early Settler in Western Australia and also A Descriptive Vocabulary of the Language of the Aborigines* (Nedlands, Australia: University of Western Australia Press, 1978), originally published in 1884; John Charles Ryan, "The Six Seasons: Shifting Australian Nature Writing Towards Ecological Time and Embodied Temporality," *Transformations* 21 (2012), accessed September 1, 2018, www.transformationsjournal.org/issue-21/.

6. Neville Green, ed., *Broken Spears: Aborigines and Europeans in the Southwest of Australia* (Cottesloe, Australia: Focus Education Services, 1984); Rosemary Van den Berg, *Nyoongar People of Australia: Perspectives on Racism and Multiculturalism* (Leiden, The Netherlands: Brill, 2002); South West Aboriginal Land and Sea Council, *"It's Still in My Heart, This Is My Country": The Single Noongar Claim History* (Crawley, Western Australia: University of Western Australia Press, 2009).

7. Martin Heidegger, *Poetry, Language, Thought*, trans. Albert Hofstadter (New York: Harper Perennial, 1971), 143–159.

8. Heidegger, *Poetry, Language, Thought*, 163–180.

9. Maurice Merleau-Ponty, *Phenomenology of Perception*, trans. Colin Smith (New York: Routledge, 2012).

10. Barbara Bender, "Time and Landscape," *Current Anthropology* 43.S4 (2002): 103–112; Christopher Tilley, *A Phenomenology of Landscape: Places, Paths and Monuments* (Oxford: Berg, 1994); Christopher Tilley, *Interpreting Landscapes: Geologies, Topographies, Identities* (Walnut Creek, CA: Left Coast Press, 2010), 25–40.

11. Ryan, "The Six Seasons."

12. Will Steffen, Andrew Burbidge, Lesley Hughes, Roger Kitching, David Lindenmayer, Warren Musgrave, Mark Stafford Smith, and Patricia A. Werner, *Australia's Biodiversity and Climate Change* (Collingwood, Australia: CSIRO Publishing, 2009), 68; CSIRO, "Indigenous Seasons Calendars," n.d., accessed September 1, 2018, www.csiro.au/en/Research/Environment/Land-management/Indigenous/Indigenous-calendars.

13. Heidegger, *Poetry*, 143–159.

14. Heidegger, *Poetry*, 163–180.

15. Heidegger, *Poetry*, 144.

16. Heidegger, *Poetry*, 145.

17. Heidegger, *Poetry*, 145.

18. Heidegger, *Poetry*, 147.

19. Heidegger, *Poetry*, 148.

20. Heidegger, *Poetry*, 149.

21. Heidegger, *Poetry*, 159.

22. Tilley, *A Phenomenology*, 13.

23. Tilley, *A Phenomenology*, 13.

24. Heidegger, *Poetry*, 166.

25. Martin Heidegger, "The Question Concerning Technology," in *Martin Heidegger: Basic Writings*, ed. David Krell (New York: Harper & Row, 1977), 284–317.

26. Heidegger, *Poetry*, 166.

27. Heidegger, *Poetry*, 172.

28. Heidegger, *Poetry*, 178.

29. Heidegger, *Poetry*, 180.

30. Merleau-Ponty, *Phenomenology*, 95–205.

31. Merleau-Ponty, *Phenomenology*, 61.

32. Merleau-Ponty, *Phenomenology*, 86.

33. Merleau-Ponty, *Phenomenology*, 96.

34. Simon Glendinning, *In the Name of Phenomenology* (London: Routledge, 2007), 134.

35. Glendinning, *In the Name of Phenomenology*, 135.

36. Bender, "Time," 103.

37. Ryan, "The Six Seasons," sect. "(De)colonising the Australian Seasons," para. 5.

38. Philip Clarke, *Aboriginal People and Their Plants* (Dural Delivery Centre, Australia: Rosenberg, 2007), 47–59.

39. Tilley, *Interpreting*, 25.

40. Tilley, *Interpreting*, 26.

41. Tilley, *A Phenomenology*, 12.

42. Aaron Hawkins, *The Gregorian and Julian Calendars, or, The New and Old Stiles, Arithmetically Explained* (London: M. Cooper, 1751).

43. Denis Feeney, *Caesar's Calendar: Ancient Time and the Beginnings of History* (Berkeley: University of California Press, 2007), 150.

44. L. E. Doggett, "Calendars," in *Explanatory Supplement to the Astronomical Almanac*, ed. P. Kenneth Seidelmann (Mill Valley, CA: University Science Books, 1992), 575–608 [580].

45. Aveni, *Empires*.

46. Aveni, *Empires*, 176.

47. Aveni, *Empires*, 176.

48. Aveni, *Empires*, 177, 181.

49. Agnes Kirsopp Michels, *The Calendar of the Roman Republic* (Princeton, NJ: Princeton University Press, 1967), 9.

50. Doggett, "Calendars," 575.

51. Aveni, *Empires*, 6.

52. Aveni, *Empires*, 6.

53. Aveni, *Empires*, 123.

54. Michels, *The Calendar*, 9–10.

55. Michels, *The Calendar*, 9–10.

56. Bede, *Bede: The Reckoning of Time*, trans. Faith Wallis (Liverpool: Liverpool University Press, 1999), 100.

57. *Bede*,100–101.

58. Leofranc Holford-Strevens, *History of Time: A Very Short Introduction* (Oxford: Oxford University Press, 2005), 80.

59. Ernest J. Fredregill, *1000 Years: A Julian/Gregorian Perpetual Calendar, A.D. 1100 to A.D. 2099* (New York: Exposition Press, 1970), 13.

60. Fredregill, *1000 Years*, 14.

61. E. G. Richards, *Mapping Time: The Calendar and Its History* (Oxford: Oxford University Press, 1999), 239.

62. Fredregill, *1000 Years*, 14.

63. Richards, *Mapping*, 239.

64. Richards, *Mapping*, 352.

65. Richards, *Mapping*, 249.

66. David Ewing Duncan, *Calendar: Humanity's Epic Struggle to Determine a True and Accurate Year* (New York: Avon Books, 1999), 261–289; Charlotte Methuen, *Science and Theology in the Reformation: Studies in Theological Interpretation and Astronomical Observation in Sixteenth-Century Germany* (London: T & T Clarke, 2008), 61–73; Richards, *Mapping*, 239–256; John Willes, *The Julian and Gregorian Year, or, The Difference Betwixt the Old and New-Stile* (London: Richard Sare, 1700).

67. Richards, *Mapping*, 241.

68. Duncan, *Calendar*, 261–262.

69. Richards, *Mapping*, 241.

70. Richards, *Mapping*, 243.

71. Fredregill, *1000 Years*, 14.

72. Doggett, "Calendars," 583; Richards, *Mapping*, 352.

73. Arno Borst, *The Ordering of Time: From the Ancient Computus to the Modern Computer* (Cambridge, England: Polity Press, 1993), 103.

74. Duncan, *Calendar*, 289.

75. Richards, *Mapping*, 256.

76. Bonnie Blackburn and Leofranc Holford-Strevens, *The Oxford Companion to the Year: An Exploration of Calendar Customs and Time-Reckoning* (Oxford: Oxford University Press, 1999), 682.

77. Mike Donaldson, *Taking Our Time: Remaking the Temporal Order* (Nedlands, Australia: University of Western Australia Press, 1996), 95.

78. Richards, *Mapping*, 252–256.

79. Quoted in Richards, *Mapping*, 253.

80. Richards, *Mapping*, 253.

81. Feeney, *Caesar's*, 151, 281; Duncan, *Calendar*, 277–278.

82. Australian Bureau of Meteorology, *A Century of Science and Service: The Australian Bureau of Meteorology 1908–2008* (Melbourne, Australia: Bureau of Meteorology, 2008), 7.

83. Australian Bureau of Meteorology, "Australian Weather Calendar," 2018, accessed September 1, 2018, www.bom.gov.au/calendar.

84. Quoted in Donaldson, *Taking*, 204.

85. Alfred Gell, *The Anthropology of Time: Cultural Constructions of Temporal Maps and Images* (Oxford: Berg, 1992), 313.

86. Suzanne Prober, Michael O'Connor, and Fiona Walsh. "Australian Aboriginal Peoples' Seasonal Knowledges: A Potential Basis for Shared Understanding in Environmental Management," *Ecology and Society* 16.2 (2011): 1–16 [2], accessed September 1, 2018, www.ecologyandsociety.org/vol16/iss2/art12/.

87. Peter J. Usher, "Traditional Ecological Knowledge in Environmental Assessment and Management," *Arctic* 53.2 (2000): 183–193, accessed September 1, 2018, http://citeseerx.ist.psu.edu/viewdoc/download?doi=10.1.1.474.5055&rep=rep1&type=pdf.

88. Clarke, *Aboriginal People*, 54–59.

89. Prober, O'Connor, and Walsh, "Australian Aboriginal Peoples,'" 2.

90. Clarke, *Aboriginal People*, 54.

91. Bates, *The Native Tribes*; Moore, *Diary*; Scott Nind, "Description of the Natives of King George's Sound (Swan River Colony) and Adjoining Country," in *Nyungar, the People: Aboriginal Customs in the Southwest of Australia*, ed. Neville Green (North Perth, Australia: Creative Research in association with Mt. Lawley College, 1979), originally published in 1831, 14–55; Ryan, "The Six Seasons."

92. Clarke, *Aboriginal People*, 54.

93. Philip Clarke, "Australian Aboriginal Ethnometeorology and Seasonal Calendars," *History and Anthropology* 20, no. 2 (2009): 79–106 [94].

94. Clarke, "Australian Aboriginal Ethnometeorology, 95.

95. Noel Nannup and David Deeley, "Rainfall and Water as Cultural Drivers," in *1st National Hydropolis Conference Proceedings*, ed. Stormwater Industry Association (Perth, Australia: Stormwater Industry Association, 2006), accessed February 4, 2012, www.hydropolis.com.au/Papers/SIA_NANNN2.pdf; Eleanor May Rusack, Joe Dortch, Ken Hayward, Michael Renton, Mathias Boer, and Pauline Grierson, "The Role of Habitus in the Maintenance of Traditional Noongar Plant Knowledge in Southwest Western Australia," *Human Ecology* 39.5 (2011): 673–682; Glen Stasiuk and Ash Sillifant, dirs., *Noongar of the Beelier or Swan River*, prod. Glen Stasiuk (Murdoch, Australia: Kulbardi Productions, 2005), 20 mins., 28 secs.; Lois Tilbrook, *Nyungar*

Tradition: Glimpses of Aborigines of South-Western Australia 1829–1914 (Nedlands, Australia: University of Western Australia Press, 1983), 3.

96. Tilbrook, *Nyungar Tradition*, 145.

97. Prober, O'Connor, and Walsh, "Australian Aboriginal Peoples,'" 2.

98. Green, *Broken Spears*, 10–11.

99. Green, *Broken Spears*, 10–11.

100. Dom Rosendo Salvado, *The Salvado Memoirs: Historical Memoirs of Australia and Particularly of the Benedictine Mission of New Norcia and of the Habits and Customs of the Australian Natives*, trans. E. J. Stormon (Nedlands, Australia: University of Western Australia Press, 1977), originally published in 1853, 131.

101. Nind, "Description," 35.

102. Nind, "Description," 54.

103. Nind, "Description," 54.

104. Mike Donaldson, "The End of Time? Aboriginal Temporality and the British Invasion of Australia," *Time and Society* 5, no. 2 (1996): 187–207 [193].

105. Donaldson, "The End of Time?," 200–201.

106. Salvado, *The Salvado Memoirs*, 289.

107. Ryan, "The Six Seasons."

108. The Perth Gazette, "The Natives: Interesting Interview," *The Perth Gazette and Western Australian Journal* September 7 (1833), 142, *National Library of Australia Trove*, accessed September 1, 2018, http://nla.gov.au/nla.news-article641889.

109. John Charles Ryan, "Towards Intimate Relations: Gesture and Contact between Plants and People," *PAN: Philosophy Activism Nature* 9 (2012): 29–36.

110. Sylvia J. Hallam, *Fire and Hearth: A Study of Aboriginal Usage and European Usurpation in South-Western Australia* (Canberra, Australia: Australian Institute of Aboriginal Studies, 1975).

111. George Fletcher Moore, *The Millendon Memoirs: George Fletcher Moore's Western Australian Diaries and Letters, 1830–1841*, ed. J. M. R. Cameron (Carlisle, Australia: Hesperian Press, 2006), 292.

112. Adolphus Peter Elkin, *The Australian Aborigines: How to Understand Them* (Sydney, Australia: Angus and Robertson, 1943), 36.

113. Moore, *The Millendon Memoirs*, 315.

114. Kurongkurl Katitjin Centre, "Wongi Nyoongar—Talking Nyoongar," *Our Place: Official Newsletter of Kurongkurl Katitjin Centre for Indigenous Australian Education and Research* (Makaru [June and July] 2011): 1–10 [5].

115. Kurongkurl Katitjin Centre, "Wongi Nyoongar—Talking Nyoongar."

116. Stasiuk and Sillifant, *Noongar of the Beelier*.

117. Collard quoted in Stasiuk and Sillifant, *Noongar of the Beelier*.

118. Kurongkurl Katitjin Centre, "ECU and BOM Launch Nyoongar Weather Calendar," *Our Place: Official Newsletter of Kurongkurl Katitjin Centre for Indigenous Australian Education and Research* Birak (December and January) (2012–2013): 1–10,

accessed September 2, 2018, www.ecu.edu.au/__data/assets/pdf_file/0007/694546/
Our-Place-Newsletter_Birak13-Edition.pdf.

119. Australian Bureau of Meteorology, "Indigenous Weather Knowledge."

120. Australian Bureau of Meteorology, "Indigenous Weather Knowledge."

121. Australian Bureau of Meteorology, "Indigenous Weather Knowledge."

122. Australian Bureau of Meteorology, *Reconciliation Action Plan 2012–2015* (Melbourne, Australia: Bureau of Meteorology, 2012), 2.

123. Australian Bureau of Meteorology, *Climate of Australia* (Melbourne, Australia: Bureau of Meteorology, 2008), 10.

124. Douglas Harper, "Phenology (n.)," *Online Etymology Dictionary* (2018), accessed September 2, 2018, www.etymonline.com/index.php?term=phenology.

125. Mark Schwartz, "Introduction," in *Phenology: An Integrative Environmental Science*, ed. Mark Schwartz (Dordrecht, The Netherlands: Kluwer Academic Publishers, 2003), 3–8 [3].

126. Marie Keatley and Irene Hudson. "Introduction and Overview," in *Phenological Research: Methods for Environmental and Climate Change Analysis*, eds. Marie Keatley and Irene Hudson (Dordrecht, The Netherlands: Springer, 2010), 1–22 [1].

127. Anon. (1884) quoted in Keatley and Hudson, "Introduction," 1.

128. Leith quoted in Keatley and Hudson, "Introduction," 2.

129. Clarke, "Australian Aboriginal Ethnometeorology."

130. Clarke, "Australian Aboriginal Ethnometeorology," 101.

131. Heidegger, *Poetry*, 152.

ANTHROPOLOGY AND THE ARCTIC

6

Arctic Summer

ALPHONSO LINGIS

Fire and Ice

Super-hyper-*über*summer in Merrieland: when I stepped out the door, I couldn't breathe. There was no air; it was all space quivering with radiation. In front of the house the last weeds had died. The ground roasted into broken tiles, mineral molecules sizzling in the cracks. Song sparrows and crows flapped down to the pond and stayed there, dunking their heads in the hot slimy water and panting. Flies and wasps clung to the windows, pressing their black and yellow bellies against the glass that was holding in the farcical air-conditioning. Set on maximum, its thermostat read 85°F. The Baltimore City Department of Health broadcast a Code Red Heat Alert; ambulances wailed through the streets.

I sat in the cellar and thought: ice. Ice cubes. Iced tea. Icicles, sleet, hail. Plate ice, pack ice, ice floe, frazil ice, grease ice, transition ice, congelation ice, shuga ice, ice rind, nilas ice, slush ice, brash ice, ice cake, pancake ice, floeberg ice, floebit ice, ice breccia, ice shelf, tabular berg, bergy bits, growler ice. I was hallucinating. Ice sheets, ice shelves, ice caps, ice streams, icefields, mountain glaciers, valley glaciers, piedmont glaciers, cirque glaciers, hanging glaciers, tidewater glaciers, icebergs. I booked a flight to the Scandinavian Arctic.

Achieving independence and adulthood means settling down. Having a post in the economic system, a place of one's own, a layout of paths one takes and returns from. Besides the efficiency, the economy of energy and the securing of skills, there's a specific contentment in bonding with a stable place. It's a shelter and nourishing medium, a womb. Weekends, holidays, vacations, we take day trips to the beach. On trips we go to the homes of relatives; we buy a camper to stay in the same room everywhere; we study the photos of hotel rooms on the internet before selecting them. The birth of civilization is the end of nomadism; civilization means sedentary life; *civitas* in Latin means city.

Sedentary existence shapes time. The tasks of the day, in the house, in the factory, or in the office recur; they are equivalent to those of the day before and the day after. Life is not a trajectory but a pacing, an amplification of the heartbeat, the pulse of breath, the steps in walking.

Norwegian Summer

The idea was summer. I had been to Antarctica during its summer; on the edge of the peninsula where you could get off the ship it was 36°F maximum. Not *summer*. But Norway is warmed by the Gulf Stream, and even at the top, Nordkapp, I read the average summer temperature is 53°F.

The flight ended in Bodø, Norway. I was starting ass-backwards, but the next morning I did go to the town of Å. Aye-oh! I skipped the bypass to the town of Drag. Also passed on the town of Moan. (In Mali, Ken and I came upon a town called Blah. A quite pretty place in fact, we stopped for lunch and strolled about the town, admiring its cubist adobe houses, their edges decorated in intricate geometric patterns. The lunch was, well, blah.)

Norway did not look laid back or lethargic by the summer. Enormous cliffs stood defiant as the ocean snarled against them. Dense armies of pines were storming the mountain ramparts, holding their pikes vertical against the winds that furled black flags of thunderclouds in the sky. Marshes foamed violet with flowering stalks of rosebay willowherb. Energy poured on the waters of lakes, shaking silver flakes off them. The sky was agate blue and vast, the sun paddle-balling around the horizon, not lowering to rest under it. "Summer" from Sanskrit *samā*: year, season. Summer here was enormous, imperial: *the* season, *the* year.

Affirmation

Staying put, doing the same things day after day, year after year is monotonous; it needs its nightly injections of melodrama and crime, like that contained in the television. Water pouring over rocks in the river removes their rough edges, but it also wears them down. Love may deepen as the years go by, but sexual excitement wilts after a year or two. Yet we cling to the monotonous; contentment lies there.

Philosophers have identified life with will, decision, and initiative and have not taken account of all in life that is repetition and of the specific pleasure found therein. Freud understood repetition compulsion to result from a trauma to "unkink." But breathing, nourishing oneself, and using one's muscles are repetitive actions. Freud claimed the deepest pleasure we can know is orgasm; it is explosive, a shattering of the armature of identity and an impersonal surge of natural and nocturnal energies. However, orgasms not only forget sense and rationality, and decency and self-respect; they also do not remember past orgasms or build on them. When orgasm comes to an end, it is an end and not a means to something further, not even to a higher orgasm. Our animal body only anticipates repeating it.

Orgasm is a will-less state to which the will says "yes" unreservedly. "What if some day or night a demon were to steal after you in your loneliest loneliness and say to you: 'This life you now live and have lived, you will have to live it once more and innumerable times more; and there will be nothing new in it, but every pain and every joy and every thought and sigh and everything unutterably small or great in your life will have to return to you, all in the same succession and sequence.' . . . Have you once experienced a tremendous moment when you would have answered him: 'You are a god and never have I heard anything more divine!' "[1] It is the test, for Nietzsche, of the possibility of total affirmation of the will, the unconditional and complete adherence of our will to life.

Å

Å is on the tip of the Lofoten—"Lynx Foot"—Islands. Starting with the maelstrom: off Å is Moskenesstraumen, whose description in the 1714 account of it by Jonas Danilssønn Ramus inspired tales by Jules Verne and Edgar Allan Poe. Here, "islands" are enormous slabs of rock set vertically in the sea. I was gobsmacked: every slice of mountain stuck out there in the water made my head sputter. What the . . . ? Why? How?

Down in continental Europe—walking around France, Italy, Spain—you see history, see city squares, country towns, churches marking epochs, see the archaic and recent and now mechanized methods with which every stretch of land has been and is possessed. There's more history in any Cleveland suburb than here in the Arctic; in 1945, the Nazis, retreating from the advancing Soviet army, performed a scorched earth on them: burned every bridge, store, and town; burned every farmhouse and stable in Arctic Finland and Norway. Here, where Earth's crust buckles into mountains and pieces broken off are stuck upright out in the ocean, you see things in geological time. I brought a couple of geology books with me and spent sleepless sunny nights reading them.

The last glacial period of the Ice Age began one hundred and ten thousand years ago, peaked eighteen thousand years ago, and ended ten thousand years ago. Year after year, it snowed until Scandinavia, the North Sea, and much of Germany and Poland were covered with compacted ice up to three kilometers deep. Immense glaciers shuddered and slid, scraping along piles of rock, widening deep cracks in the mountains—the fjords. The weight of all that ice squashed Scandinavia down in Earth's fluid mantle.

Then temperatures warmed up and the ice started to melt. Water that had fallen from the sky and stuck frozen on the peninsula for thousands of years poured into the ocean. Racing torrents deepened cracks on Norway's coast and pushed chunks of it into islands. The sea level rose some 300 feet.

The landmass that had been pushed down in Earth's fluid mantle began rising. The whole of Scandinavia has by now risen 275 meters—nine hundred feet. A postglacial isostatic rebound, the geology books call it. "Rebound"—one day I stood on top of one of the mountains looking far and wide and imagined it all whooshing up nine hundred feet, my stomach wrenching. But the rebound was slow, nine hundred feet in ten thousand years. It will continue for at least another ten thousand years. Currently, the Scandinavian Peninsula is rising from one to three feet per century. Finland is getting bigger; its submerged edges are rising such that the surface area of the country is expanding some seven square kilometers annually.

Nomadism

For their first two hundred thousand years, *Homo sapiens* were on the move, following other species of animals. Ten thousand years ago, they began to domesticate some of them and became themselves sedentary. The nomadic people of today follow other animals in Amazonia and Australia. The Sámi of the Scandinavian Arctic follow migrating reindeer.

The vast majority of people now migrate independently of other species. They are fleeing persecution, famine, and poverty. At the time of this writing, there are about 200 million immigrants, 62 million refugees, and 34 million people displaced by war.

Among the secure, settled, and sedentary, the nomadic instinct returns. We travel, we say, to learn, to discover the wide world, to know the pleasures of magnificent landscapes, grand human constructions, and share the pleasures of other ways of life. Beneath all that there is the pleasure of just moving. See our feet, Bruce Chatwin says, they are long and set parallel; they are made to move on ahead.[2] The sense that we have gone somewhere is especially marked by seeing species of animals we don't see back home—water buffalo, zebras, sea lions, koalas, reindeer.

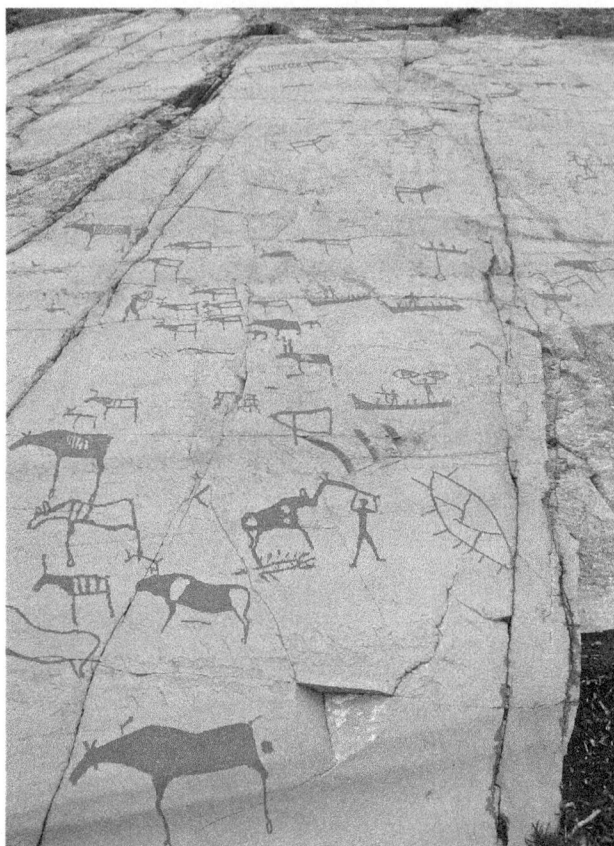

Sámi

Alta is a small town some five hundred kilometers north of the Arctic Circle where they fish and quarry slate. I spotted a small museum a few kilometers outside of town and went to look. Inside, I found cabinets of Stone Age crusted iron tools, maps, and historical explanations. Rock carvings were discovered here in 1972. They cleared the rocks of the thick mats of lichens and mosses stuck upon them, and eventually revealed three thousand carvings. In four other sites around Alta, they found three thousand more carvings. The most recent studies conclude that the first ones were made 7,200 years ago, when the rocks were on the beach; as the land rose with the "postglacial isostatic rebound" rocks at the new lower beach level were carved; the last ones 2,200 years ago.

I thought of small bands of humans drifting out of Africa, wandering along the French Riviera, painting hundreds of caves in Provence, and then coming up here to the edge of the colossal ice sheet that was melting. People with big horizons. And big appetites; they are blamed with killing off the last of the wooly mammoths.

Behind the museum, a boardwalk snakes around huge rocks down the slope toward the bay. At fourteen stops, the cleared flanks possess dozens, even hundreds, of carvings that have been filled in with red ochre to make them visible. I note incised pictures of reindeer, moose, bears, dogs, wolves, foxes, hares, geese, ducks, swans, cormorants, whales, and halibut. Pregnant reindeer and moose have carvings of their calves standing inside them, while pregnant women have their children standing within them. There are corrals with reindeer inside. Stick figures of humans hold spears, bows and arrows, and fishing lines. Boats contain many people on panels lower down. Carved bears leave tracks across scenes and even across other animals.

In the late afternoon, I was the only one on the boardwalk, and lingered long. What did the people who carved these panels have in mind? I had read books about the cave art of Lascaux, Cosquer, and Chauvet in southern France. Scholars argued about a succession of explanations: hunting magic, totem animals, initiation rites, structural representations of social hierarchies, and shamanist visions. Philosophers joined in—I read Georges Bataille's work on Lascaux soon after it was opened. Back at this museum, all the signs emphasized expert ignorance. Fish and fishing scenes are few, although archaeological digs have revealed that most of the food of these ancient people came from the sea. Did they depict bear, moose, and reindeer because these animals were difficult to hunt and so success merited record or required rituals? Archaeologists now doubt that they indicate simply belief in symbolic magic. Perhaps the great land animals played a larger role in cults. Were they instead totemist symbols for individual tribes and the real or wished-for interrelations among them? Were the scenes showing a dance, preparation of food, or sexual concourse depictions of rituals or fertility rites? Were the human images priests or tribal chiefs? If figures with headgear were chiefs, were these presentations of the ascension of a ruler, royal marriages, or diplomatic relations between tribes? Or historical records of important events? Were these animals icons used in shamanist trance rituals? Were the bears whose tracks wander across scenes supernatural beings crossing the three levels of reality? To understand the figures, would we not have to know the myths that told of regions of reality and of cosmic events? To what extent was simple artistic pleasure at work?

In Narvik, there is a rock carving within the town. It is a very attractive site: secluded, shady trees and plants, a path descends to the fjord. On the face of a big rock there is a full-sized moose in outline. It is very impressive, large, and there all by itself. A sign indicates experts have dated it five thousand years old. At Saltstraumen, some five hundred kilometers away, there is another moose carved alone on a rock. This one is eight thousand years old. Carved alone, these two are without narrative or mythical context. Whatever other function they might have had, it was clear to me that the realism and stately profile of the carvings reveal the aesthetic skill and pleasure of the solitary artist.

Archaeologists called all this "Fosna Culture." What happened to these people? Their descendants are the indigenous people of the Scandinavian Arctic, the Sámi. (The term *Laplanders* is considered derogatory.) About 10 percent of the Sámi live by herding reindeer; the others live along the coast on small farms and engage in fishing. On the edges of their mown fields, the hay has been compressed into big cylinders and tightly wrapped in white plastic by a machine I never saw—they look like the cheeses made by the Sámi in winter.

In the little town of Inari in Arctic Finland, there is the Siida, a Sámi museum. There, I learn that the Sámi were Christianized starting in 1720, with forced destruction of their sacred objects and places. The museum has three of the shamans' drums out of only seventy that collectors have saved. In the eighteenth century, the civilizers in Oslo and Stockholm sought to wipe out Sámi culture; between 1900 and 1940 one had to speak Norwegian or Swedish in order to buy or lease land. Since 1990, the Sámi have been allowed to school their children in their own languages and have acquired measured rights to their lands; they have set up political organizations. Now entire Sámi families no longer accompany reindeer herds on their traditional migrations. Instead, one member of the family follows the herd with car, motorcycle, or snowmobile. In every town, signs direct tourists and me to a museum with its collection of canoes, reindeer skin boots and jackets, woven dresses and coats, cradles, knives with carved reindeer-antler scabbards, and delicate cups and bowls cut out of birch burls that the Sámi ceased making around 1950. The Nordlandmuseet in Bodø that I strolled through features a collection of thirty-four radios along with these traditional items.

Seasons and Periodicity

Periodicity is a combination of movement and repetition. The sequence of day and night repeats. Our life as an arc rising at birth and descending toward death is spanned by the periodicity of seasons. We sedentary animals, however, restructure life as a linear plateau, where a day is followed by another day with equivalent tasks and forms of contentment. Even as our tasks and pleasures at home and at work repeat day after day, our metabolism, our initiatives, and our mental horizons are seasonal. The diseases and accidents that arrive at the hospital give the everyday work of doctors and nurses a seasonal pattern.

Day and night and seasons are planetary periodicities. There is the periodicity of El Niño and La Niña. Hindus, Buddhists, and the Maya have depicted cosmic periods. In 1824, the Danish-Norwegian geologist Jens Esmark proposed that the world had undergone a sequence of ice ages. Since then, geologists, chemists, and paleontologists have determined that there have been at least five Ice Ages. Their conclusions come from extensive research on things that almost any traveler has wondered about. We see sidewalks crack from the winter and stones washed down rivers. But what scattered huge boulders around? What cracked open the Norwegian fjords not traversed by rivers but by the ocean tides? We find or receive a few fossils of plants or animals and wonder what happened to them. What happened to those dinosaurs we see in natural history museums, those giant moa birds, those giant kangaroos, sloths, armadillos, and sharks, those guinea pigs whose fossils were found in 1987 in Uruguay that weighed between 1,700 and 3,000 pounds?

Summer Migration

Does the moon have seasons? It has its seasons on earth. When the moon is full or new, the high tides are very high and the low tides very low; they are called spring high tides. Astronomers explain this phenomenon when the

moon lines up with the sun and their gravitational pull is combined. There are some four thousand fjords in Norway, cracks in Earth's crust gouged out by glaciers. Sognefjord extends 205 kilometers (127 miles), with a maximum depth of 1,308 meters (4,291 feet) below sea level. I went to Saltstraumen, where a narrow three-kilometer-long strait connects two wide sections of the fjord. Every six hours the tide pours in and rushes back, shooting (the sign says) 372 million cubic meters of seawater through the strait, creating maelstroms up to ten meters in diameter and five meters deep. Edgar Allan Poe describes the scene:

> Here the vast bed of the waters, seamed and scarred into a thousand conflicting channels, burst suddenly into phrensied convulsion—heaving, boiling, hissing—gyrating in gigantic and innumerable vortices, and all whirling and plunging on to the eastward with a rapidity which water never elsewhere assumes except in precipitous descents. . . . The edge of the whirl was represented by a broad belt of gleaming spray; but no particle of this slipped into the mouth of the terrific funnel, whose interior,

as far as the eye could fathom it, was a smooth, shining, and jet-black wall of water, inclined to the horizon at an angle of some forty-five degrees, speeding dizzily round and round with a swaying and sweltering motion, and sending forth to the winds an appalling voice, half shriek, half roar, such as not even the mighty cataract of Niagara ever lifts up in its agony to Heaven.[3]

The seawater instinctually wants to get back into Scandinavia, freeze there, and cover it all over again.

Seasons mean migration. Twice, peering with binoculars, I spotted Arctic terns skimming the ocean. These little birds, weighing but three or four ounces, nest on isolated islands in the Arctic summer, then take off for the Antarctic, making a round trip of seventy to eighty thousand kilometers every year. They fly offshore, not making land, and linger for twenty-five days in the mid-Atlantic on the way. They spend the first half of the year in Antarctica, and the second in the Arctic, their year consisting of two summers. Nobody enjoys more sunlight than they.

The greatest migrators among terrestrial mammals are reindeer; some populations travel five thousand kilometers a year, swimming across many swift and icy rivers. There are tundra and forest reindeer in Scandinavia, North America (where they are called caribou), and Siberia, along with nine subspecies. Wild forest reindeer were extinct in Finland, but now a few hundred have wandered in from Russia. I saw some of them in a zoo in Ranua, Sweden; they are taller and darker, and possess a third high branch on their antlers.

It's summer, and the reindeer look wooly and disheveled, still with patches of their winter hair. They are not sleek like the white-tailed deer of Merrieland, and have splayed hoofs like outsized galoshes, but they own the most impressive antlers—up to four-and-a-half feet high and more than three feet wide. They all have them, though the cows shed theirs after bearing calves, and they are re-growing the antlers now. Young bulls shed their antlers in early spring, but mature bulls shed theirs in December. (So that old patriarch Santa is pulled about by women and adolescents.)

At midday, the reindeer take refuge from too much ultraviolet light inside the entrances of highway tunnels, where you may run into fifteen or twenty of them. You are not supposed to honk the car horn at them, but they ignored it when I did. I stepped out of the car and physically pushed some aside to get through.

Eight Seasons

I feel guilty going to a bar at midnight for a drink when it looks like midmorning. Some tourist guys sit around a table; a couple of loners sit at the bar. An old man in a plaid shirt approached, his face in pleats of wrinkles, slid his eyes at the beer and then at me. In exchange, he gave me some information. Said his name is Aili. "Here there are eight seasons," he explained. "Pakkastalvi: when you move the reindeer to the forest where they can find enough lichens. That's your January-February. Kankikanto, when the reindeer begin to move from the forest to the calving grounds in the mountains, is your March-April." "Wait," I said, "let me write that down." I looked around, spotted an empty cigarette package on the floor, tore it open. He pronounced the names a couple of times and I wrote down something approximate; made a note to look it up later on the internet. "In Jäidenihtökevät—your April-May," he went on, "the reindeer are eating leaves, grass, some plants, and the calves are born. Keskiyönauringon Aika—that means Unending Sun—is when we earmark the calves. June. Sadonkorju-unaik is when the reindeer build up muscle and fat; it's July-September. Then comes Ruska, reindeer courtship season. The bucks use up their stored fat and lose much of their muscle weight. Your September-October." "Lose weight?," I butted in. "Too busy sparring and showing off to eat," he said. "Then?" I said. "Then Mustalum, means 'Black Snow'—the ground freezes into a black crust before the snow covers it. October-November. Then Jou-lukaamos, when the reindeer are moved to the forests where they can feed on lichens in the branches and dig grass, twigs, and moss out of the snow. Your December-January," he finished. "How long you going to be here?" "Seven weeks," I said. "Keskiyönauringon Aika and Sadonkorjuunaik," he figured. "The time to muscle up in the unending sun," he grinned. "And fatten up," I muttered and signaled the bartender for more beers.

The Lemming Year

Summer it was; even when huge clods of black clouds drifted low, the sky between them spread cerulean blue, kingfisher blue. Big puffy mats of cumulonimbus hovering low and blackening within, white smears of stratus clouds, wispy strokes of cirrus, high-altitude cirrocumulus, like throws of feathers. The sun radiates them into shovels of silver dust. "How is it that

the sky opens so vast here?" I wondered. I figured it's seeing the banks and
strata of clouds so precisely outlined at great distances in the pellucid blue of
the sky. The sky gives its measure to everything in view, even the mountains
and the lakes. At ground level your eye recognizes shapes and repetitions
and regularities; the shapes of the clouds are unnamable and shape-shifting,
ensnaring your observation and thwarting it. On this ruggedly dramatic
peninsula you do not so much walk the earth as walk under the sky.

I put down my bags in a room in Inari and went out to look at
the lake. Sat down on a big rock, contemplated the pines doubled on the
unrippled plate glass of the lake and the mountains whose slow postglacial
rebound I could not see, rising with them. A faint rustle in the stillness; I
turned and saw a bit of animal like a small chipmunk scuttling along the
shore. Spotted brown and yellow ocher like a bit of a fawn. I saw it was
coming straight toward me; I lifted my camera and immobilized myself,
intent on quieting my breath. When it was but a foot away, it looked
up and—instead of being spooked by the massive animal hovering over
it—it squeaked, squeaked, and squeaked louder in a squall of outrage. "I
am sitting over your burrow and family?" I translated, then got up and
moved back. It then scuttled across where my feet had been and went on
down the shore. All that rage simply because I had been in its way. What
was this headstrong little chipmunk? Wee and pretty and with vehement
emotions and determination; what self-assertion. I sat back down to the
serenity of the lake. Eventually, I too got up to walk the shore. Heading
back, I came upon four people dragging suitcases to the lodge. I felt that
hackneyed reaction, which I now feel very rarely, of resenting "tourists" in
enchanting places I want as my own, and momentarily imagined marching
up and snarling until they got out of my way. Two days later, while waiting
for a rain to pass, I sat on a chair with Martti, the red-faced, wiry owner
of the lodge. He said that this was a "lemming year," the phase in a usually
four-year cycle when the population of these rodents explodes, only then
to diminish to near extinction. "In lemming years," he said, "millions of
them take off to new areas where they can find food." "How far can they
get, with all those rivers and streams everywhere?" I asked. "Oh they can
swim," he said. "Up to two hundred meters. Though in rough water many
drown." Then it occurred to me that what I had seen was a lemming;
I had never seen one in a zoo; I had never even seen a picture of one,
and they had become colorless and de-individualized to me as they are in
clichés.

Vertical and Horizontal

Summer it was; the pine and birch forests, laundered clean, extended lime green new twigs and shook their needles to get them strobe-chromed in the sun. The vegetation did not mound; it was vertical or horizontal. I remembered the architect Gaudi declared that there are no straight lines in nature; across the Arctic, there are millions of pines and spruces that have for so many generations grown straight up with no space to spread their limbs so that even when they are quite alone they do not venture a branch out further than a few feet. The white trunks of the birches are as plumb as the flagpoles in the White House lawn. On ground level, everything goes horizontal—the twiggy little plants covered with oval leaves that rise but a foot and cover floors by the kilometer and the mosses that creep across the tops of mountains. Since the lower branches of the pines have long died and disintegrated, and since there are not, as in the forests back in Merrieland, bushes with branches arching and tangling, you can stroll the moss-, crowberry-, and cloudberry-carpeted forests as nonchalantly as if they were the lawns of suburbia. The reindeer don't have to think about getting their antlers snared in brush and so have been able to grow them splayed four feet high. In the mountain passes, there were curtains of rain; then the sun blossomed above, and half rainbows glowed.

Braving the higher levels of the mountains are the contorted, kinked efforts—broken by the ice, chewed by reindeer—of dwarf, alpine, and downy birch; their shoots are covered with down, as in pubescence: *Betula pubescens*, subspecies *tortuosa*. They straggle on in the far north; I see them on the way to Nordkapp; they give up in the final stretch. I read that they are the only native tree in Iceland and Greenland.

Winter in the Summer

Summer here, they say, but I see winter right up in the mountains. Ice clouds in high altitudes, swollen dark clouds so low they engulf you on the mountains, but they only sprinkle rain on and off, saving up for when they can unload ice. Winds scramble and scrap over the tundra. You see winter underfoot. In lower elevations, during the summer the permafrost thaws just enough to let plants grow and reproduce, but the ground below is frozen; the water cannot sink any lower, and spreads in bogs. The tapestry of so many hues of green

looks pretty; you walk, sinking in the spongy carpet. Then comes winter; the plants die down but do not decay; new growth in summer surfaces on top of eventually deep peat bogs. In fact, winter toys with each summer day: dark, mattressy clouds in the morning; sprinkling drizzle around midday; clouds lumbering off around 2:00, in time for a summer afternoon; vast, transparent sky full of radiation; then the end of the day, when the seagulls settle to sleep on the waves and it feels like night in sunlight.

Nordkapp was named by an English explorer back in 1553, and it was taken to be the northernmost point in Europe (although a nearby cliff extends further). The road, open from May to October, was built in 1985, careening around cliffs and through tunnels. One tunnel opened recently, more than four miles long, it descends 696 feet below sea level under the fjord. The last scrub birches have been passed, and the road ascends a high mountainous plateau that levels off at the promontory. At the brink, the ocean below is not visible through the swirling mists; tossing pebbles below provides a sense of the height. At midnight the sun has swung around to the north. Beyond, nothing but icy waters until the solid ice of the North

Pole. What a place for suiciders; nevermore! A big raven hangs out there; he blackly scorned the bread I tossed to him.

Seasons, Species, and Sagas

We are not simply upright apes; our bodies line up with things about us. Among the pines we stand tall; we lay on the banks of rivers and flow down them; we nestle in combes and crouch against the walls of caves; we rise, and our sensibility soars into the sky. Summer opens our bodies, sends us strolling and climbing. The last days of my stay, the whole sky was overcast and dark and the winds were strong, winter wanting me. I wanted to return here during the months of the polar night. Stay at the five Ice Hotels across the Arctic and watch the aurora borealis opening curtains upon celestial night. Years ago I had stayed at the Hôtel de Glace north of Quebec; it was the most enchanting place to sleep, in domed rooms of compacted opaque snow carved by artists in bas-relief. The chapel and common rooms were constructed of transparent ice, with ice chandeliers.

Other species match their outer appearance to the seasons. Arctic foxes, Arctic hares, ermines, and collared lemmings molt and grow all-white fur for the winter. Reindeer, which are sometimes white and usually have white necks, extend winter white further across their bodies. The huge male snowy owls are like soft snowmen; the females are white with some black scalloping year-round. The entire species prefers the northernmost regions of the Scandinavian Arctic tundra where there is always some snow. I wondered why birch trees, the dwarf Arctic birch braving the mountain heights and the northern tundra, made their trunks and limbs white. White reflects and does not absorb heat.

Ocean tides rush in and out of the fjords. The Alta rock carvings show men in boats seven thousand years ago. The Vikings took to boats—raiding, looting, taking slaves, trading, colonizing the Baltic, and what is now Germany, Scotland, England, Normandy, Portugal, and Sicily. In the Icelandic sagas, the phrase "to go Viking" means piracy and raiding. They colonized Iceland and Greenland, then, in the year 985, reached Newfoundland. Bjarni Herjólfsson, Leif Ericsson, Thorvald Ericsson, Thorstain Eiricsson, Þorfinnr Karlsefni, Freydis Eiriksdottir, Snorri Guðriðsson, Eric Gnupsson, and thousands of their companions. Coming from North America, I thought they knew that land; I wanted to know why, after going there for four hundred years, they gave up on North America. They got to Constantinople in 839

CE, where they served as mercenaries for the Byzantine court and, a little later, arrived in Baghdad. Did Orientalism sway their thinking?

I went down to Stiklestad, where King Olav II, known in his lifetime as Olav the Stout and after his death as Saint Olav, fought his last battle. There is a marker where he died, a small stone church, and a big hotel with an amphitheater seating seven thousand where each July they put on, in Viking costume and with a cast of hundreds, the Saint Olav Drama. Born in the year 995, Olav took part as a youth in raids, plundering and pillaging in the Baltic Sea and England; then he raided, plundered, and pillaged with the Norse in Normandy. There, he came to idolize Charlemagne and was baptized a Christian in Rouen in 1013. He returned to Norway two years later, declared himself king, and set out to subdue rivals and impose Christianity by force. He made himself head of the Church. He married Astrid, the illegitimate daughter of Swedish king's Olof Skötkonung, and kept concubines. Finally driven out by his tormented subjects, he returned to Stiklestad with Swedish recruits in 1030 and was confronted by a peasant army and killed. The English bishop he had imported canonized him a year later in Trondheim, and declared him Eternal King of Norway. His canonization was confirmed by Pope Alexander III in 1164, and, requisite miracles attested, confirmed again by Pope Leo XIII in 1888. The oldest surviving picture of Saint Olav is a twelfth-century painting on a column in the Nativity Church in Bethlehem.

I further learned that Magnus (after Carolus Magnus—Charlemagne), Olav's illegitimate son by Alvhild, one of his concubines, did acquire the throne in 1035. Magnus never married. A daughter out of wedlock, Ragnhild, was the great-grandmother of Eric III, who became ruler of Denmark in 1137. He resigned in 1146, entered a monastery, and died soon after.

I spot a little item in a newspaper: In 2010, statistics revealed that 2 percent of Norwegians go to church regularly.

Place and Displacement

It is not only the planet that has space and geographic regions: there are strata in our experience, and smooth nomadic and striated spaces.[4] There are also mountain peaks and glaciers, rivers and lakes and swamps in our experience and life. What would we be if we lived in one place only, or outside of places?

For the lichens, mosses, flowering herbs, trees, lemmings, wolverines, and reindeer, summer is the season of reproduction, growth, and maturation. Summer is also the season of growth and maturation for us. Long hours for work, warmth, and sunlight for physical exertion, ripe fruit, and vegetables, and a time when our bodies relax and our minds remember and ruminate. What would we be if we lived outside of seasons?

Eugène Ionesco tells of a man who one day comes upon a radiant city. He wanders its streets, marveling over the beautiful homes. Each has a different architectural design, surrounded by gardens all flowering in marvelous variety. Great concealed heaters and air-conditioners maintain the city in a perpetual springtime. But as he wanders he sees that no children are playing and laughing in the gardens and parks; no couples are wandering the streets; all the houses are closed, their windows shuttered. He eventually learns that there is a killer loose in the city, killing for no discernible reason people of any age, any condition. In this city where technology has provided for all needs and pleasures, the inhabitants are living in unremitting terror. One day on the street the traveler finally encounters the killer, a puny, gnarled individual who comes for him. He argues with the killer: "Why? Why me?" He appeals to every principle of goodness, of humanity, of simple meaning and utility. Each time the killer responds with a snicker or guffaw.[5]

The reader understands that the killer is death itself. Understands that in this future city where science and technology have provided for all needs and pleasures, the inhabitants can no longer distract themselves with immediate concerns and problems from the inevitability, the incomprehensibility of death.

The reader also understands that the technicians and architects who designed the radiant city maintain an institute of theoretical physicists upon which their work depends. These physicists work to understand the laws governing the mineral and energy resources with which the city is built. They have come to understand that these resources, and the city, are doomed to disappear in the oncoming explosion and extinction of the sun.

No Seasons

I took the road up Norway, across Finland and Sweden, then back to Norway again, stopping two to five days where I found lodging—some three thousand miles, but mountains, fjords, cliffs, always the sky, and the very peninsula rising; it was a summer of verticality. So many bald mountains and cliffs, tundra covered with boulders, eight-thousand-year-old rock carvings; rock was the fundamental. At Kiruna, the northernmost town in Sweden, I went vertically down a kilometer into the rock.

Stuck in Mount Kiirunavaar is a huge slab of iron ore that is four kilometers long, two-and-a-half kilometers deep, and an average of 262 feet wide—the biggest such slab in the world; 70 percent pure magnetite-apatite. In the nineteenth century, some ore was extracted in summer and transported in winter, using sleds drawn by reindeer and mules. In 1888 a train line was finished to Luleå on the Baltic Sea, and in 1902 to Narvik on the Norwegian coast. At first the ore was taken from the top of the mountain, and the slag fashioned into spiraling terraces down which it was moved. Then in 1960 the mining went underground. It is the now biggest and most modern underground iron ore mine in the world. The working tunnels are currently 1,045 meters (3,428 feet) underground; next year the depth will be 1,365 meters (4,478 feet). The guide showed us the technicians stationed in front of TV screens who by remote control operate the huge machines that drill and scoop the ore and load it onto trains. Ten trains with sixty-eight cars leave daily, each car holding a hundred tons of ore. Down in the mine, there are no seasons; the twenty-four-hour days are artificially lit, and the temperature is constant. I strolled around the behemoth drills, scoops, and loading machines while wearing a sweater.

In 1900, Director Hjalmar Lundbohm assembled architects to lay out the town of Kiruna; the existing shantytown was demolished. His house is open to visitors. He was a close friend of leading artists of the day and writers such as Strindberg; the house displays his impressive art collection. Nearby is the Kiruna Kyrka; in 2001 it was voted Sweden's most beautiful church. After World War II, the town was completely renovated, and most pre-1920 buildings were demolished. A city hall was built; in 1964 Swedish architects voted it the most beautiful public building in Sweden. The town center clusters high-rise residential buildings and a six-floor luxury hotel built in the last two decades.

I was reading about the mine one night when a rumbling shook my room. The night clerk said it was the mine. Every morning at 2:30, high explosives detonate, breaking thousands of tons of iron ore from the heart of the mountain. Scooped out, the resulting caves are filled with rubble.

Conversation in the tourist office. In 2003, huge crevasses appeared in the surface area below the mountain; the wall that tilted at a 60° angle overhanging the extractions was found to be fissioned, with cracks spreading. Experts determined that crevasses were going to open across the town. The tourism person on duty showed me some leaflets, maps, and diagrams.

In 2004, the city government decided to move Kiruna because the geological situation threatens the modern town center, with its new luxury hotel and apartment buildings. Some houses that can be moved will be, but most buildings will be demolished. The City Hall will be sliced into four or six pieces and transported to the new site; the church as well. A new town for the 25,000 inhabitants will be built, at a cost of more than $4 billion U.S. dollars.

The experts involved in this project think big. In the coming decades, climate change and the predicted sea level rise will require the world's biggest cities, most of which are on ocean coasts, to move populations to higher ground. In 2008, the Kiruna officials organized a conference that brought in experts from everywhere to discuss this coming nomadism of the sedentary centers in the new planetary epoch we have produced. I was given some brochures left over from that meeting.

Outer Space and Home

Outside of Kiruna is the Esrange Space Centre, where the Swedish Space Corporation tracks satellites. Billionaire Richard Branson has determined that it will be the European spaceport for spacecraft that his Virgin Galactic is building for tourism in outer space. "We would love to send up people in a rocket so that they get to experience the northern lights from space," Branson told the press. I learn that launches are set to start soon, tickets set at $200,000. There will be take-offs summer and winter in Kiruna, to outer space where there are no seasons.

My plane just flew at thirty-five thousand feet and landed in the afternoon. It was 81°F—a normal summer day in Baltimore. Strolled around my house; the weeds had begun to fill in the yard again. Then it got dark; I couldn't see things anymore. Went into the house. Couldn't think of what to do.

Notes

1. Friedrich Nietzsche, *The Gay Science*, trans. Walter Kaufmann (New York: Vintage, 1974), §341.

2. Bruce Chatwin, *The Songlines* (New York: Penguin Books, 1988).

3. Edgar Allan Poe, "A Descent into the Maelstrom," *The Complete Tales and Poems of Edgar Allan Poe* (New York: Vintage, 1975), 129.

4. Gilles Deleuze and Félix Guattari, *A Thousand Plateaus*, trans. Brian Massumi (Minneapolis: University of Minnesota Press, 1980).

5. Eugène Ionesco, *Exit the King and Other Plays*, trans. Donald Watson (New York: Grove Press, 1994).

7

Seasonal Affective Order

The Passage of Sense in Circumpolar Religion

JOSEPH BALLAN

Affective and Natural Orders

An entry in the journal of early nineteenth-century sensationalist philosopher Maine de Biran articulates a rather common thought about the way
humans experience the natural patterns of the year: "Each season has, not
only its own kind or order of sensations, but also a fundamental feeling
of existence which is both analogous to it and which is reproduced rather
uniformly with each return of the same season."[1] In ordinary discourse, it
is readily admitted that each season is associated with a particular set of
emotions or affective tonalities. But if the correspondence between an order
of feeling and an order that obtains in the physical world, which is to
say, between an affective order and a natural order, is an *analogy*, as Biran
claims, who or what constructs such an analogy? How does it come about
that affects get attached to regular, patterned changes in the environment?
Such a process doubtless involves natural, social, individual, and even poetic
forces, and is therefore a great deal more complex than Biran's observation
indicates. Religion represents one relevant set of social and poetic forces for
understanding how a seasonal affective order originates, gets perpetuated, and
changes. Operating at the nexus of ritual, story, and seasonal patterns of the
environment, religions determine a way of experiencing the world and its
alterations. In this way, religions are one of the social, but also poetic, means
by which an analogy between affective and natural orders gets constructed.

The present paper attempts to elaborate upon this thesis, taking as a kind of case study the religious lives of some circumpolar peoples. It has long been observed that social life in the Arctic regions, including the rituals enacted in and the stories transmitted by religious life, connects strongly to the extreme alternation between winter days in which there is very little sunlight, and summer days in which the sun sets for only a very short period every day. Additionally, these regions have, in the past century alone, experienced significant changes in both the physical environment (the effects of climate change are perhaps nowhere as tangible as in the Arctic) and religious life (a result of Christian missionary work has been the conversion of many Inuit, for example, to Christianity). For these reasons, the question of the "analogy" between seasonal patterns in the natural world and the sensations tied to religious life is especially pertinent for an interpretation of human life in the earth's circumpolar regions. In the second half of the paper, we turn to some examples of life in these regions with our questions about seasonality in mind. First, however, it is necessary to make clear what exactly we might expect to learn about natural and affective orders from these examples, in the context of this brief essay. Many of us likely have a rough sense of what Biran means when he speaks about an analogy between the natural order and an order of feeling or sensations. But how can we make this intuitive sense of a connection between the experience of the natural world and affective life more precise?

In this paper, I wish to outline the elements of a theoretical framework—a set of concepts, questions, and concerns—for interpreting the relationship between affective order and natural order. Specifically, I argue that Henri Lefebvre's idea of rhythmanalysis and Augustin Berque's idea of mesology hold particular promise for identifying what is at stake in the kinds of questions raised in the previous paragraphs. But the goal is not so much to offer a new methodology for empirical research as it is to investigate the conditions of and constraints upon any circulation of meaning (and thus of any analogy) between social, natural, and affective temporal worlds. How does it come about, we ask, that religion gets inscribed upon the very bodies of individuals dwelling within particular natural realms?

Rhythmanalysis and the
Critique of Everyday Life in the Modern World

Among the possible reasons for the general neglect of Henri Lefebvre's idea of rhythmanalysis, developed toward the end of his long career, is the unusual breadth and wildness of the interdisciplinarity that it imagines, bringing together, according to one list, "history, climatology, cosmology, poetry, etc."[2] From Lefebvre's perspective, such interdisciplinarity is necessitated by the object he gives himself to think: human life as a site of complex interactions between a multiplicity of rhythmic forms, between "rhythms of the self" and "rhythms of the other," but also between natural rhythms and the rhythms fashioned by social imaginaries.[3] Nowhere in his fragmentary reflections on rhythmanalysis does Lefebvre reflect on exactly what contribution to that field cosmology or climatology might make, which leaves a question for those working in the wake of his project. Given that he includes poetry alongside these two fields, and given that rhythmanalysis is the study of interactions and interferences between different rhythmic measures, however, it would seem to be faithful to the original spirit of Lefebvre's inquiry to develop a relatively expansive understanding of cosmology and climatology.[4] Such an idea of cosmology would include poetic, cultural, or religious *and* natural or physical senses of these words, and it might also point to the inseparability of nature from cultural fields like ritual religion.

In his classic study of collective memory, Maurice Halbwachs observes that religions often "adapt themselves to seasonal variations," but Halbwachs does not raise as a theoretical problem the medial form of life established by the interaction between the cultural rhythms of religion and the natural cycles of seasonal time.[5] What Lefebvre calls *interaction*, Augustin Berque calls *médiance*. He makes this neologism a term of art, defining it as a "passage of sense between nature and society, between the physical world and the phenomenal world."[6] Take the notion of a "passage of sense [*sens*]," or meaning, as that which makes possible any metaphor or analogy between the natural order and the affective order. Berque wants to move away from a conception according to which humans and the natural world within which they dwell are taken as entities exterior to each other and subsequently coordinated by thinking, and to move toward a better understanding of the earth "*insofar as* it is inhabited by humanity."[7] Such an approach leads him to study "ecosymbolics," understood as the appropriation "at once material and semantic" of the physical world.[8] Religions once furnished the semantic elements out of which an ecosymbolics could be fashioned, and the weakening hold of such elements constitutes part of the crisis of modernity, according to Berque.[9] Under the rubric of a new mode of thought that he calls *mesology*, drawing inspiration from the Japanese philosopher Watsuji Tetsuro's notion of *fudosei*, Berque's work attempts to study the ambiguities that constitute the milieux within which humans dwell.[10] In this section, we will first clarify the significance of seasons for Lefebvre's project before showing how Berque's idea of *médiance* provides a helpful corrective to some of Lefebvre's simplifications and shortcomings.

Although the field of cultural studies has generally neglected the investigation of the seasons, one of its founding texts, the first (1947) volume of Lefebvre's *Critique de la vie quotidienne*, gives an interpretation of the cultural significance of seasonal cycles that is also a meditation on religion in the modern world and perhaps the earliest anticipation of his rhythmanalytical project. As such, it demonstrates in exemplary fashion the theoretical connection between seasonal variations and religious life. There is an uneven quality to the volume in question, with technical discussions of Marx as a philosopher flanked by comparatively more free-wheeling excursions into the worlds of literature and culture. Chapter 5, which follows on the heels of an account of Marxism as critical knowledge of "how we live" and even, strikingly, as a contribution to an "art of living,"[11] marks a somewhat abrupt shift in analytical modality, as Lefebvre begins to reflect on rural community life, culminating in a poignant, personal reflection on the shape of the Christian rite as celebrated in a church close to where Lefebvre himself grew up. The chapter evokes a qualitatively rich world of everyday life with origins in ancient societies, but one which persists today in (often threatened) rural communities. This richness stands in stark contrast to the level of everyday life as Lefebvre perceives it in the postindustrial world. Ancient and rural societies, Lefebvre asserts, are more attuned to forms of cyclical time than are modern societies, dominated as they are by the temporality of the atomic clock. Two forms of cyclical time, broadly construed, are pertinent here, and they are connected to each other: rite or ritual and the seasons.

The question of cyclical time in these forms is one that traverses Lefebvre's oeuvre. In his outline of rhythmanalysis as a mode of inquiry, he describes rites and rituals (both religious and secular) as being doubly rhythmic: their periodic recurrence in everyday life grants a rhythm to social time in a given community, and they themselves are also marked by a rhythm internal to them.[12] That is to say, their own rhythm interacts with the other rhythms constituting the fabric of the ordinary in a given place and time. Forty years earlier, in a rural rather than an urban context, Lefebvre was meditating on the ways in which communities bind the time of their lives to the times of the physical world. By establishing a particular form of social time on the basis of the "material," so to speak, of the natural world, communities establish a regularity that would be common to the calendar of festivals and to the astronomical seasons.[13] Here is perhaps the one topic pertaining to religiosity in Lefebvre's oeuvre to which he does not apply a form of a standard Marxist critique. Because "ritual" and "magic" are primary tools by which the societies in question give this form to lived time, they contribute to the richness of everyday life that Lefebvre celebrates (and whose slow disappearance he mourns) in this chapter, evoking a time when "man [sic] cooperated with nature; he maintained and regulated its energies, both by his real work and by the (fictitious) effectiveness of his magic."[14]

Even in the age of secular modernity, Lefebvre thinks, a cultural memory of the lived significance of the seasons (especially the winter solstice and the return of spring) persists, but without the "Dionysian joy" that characterizes archaic and rural celebrations. Marcel Mauss seems to make a similar observation in reviewing his friend and colleague Henri Hubert's 1906 essay on representations of time in religion and magic. There he suggests that the contemporary European problem that solicits Hubert's transhistorical and transcultural study of the ways in which religious symbols and practices construct social time is the problem of the secular. Hubert's essay ends with the startling claim that the original function of calendars is essentially religious. Despite the apparent rigidity with which calendars organize time, despite the *homogeneity* they seem to impose, their real purpose is actually the marking of those days and seasons that are *heterogeneous* in relation to quotidian time. In his review, Mauss takes the step that Hubert does not: he considers the impact of the advent of secular modernity on this immemorial function of the calendar. "Today," Mauss writes, "religious chronology remains caught in . . . limbo, for a significant part of our mental activity continues to depend on old ways [that is, theological or ecclesiastical ways] of counting and classifying"[15]—old ways, that is, of marking time, of endowing the inexorable flow of the irreversible with rhythms that are experienced, learned, and that become the basis of expectations and desires. Even in an era over which homogeneous time holds sway, old modes of time-reckoning and synchronizing communal life with the physical rhythms of the seasons persist.

Mesology and the Philosophical Dignity of the Sensible

We shall return to Mauss, who establishes the seasons as a question of the social in an early study of Eskimo life, in the following section. First, however, I wish to suggest a slight corrective or revision to Lefebvre's rhythmanalytical project, beginning from Berque's work. Lefebvre presents his project as one of recovering the "dignity" of the "sensible" within philosophy.[16] To accomplish this task, however, more is needed than a simple empiricist reversal, whereby physical and natural along with cultural objects and phenomena become the objects of discourse. Instead, Lefebvre needs (and lacks) an idea of sense and the sensible that would attune us to the ambiguities constitutive of sense itself as a bearer of human existence on the earth. A symptom of this theoretical lacuna is that Lefebvre associates symbols and symbolisms with the "cosmic rhythms" of rural life without accounting for this connection between a form of lived time, a form of social life, and a symbolic form.[17] "Sense" itself, as Jean-Luc Nancy has suggested, commenting on Hegel, is a kind of "transport" or "passage" between *sense* construed as immediate intuition of a sensory manifold "out there" and *sense* construed as the meaning or thought of what is thus apprehended.[18] Likewise, as we have already seen, for Berque, a human *milieu* is a "passage of sense between nature and society, between the physical world and the phenomenal world." By virtue of its object, mesology gives itself the paradoxical task of "raisonner la sensibilité, sensibiliser la raison."[19]

Berque gives us a richer vocabulary for talking about interaction and interference than Lefebvre's rhythmanalysis provides because he shows how these kinds of relationships between varying rhythmic measures and time scales result in a *meaning* or *sense* of a given milieu that is nonetheless irreducible to a semiotics.[20] The sense of a milieu, as we have noted, is its *médiance,* but Berque does not limit this relationship to ancient and rural societies (which is not to say that he would not agree with Lefebvre's analysis of a significant shift, for the worse, in this natural-social relationship), making it instead a veritable anthropological principle: *médiance* determines a way of "being human on the earth." It defines a movement of existing, in the strong sense of holding oneself [*sistere*] outside [*ex*] in the open, of moving outside of oneself.[21] An understanding of this middleness, intermediarity, and relatedness is necessary to account for seasonality as a condition of human existence, as identified in the comment by Biran cited in the introduction. Berque's work indicates a powerful approach to this sensory significance of the seasons because it brings into focus the more general fact of "being-between" nature and culture as a "power of movement" that characterizes human life. We shall therefore let it inform our discussion in the final sections of the paper.

The Rhythmanalysis of Eskimo Societies by Mauss and Beuchat

Let us now consider the stakes of these theoretical perspectives on seasonality and the relation between phenomenal and physical orders of things by turning to a concrete example: the seasonal variations characteristic of Northern peoples, especially the Inuit of Canada and Greenland. As noted above, this region is particularly pertinent for the problem of seasonality for several reasons. This problem is the subject of a 1906 study written by Marcel Mauss with the help of Henri Beuchat, itself the product of a seminar given at the Sorbonne in 1904-05 on the basis of European and North American texts about Eskimo life. The basic fact that they give themselves to think in that book is a phenomenon identified by many of the explorers, ethnographers, and missionaries who wrote about circumpolar life before them: Eskimo life is characterized by winters filled with intense social, festive, and religious activity, with all the members of a community living very close to one another in a settlement, and summers when families disperse to spend time away from the rest of the community and the only rituals observed are those associated with birth and death.

Together with this division of activities goes a concomitant division of all material objects and persons into categories according to their association with "winter" or "summer."[22] In the Arctic, a place of extremes, a very dark winter gives way rather quickly to summer days marked by very long sunlight. Correlatively, there is an alternation between a very concentrated social life and a relaxation or reversal of this concentration that corresponds exactly to the seasons of winter and summer. The core thesis put forward by Mauss and Beuchat is that this "rhythm of concentration and dispersion"[23] fulfills a "natural need" of human beings, who cannot sustain an intense communal life indefinitely.[24] Insofar as they ascribe to "each social function" a "rhythm of its own," the book can be seen as a precursor of Lefebvre's idea of rhythmanalysis.[25] Like Lefebvre, they also emphasize the survival of these rhythmic forms of concentration and dispersion in modernity (e.g., those brief times of year, usually during the summer, when it seems that everyone leaves the cities to go on holiday[26]). Moreover, they provide an example of the sort of temporal binding-together of social life with the life of nature that Lefebvre mourns in the chapter from the *Critique of Everyday Life* discussed above. Lefebvre seems to mourn, in particular, the loss of the ancient and rural "festival" in the quotidian modern world. Winter festivities, more than anything else, Mauss and Beuchat explain in their account of the effect of seasonal variations on Inuit religious life, express "the feeling which the community has of itself."[27]

Mauss and Beuchat's central question is the following: what is the *function* of this seasonal variation common to communal and natural life? Their conclusion is that "the seasons are not the direct determining cause of the phenomena they occasion; they act, rather, upon the social density that they regulate."[28] This statement, which is meant to clarify the relationship between a material (seasonal) substratum and the stratum of social life that overlays it, so to speak, is itself dense and demands further reflection and clarification. This is especially true given the anthropological ambition of the concluding chapter in which it appears, that is, its ambition to say something about an inherent human need for a social life that expands and contracts, as it were. What does it mean to claim that, in relation to social time, the cyclical time of the seasons does not function *causally* but nevertheless has a *regulatory* purpose? That life among the Inuit is characterized by what we could call seasonal affective *order* is unquestionable, but what is the seasons' mode of acting upon social life, if it is not causal? It is here, I think, that the basic theoretical gesture of Berque might be of use. Recall that this basic gesture consists in attempting to formulate a "principle of integration that takes account of both subjective or phenomenal transformations (metaphors) and objective or physical transformations (metabolisms, ecological cycles), which converge in giving a unitary sense to a milieu."[29] This principle accords with the unwillingness of Mauss and Beuchat to make claims about causation. Rather than a unidirectional determinism, Berque's work prompts us to consider the possibility that the seasonally regulated or "rhythmed" life of circumpolar peoples is a more complex mediation between the specific space-time of a community and its material substratum.

Some Passages of Sense

But to advance this line of thought, more work on the side of "subjective or phenomenal transformations" among the Inuit would be needed. In the final section of this essay, we outline some areas of cultural life that illustrate the circulation between social, poetic, natural, and affective registers that rhythmanalysis and mesology bring into view. Such a perspective could effectively supplement the framework of Mauss and Beuchat. Nowhere in their book do Mauss and Beuchat discuss, for example, the important Inuit concept of *sila*. As the work of Bernard Saladin d'Anglure, who himself acts as a kind of go-between or mediator between cosmography or astronomy and cosmology, has shown, this concept endows the seasons with a symbolic and ritual significance essential for understanding the seasonal regulation of religious and social life in the Arctic regions. Mauss and Beuchat themselves recognized that there must be more fine-grained rhythms than the binary alternation they discuss, and Saladin d'Anglure shows how, even within the single season of winter, the rhythm of the moon and its declination is of social significance. The Inuit calendar "is a lunar-solar one [in which] the moon and the sun form a system, as much in physical reality as in symbolic representations," a system that furnishes an example of "the dynamic unity of opposites in *sila*, which remains the great cosmic referent of the universe."[30] The function of the winter religious festivals is not merely to ensure the "continued subsistence" of the collective, but to restore this unity of *sila* through a linking of "the myths and rites of shamanistic space-time to the social time of the people" at a time of year when "the great equilibrium of *sila* and the universe seemed challenged."[31] Saladin d'Anglure shows how this process is understood according to a mythologization of the sun, moon, and the polar bear as a creature that passes easily between the worlds of land and water. We shall not go into these details here, simply noting instead the integration of astronomical "selenocentric computation" and a metaphorical or mythological understanding of reality. In this instance, observation and narrativization of the natural world interpenetrate each other in a passing of sense between human communities and the terrestrial firmament.

Yet there is another, perhaps even more telling respect in which *sila* is a relevant concept for our discussion of seasonality and *médiance*. According to A. Nicole Stuckenberger, who has done extensive ethnographic work with Inuit in Canada, this concept demonstrates that weather and climate are irreducible to the plane of the natural world, according to the traditional Inuit understanding. She explains that *sila* has as connotations "universe," "sky," and "weather" alike,[32] enumerating, in addition, a number of composite Igloolik expressions that include this term. To cite a few: "*Silatuvuq*: S/he is intelligent, has understanding/sense . . . *Silaujualuq*: A very intelligent or reasonable person . . . *Silaap Inua*: Spirit master of the universe . . . *Silaluttuq*: Bad weather."[33] It would seem that the understanding or intelligence in question here depends on a relationship to the natural and spiritual order of things, rather than being intellect in the abstract sense. The semantic richness of the morpheme *sila* highlighted by Stuckenberger seems to accord well with *médiance* taken as a *sense* of the milieu that we have been working to develop throughout this essay, as a passage between natural and subjective or phenomenal forms of sense, between sense as apprehension and sense as understood meaning.

Now, by allying rhythmanalysis with sociology, Lefebvre runs the risk of "recasting the arbitrary as necessary" that is common to all sociological projects.[34] Yet Lefebvre is in fact concerned—perhaps above everything—with possibility, both with understanding what in the past made the present possible, and with nurturing the emergence of the new. The burden of his critique of everyday life is to display the non-immutability of a specific level of existence within the order of things, to analyze "what can and ought to change in human reality."[35] The ultimate object of this critical project is the changeable, the possible. Therefore, it is appropriate that we conclude our study by taking note of some of the notable *changes* that are taking place and that have already taken place in the kinds of Arctic cultures we have been discussing and that are relevant for the issues raised in this essay.

One of the reasons we gave at the outset for focusing on the seasons in circumpolar life was the remarkable changes the circumpolar regions have undergone even in the hundred years that have passed since the publication of Mauss and Beuchat's classic study. Stuckenberger's work allows us to register a few such changes. For example, she notes that, for the Inuit, seasonal change is not strictly regulated according to the calendar, but is instead connected to the formation and break-up of ice floes.[36] Therefore, as reduced sea ice continues to be observed as an effect of the general warming of the Arctic, this alteration of the landscape has consequences for the rhythms that regulate social life among the Inuit. Another major cultural change is contact with Europeans and the Christianization of the Canadian Inuit. The work of Frédéric Laugrand and Jarich Oosten has shown that the Inuit adoption of Christianity, though resulting in major changes especially with respect to shamanistic practices, did not cause a simple cultural "loss," but illustrates instead the "amazing creativity" and "cultural innovation" on the part of the Inuit who integrated Christian symbols and practices into their traditional belief system.[37] On the basis of interviews with community elders, they discern a number of Christian ideas that the Inuit themselves seem to have found attractive.[38]

As for post-contact seasonal variation more generally, Stuckenberger suggests that in the century since they organized and interpreted the existing ethnographic data on the topic, the patterns described by Mauss and Beuchat with respect to the seasons is precisely the reverse of what they observed in the literature of their day: "Whereas the winter camp was the ideal social configuration in Mauss & Beuchat's description, it is the spring/summer camp that is perceived by Inuit to be the ideal configuration at present."[39] One possible explanation for this reversal lies in the association of life on the land in the summer camps with older, traditional practices that have been occluded if not forgotten in post-contact modernity.[40] Movement[41] and rhythm characterize traditional Inuit community, and among the effects of contact with Europeans was an interruption of this movement in the form of "programs for the sedentarization of the Inuit."[42] Social life in winter settlements, then, becomes associated, to some extent, with colonization, and social life in summer camps becomes an escape from the sedentarization effected by colonization, a reconnection with traditional ways of life, and a time for visiting and socializing with people outside the family unit. There is still a rhythm of concentration and dispersion associated with particular seasons, but the social signification or valuation has changed slightly.

Nonetheless, winter festivity retains the "intimacy" observed and summarized by Mauss and Beuchat a century ago, although it now employs the Christian symbols of Christmas (*Quviasuvik*, literally, "place/time of joy"). Laugrand and Oosten give as an example of Inuit creativity and innovation the integration of Christian symbols and imagery into the traditional winter celebrations.[43] It would be incorrect, they show, to elide the processes of colonization and Christianization too closely in this case. Unlike instances of missionary activity in other times and places, as Stuckenberger also emphasizes, the Canadian Inuit were not forced to become Christian; they were not passive recipients of an alien theological system, but savvy cultural innovators. For example, in addition to reinventing the traditional winter feasts in the image of Christmas, they developed their own ceremony (*siqqiqtirniq*) to mark an individual's transition to Christianity, which involves the eating of a food that was not permitted by traditional mores: the heart of a seal.[44] As Laugrand and Oosten put it, with such rituals, "Inuit shaped their own conversion."[45]

Needless to say, however, circumpolar cultures and religions, along with their experiences of contact with Europeans, differ widely. So do reactions to these experiences. What anthropologists Oosten and Laugrand characterize as creative adaptation of Christian symbols, Greenlandic activist Aqqaluk Lynge describes as a "manipulation of the mind and spirit" more powerful than any "military force."[46] His poetry poignantly attests to a resentment of the changes brought by Europeans to his island. He speaks, for example, of the contemporary practice of Inuit traditions as an *imitation* of the "life that was ours / that was once our own."[47] Today, the social life of native Greenlanders is subjected to the indifferent "calendar without days" by which the Danish colonizers organized their own time (in Greenland).[48] An analysis of the variety of possible perspectives that could be taken and that have been taken on the history of contact between Inuit and Europeans would constitute a task for an entirely different paper. As Lynge himself notes, the "spiritual invasion" of Christian missionaries, because it resulted in both positive and negative effects, "is difficult for posterity to pass judgment on."[49] However the process according to which traditional practices were transformed to accommodate Christianity and European cultural patterns is interpreted, what is unquestionable is the transformation effected by this process on macro time scales.

In conclusion, one reason for preferring to describe the relation between the natural world and social life as regulatory (or rhythmic) and not as causal in a straightforward, unidirectional way is that a causal model presumes that the two terms in the relationship—the material substratum and the social realm—stand over against each other. Berque's mode of thinking attunes us to the middleness characteristic of every human milieu, the spacing and relatedness characteristic of human life vis-à-vis its earthy support. Lefebvre's rhythmanalytical project encourages us to think about this relation in terms of time, especially insofar as societies produce qualitatively different times (different in comparison to other societies, but also different inasmuch as different segments of the calendar year are experienced as having differing affective tonalities). It also reminds us of the mutability of such forms of time. While we can be grateful to scholars like Laugrand and Oosten for the work they have done on this question in the Canadian context, the history of modern religions in the circumpolar region, taken as a whole, still remains to be written. Such a history would need to include an account of the profound transformations on this particular level of forms of time and forms of life, of seasonality as a relation between temporal physical changes and the organization of meaning and affect on individual and collective levels. We hope that the perspective developed in this paper at least poses some of the questions that such future investigations might begin to answer in more detail.

Notes

1. Maine de Biran, *Journal*, ed. Henri Gouhier (Neuchatel: Baconnière, 1954), 77–78.

2. Henri Lefebvre, *Rhythmanalysis: Space, Time, and Everyday Life*, ed. and trans. Stuart Elden (New York: Continuum, 2004), 16.

3. Lefebvre, *Rhythmanalysis*, 95.

4. Lefebvre, *Rhythmanalysis*, 76.

5. Maurice Halbwachs, *On Collective Memory*, trans. Lewis Coser (Chicago: University of Chicago Press, 1992), 92.

6. Augustin Berque, *Médiance* (Paris: Belin, 2000), 33.

7. Augustin Berque, *Être humains sur la terre: Principes de l'éthique de l'écoumène* (Paris: Gallimard, 1996), 78.

8. Berque, *Être humains sur la terre*, 79.

9. Berque, *Être humains sur la terre*, 80.

10. Berque, *Médiance*, 80.

11. Henri Lefebvre, *The Critique of Everyday Life*, vol. I, trans. John Moore (New York: Verso, 1991), 196–200.

12. Lefebvre, *Rhythmanalysis*, 94.

13. Lefebvre, *The Critique of Everyday Life*, 204.

14. Lefebvre, *The Critique of Everyday Life*, 205.

15. Marcel Mauss, "Review of Hubert's Essay on Time," *Essay on Time: A Brief Study of the Representation of Time in Religion and Magic*, trans. Robert Parkin (Oxford: Durkheim Press, 1999), 94.

16. Lefebvre, *Rhythmanalysis*, 21.

17. See Henri Lefebvre, *The Critique of Everyday Life*, vol. II, trans. Gregory Elliot (New York: Verso, 2002), 302.

18. Jean-Luc Nancy, *Hegel: The Restlessness of the Negative*, trans. Jason Smith and Steven Miller (Minneapolis: University of Minnesota Press, 2002), 46.

19. Berque, *Médiance*, 86.

20. Berque, *Médiance*, 42.

21. Augustin Berque, *Ecoumène: Introduction à l'étude des milieux humains* (Paris: Belin, 2000), 126.

22. Marcel Mauss and Henri Beuchat, *Seasonal Variations of the Eskimo: A Study in Social Morphology*, trans. James J. Fox (Boston: Routledge & Kegan Paul, 1979), 60.

23. Mauss and Beuchat, *Seasonal Variations of the Eskimo*, 56.

24. Mauss and Beuchat, *Seasonal Variations of the Eskimo*, 79.

25. Mauss and Beuchat, *Seasonal Variations of the Eskimo*, 79.

26. Mauss and Beuchat, *Seasonal Variations of the Eskimo*, 78.

27. Mauss and Beuchat, *Seasonal Variations of the Eskimo*, 58.

28. Mauss and Beuchat, *Seasonal Variations of the Eskimo*, 79.

29. Berque, *Médiance*, 36–37.

30. Bernard Saladin d'Anglure, "Brother Sun, Sister Sun, and the Direction of the World: From Arctic Cosmography to Inuit Cosmology," *Circumpolar Religion and Ecology*, ed. Takashi Irimoto and Takako Yamada (Tokyo: University of Tokyo Press, 1994), 207.

31. Bernard Saladin d'Anglure, "Brother Sun, Sister Sun," 208.

32. A. Nicole Stuckenburger, *Thin Ice: Inuit Traditions within a Changing Environment* (Hanover: University Press of New England, 2007), 33.

33. Stuckenburger, *Thin Ice*, 33.

34. Jacques Rancière, *The Philosopher and His Poor*, trans. John Drury, Corinne Oster, and Andrew Parker (Durham, NC: Duke University Press, 2003), 204.

35. Henri Lefebvre, *Critique*, vol. II, 97; see also 63.

36. A. Nicole Stuckenburger, *Community at Play: Social and Religious Dynamics in the Modern Inuit Community of Qikiqtarjuaq* (Amsterdam: Rozenberg, 2005), 106.

37. Frédéric Laugrand and Jarich Oosten, *Inuit Shamanism and Christianity: Transitions and Transformations in the Twentieth Century* (Montreal: McGill-Queen's University Press, 2010), 35.

38. Frédéric Laugrand and Jarich Oosten, "Shamanism and Missionaries: Transitions and Transformations in the Kivalliq Coastal Area," *Native Christians: Modes and Effects of Christianity among Indigenous Peoples of the Americas*, ed. Aparecida Vilaça and Robin M. Wright (Burlington: Ashgate, 2009), 181.

39. Stuckenburger, *Community*, 134.

40. Stuckenburger, *Community*, 122.

41. Stuckenburger, *Community*, 32.

42. Stuckenburger, *Community*, 38.

43. Laugrand and Oosten, *Shamanism*, 69–100.

44. Laugrand and Oosten, "Shamans," 171.

45. Laugrand and Oosten, "Shamans," 182.

46. Aqqaluk Lynge, *Inuit: Inuit Issittormiut Katuffiata oqaluttuassartaa* (Nuuk: Atuakkiorfik, 1993), 35.

47. Aqqaluk Lynge, *Taqqat uummammut aqqutaannut takorluukkat apuuffiannut* (Montreal: International Polar Institute, 2008), 102.

48. Lynge, *Taqqat uummammut aqqutaannut takorluukkat apuuffiannut*, 104.

49. Lynge, *Inuit*, 36.

Everyday Aesthetics

8

The Almanac Projects

Modeling the Seasons through the Material World

Jo Law

Seasons are social and cultural constructs that help humans navigate the world of things. An almanac is an ancient tool—a scientific instrument—for mapping and understanding experiences of physical environmental systems. This essay takes the almanac form as a departure point to argue how weather observations can be a creative encounter that continually defines the seasons. I present my own almanac projects: *The Autumn Almanac of Tokyo* 東京の 秋の生活暦 (2008) and *The Illustrated Almanac of the Illawarra and Beyond* (2011–2018) to illustrate how almanacs provide an active open framework that facilitates creative engagement with the living and non-living worlds. The essay argues that the almanac as a medium opens up a space for studying encounters with environmental systems at different scales. It has the potential to make perceptible an inclusive and encompassing ecology that constitutes our multifaceted experience of the seasons.

To help achieve these aims, I draw upon Jane Bennett's "vital materialism" as a central framework to consider weather, seasons, and climate as human and non-human assemblages. By constructing models of seasons from a vital materialist perspective, I argue that we may be able to conceive of the complex, entangled agencies that contribute to the experience of the seasons in different ways. From this basis I put forward the notion that the almanacs provide a medium for such aesthetic practices to be realized. I do so in two parts: first I outline the central components of Bennett's

Figure 8.1. Jo Law, *The Illustrated Almanac of the Illawarra and Beyond: September*, offset lithographic print, 76 × 56 cm, 2016.

ontology and how they may present ways of thinking about our experience of the seasons. Secondly, I show how Bennett's vital materialism and its adjacent philosophical methodologies can be applied to weather observations in general, and specifically, in the creation of almanacs. This paper asks: What elements do we incorporate into our maps of weather, seasons, and climate? What possibilities exist if we construct our conception of weather and seasons from non-human perspectives? How does an almanac construct these alternative and evolving models of seasons? And what are the implications of these models?

1.

In *Vibrant Matter: A Political Ecology of Things*, Bennett advocates for a "vital materialism" that questions the divide between non-living and living "things."[1] She argues that we ought to re-think matter in terms of the agency often afforded to living beings. Drawing from diverse sources in philosophy, critical theory, science, and literature, Bennett's project constructs a way of

小雪
しょうせつ

天氣上騰地氣下降
①②③④⑤

Figure 8.2. Jo Law, "Shousetsu: Heaven's essence rises, earth's essence sinks/ North wind, freezing rain (3 of 5)," 2008, *The Autumn Almanac of Tokyo*.

thinking that accounts for the capacities of non-human entities to affect and to be affected. She prefaces her argument by outlining her reasons and motivations:

> Why advocate the vitality of matter? Because my hunch is that the image of dead or thoroughly instrumentalized matter feeds human hubris and our earth-destroying fantasies of conquest and consumption. It does so by preventing us from detecting (seeing, hearing, smelling, tasting, feeling) a fuller range of the nonhuman powers circulating around and within human bodies. These material powers, which can aid or destroy, enrich or disable, ennoble or degrade us, in any case call for our attentiveness. The figure of an intrinsically inanimate matter may be one of the impediments to the emergence of more ecological and more materially sustainable modes of production and consumption.[2]

By aligning with the philosophies of Baruch Spinoza, Denis Diderot, and Gilles Deleuze, Bennett reinvigorates the potential of a novel approach to materialist thinking. It is important to emphasize that, for Bennett, vibrant materialism rejects the assertion of vitality being something that is *external*

to matter itself. Indeed, Levi Bryant suggests that Bennett's vitality need not
invoke something other than matter itself.[3] Unlike the critical vitalism of
Henri Bergson and Hans Driesch (who posit an *élan vital* or entelechy in
their concepts of materiality), vital materialism asserts matter's own self-or-
ganizing capacity as an agency—an active force situated within material
forms, both living and nonliving. Bryant refers to Aristotle's observation of
matter's potential to take forms, and drawing on contemporary scientific
understanding of matter, he argues that this agency (alignment of molecules
within a crystalline structure, for instance) resides entirely within the material
itself. Manuel DeLanda characterizes this tendency for entities to act in one
way rather than another as their innate properties, emerged from interactions
between constituent parts. Rather than conceiving matter as activated by
external agencies or forces, Bennett's vital materialism regards the qualities
of aliveness and affect as immanent to all matter. Bennett describes this
agency as "*Thing-Power:* the curious ability of inanimate things to animate,
to act, to produce effects dramatic and subtle."[4] In many ways, Bennett's
vital materiality awakens the magical sense of things that children often hold
when regarding the world around them without invoking extra substances
or supernatural causes historically associated with vitalist traditions. In this
political ecology of things, all matter plays a part in an interconnected net-
work that precipitates into events. She writes, "My aim . . . is to theorize a
vitality intrinsic to materiality as such, and to detach materiality from the
figures of passive, mechanistic, or divinely infused substance."[5] By re-figuring
the ontological imaginary by which we understand matter, Bennett hopes
to initiate a more ecologically sound relationship between humans and the
rest of the material world. Thus, her philosophical-political project can be
deployed to construct a model of seasons that can incorporate the enmeshed
networks of all things.

But just how do we conceptualize seasons and weather as assemblages
that are composed of vital materials? Central to Bennett's methodology is
her use of Bruno Latour's concept of actant. She explains, "[a]ctant . . . is
Bruno Latour's term for a source of action; an actant can be human or
not, or mostly likely, a combination of both"; it is equivalent to Deleuze's
"quasi-operator" which "by virtue of its particular location in an assemblage and the fortuity of being in the right place at the right time, makes
the differences, makes things happen."[6] Actants do not require things to
be capable of intentional acts, but rather presuppose "a power that is less
masterful than agency but more active than recalcitrance," and which is a
constitutive feature of all material bodies.[7] She extends Spinoza's conative
bodies "across an ontologically heterogeneous field, rather than being a

capacity localized in a human body" to capture the efficacy of all actants at work.[8] In her book, Bennett presents actual incidents to illustrate how this agency in all matter—metal, fatty acids, worms, electricity—affect other bodies in an assemblage. She writes, "Assemblages are living, throbbing confederations that are able to function despite the persistent presence of energies that confound them from within."[9] Actants and assemblages thus form the units and networks that constitute a vital materialist framework. When examining matter as an assemblage, we can ask: What actants are at work in an assemblage? What are the relationships between these actants? How do they interact with each other? What agencies do they bear on one another? And how do they affect and get affected by other bodies?

In this essay, I place my almanac projects within this new materialist framework in order to consider how seasonal experience emerges as assemblages of living and non-living things. Rather than artworks that illustrate theoretic concepts, these almanac projects enact the new materialist mode of enquiry through encounters. Unlike weather-data-driven artworks such as Tim Knowles' *Windwalk* (2008) and Cam and Yvette Merton's *The Little Optimum* (2003), the almanac projects were not derived from a mediated relationship with weather. These projects also differ from re-creation of weather phenomena such as Fujiko Nakaya's *Fog Sculpture* (1976), Olafur Eliasson's *Weather Project* (2004) and *Vær i vejret* (2016). The almanac projects pay close attention to details of everyday life and meditate on the materiality of the material world emerged from these observations. As Bryant argues in his essay "Wilderness Ontology," "The work of art allows us to encounter even the familiar things of our everyday life in their independent thingliness, seeing them, perhaps for the very first time."[10] The creation of a disjunction between objects and experiences through art is central to seeing them anew. Bryant writes, "Art seems to carry the capacity to break with meaning, to bring the alterity and thingliness of things to the fore, to allow us to see them both from their point of view and independent of our own meanings and intentions."[11] The almanac projects make manifest aesthetic experience of observation as an inherently non-passive and creative act of perception, fundamental to exploring and understanding the world of the living and non-living.

2.

The Autumn Almanac of Tokyo was conceived as a durational project and created during my Australia Council Tokyo Studio Residency in 2008. The project took place between September 5 and December 4, framing my stay

Figure 8.3. Jo Law, "Kanro: Sparrows enter the water and turn into clams/ Chrysanthemums bloom (2 of 5)," 2008, *The Autumn Almanac of Tokyo*.

in Japan within the season of autumn.[12] Inspired by Liza Dalby's *East Wind Melts the Ice*, the project adopts the Chinese solar calendar as a structuring device to affiliate the ninety days of the residency with reference to seasonal occurrences.[13] This project was followed by *The Illustrated Almanac of the Illawarra and Beyond* (2011–2018) which collected observations of phenological occurrences, weather statistics, and astronomical information pertaining to the Illawarra region on the southeast coast of Australia. This later project was completed with twelve lithographic prints that reworked the original seventy-two online entries written over one calendar year.

An almanac is an ancient tool used to organize humans' experience of the environment into familiar and predictable patterns.[14] It is an effective medium to understand the world through its material constituents. Still in use today, the Chinese Almanac is based on a lunisolar calendar, also known as the agricultural calendar (農曆). In additional to the twelve months as defined by the phases of the moon, a year is divided into twenty-four solar terms (節氣) as determined by the position of the sun on the ecliptic. Each solar term lasts fifteen days and marks a significant point in the season, such as "start of spring," "summer solstice," and "autumnal equinox." Other solar terms are named with reference to weather events or agricultural activities as observed in ancient China, for instance, "Grain Rain" in spring. Each solar term is further divided into three pentads (候 or five-day periods). Their names are derived from general observations of ecological, climatic, agricultural, and animal activities. The seventy-two pentads bear names such as "Thunder Sings" in mid-spring, "Worms Come Forth" at the start of summer, "Cool Winds Arrive" in early autumn, and "Elks Break Antlers" in mid-winter. The calendar was adopted in Japan, Korea, and Vietnam, where the solar terms remain unchanged but the pentads were modified in accordance with local observations. This ancient almanac acts as an archaic map that not only guided farmers in their agricultural activities, but more importantly, as Dalby notes, provided a divination reference for the emperor as the "the son of heaven."[15] In the context of this ancient world, it was important to pay close attention to *all things* between heaven and earth.

The Autumn Almanac consists of ninety daily multimedia online postcards, each postcard composed of materials gathered on the day: photographs, ephemerals, audio recordings, video footage, information, questions, and thoughts. The expositions drew upon things, objects, characters, and experiences encountered on the day framing ecological and anthropogenic events within the corresponding pentads and solar terms. The project has a strong basis in the diaristic form realized by Sei Shōnagon's *The Pillow Book*[16] and Lady Muraski Shikibu's diary.[17] Specifically, it takes cues from the aesthetics of interacting with the seasons and surrounds through observations. Shōnagon's text, in particular, delineates intimate interactions between things, times, places, and transitions that occurred within her world in tenth-century Japan. It is speculated that the collection of entries in her book was conceived as lists of seasonally and aesthetically appropriate objects to be used in poetic compositions. Poetry here is composed from the brief coalescence of things: a selected flower to accompany a letter, the deliberate layering of fabric, a chance view of the river. The diarist's role is to observe these temporary meetings and draw attention to the impermanence of encounters. Dalby's use of the Chinese solar calendar in her memoir creates a deliberate layering of the ancient almanac, the two Japanese versions of this calendar, her own experience of the seasons in Berkeley, on the Sonoma coast of California, and her memories of Japan. In doing so, she allows not only different geographies to overlap but also different timelines to intersect within each pentad. *The Autumn Almanac* similarly makes use of layering by contrasting the generalized perception of seasons with their materialistic experiences in order to make sense of seasonal encounters in Tokyo. Using the modern Japanese almanac, the project extends the ancient categories of things to include pampas grass, daikon, freezing rain, and typhoons as well as *kotatsu* (a type of heater) and water pipes. These things situate the experience of contemporary Tokyo firmly in relation to the tangible materials and the assemblages that make up the everyday life.

The creation of an almanac thus necessitates a direct and active inter-action with assemblages within the material world. The nineteenth-century diarist and a founder of the Royal Society, John Evelyn, was a keen gardener. Evelyn understood not only the relationship between elements—material or immaterial—but also, importantly, that future predictions can be inferred from past experiences. He aligned weather observations with botanical ones, paying close attention to the interactions between things. After Evelyn, it became customary to describe the weather at the beginning of a diary entry. Alexander Harris writes, "Weather-watching and diary-keeping would, from now on, be almost inseparable. The recording of weather and the writing of lives would occupy the same small notebooks."[18] In *A Sand County Almanac*, Aldo Leopold retells intimate accounts of activities observed in the plant and animal worlds and the varied responses to the changing seasons in Wis-consin.[19] In his almanac, humans are a bit player in the broader world of wilderness; they live alongside the other inhabitants of the world, sometimes collaborating, other times at odds with them. In developing his theory of wilderness conservation, Leopold puts forward the concept of land ethics, writing, "The land ethic simply enlarges the boundaries of the community to include soils, waters, plants, and animals, or collectively: the land . . . In short, a land ethic changes the role of *Homo sapiens* from conqueror of the land-community to plain member or citizen of it."[20] Bryant extends the concept of wilderness ontologically to "rescue this kernel from the domain of anthropocentric experience and transform it; wilderness would signify being as *a plurality* of agencies, without ontological hierarchy—one that might refuse any bifurcation of being into nature and culture."[21] Bryant echoes Bennett and Leopold when he writes, "We need to cultivate modes of thinking that help us to become attentive to the alterity of things, the thingliness of things, and the differences that things themselves contribute independent of social construction, human intention, and human meanings."[22] I argue here that the creation of almanacs also achieves this goal. *The Autumn Almanac* draws attention to the material details of each encounter and maps the experience emerged from various assemblages. An entry during the solar term, *Kanro* (寒露 or Cold Dew) (Figure 8.4) illustrates such an engagement with the urban environment of Shinjuku and the river Kandagawa:

寒露

菊有黃華

①②③④⑤

Figure 8.4. Jo Law, "Kanro: Chrysanthemums tinge yellow/ ducks migrate, 1 of 5," 2008, *The Autumn Almanac of Tokyo*.

The Kandagawa has a long and complex history—something that I am yet to learn more about. What I can gather so far is that it was originally named Hirakawa and has a number of tributaries and diversions. Many modifications have been carried out, changing its natural appearance, shape, and character. The river's source is the Inokashira pond in Mitaka (western Tokyo). The river heads East towards Shinjuku, then winds North pass Takadanobaba, then turns West again through Bunkyo-ku (ward), running through the central districts of Tokyo (and alongside part of the Chuo line from just beyond Yotsuya, to Iidabashi, Suidobashi, and Ochanomizu). Once it passes Kanda, it joins the Sumidagawa (river) and flows into Tokyo Bay.

Much of the modifications and riverworks were ordered by the Shogun, Tokugawa Ieyasu, in the sixteenth century. The purpose was to ensure that adequate drinking water could reach the growing population of Edo. Today, the Kandagawa mainly acts as an enormous drain for storm water. Maps of the river are marked by its 104 bridges, many of which have their own significant histories. We walked along the stretch between Takadanobaba and Shinjuku (around seven kilometers). The intersection between Otakibashi (bridge) and Waseda Dori (Avenue) separates Takadanobaba from Kita-Shinjuku (North Shinjuku). The Kandagawa also separates Shinkjuku-ku (ward) to the East from Nakano-ku (ward) to the West.

Between Otakibashi and Kireibashi at the top-end of Kita-Shinjuku, the riverwalk is designed for the pleasure of pedestrians (it is closed to traffic—even to cyclists). Here, people walk their dogs, jog, exercise, meander, and enjoy the greenery, the artificial stream, and abundant public seatings. We saw two old ladies discussing how their plants are doing in their gardens; a young schoolgirl stopped and said hello to them before going next door to visit her grandmother.

Near Kashiwabashi I spotted an early reddish maple, and opposite was a grumpy-looking mermaid statue outside a small villa. Just beyond Daidobashi, around eight very old ladies were sitting in a close row in the sun, tended by their carer. They were chatting and watching the birds. They said *konnichiwa* as we walked by. We crossed Ome Kaido and Yodobashi, which separates Kita-Shinjuku from Shinjuku. The vista has now completely changed to an urban one.

The river continues to divide Nakano-ku from Shinjuku-ku. We saw some ducks on the river. A man was strolling along the river with his wife. He stopped next to me and said something about *Kamo* (duck). Then he asked in English, "You call them 'ducks' in English?" We said yes. "There are many kinds, you know." I asked him what kinds those were. He said that they were from Russia. "They migrate," I said, then asked, "in Autumn?" He checked with his wife then answered, "About two months ago." I asked him whether he studied birds. He chuckled a little and said, "No, I study human beings." Then he and his wife said goodbye and left us.

Just about fifty metres beyond, a group of street cats were waiting to be fed. We turned left at Aiwaibashi into Shinjuku, leaving the river.[23]

This entry renders the encounter with seasonality by drawing attention to the enmeshed networks of things that constitute the experience: the maple tree whose leaves were beginning to turn red, the sun in which the eight old ladies were basking, the Russian ducks that recently migrated to Japan. Together with a number of other entries, these recordings form an emerging thread from *The Autumn Almanac* that can be loosely grouped under the title of "riverwalks." Instead of being guided by maps or destinations, these walks were simply led by the river courses with no particular aim or purpose. Over a number of iterations, the descriptions of each riverwalk drew out active members of a community or actants in an assemblage. The entry on September 18 during *Hakuro* (白露 or White Dew) and "Swallows leave / lycoris bloom," records an earlier encounter with the Tokyo river system:

> Walking along the Tamagawa Josui (Tamagawa channel) in Mitaka I came across stands of the *Lycoris radiata* cited by the modern almanac. They are indeed in bloom. The blooming *Higanbana* signals the presence of autumn.
>
> Along the Tamagawa towards Musashi-Sakai, we also came across what seemed to be a market garden. The main crop in season is winter melon. The vine has already started to die back, and the ripe melons were perfectly formed, waiting patiently to be harvested. An unattended counter outside the garden listed the vegetables for sale.
>
> The Tamagawa is a natural river that was once a source of fresh water for Edo/Tokyo. In the seventeenth century major work was undertaken to create artificial canals to feed water from the river to the wells in Edo. It is not surprising to learn that the needs of the growing population of Edo and later Tokyo had impacted both the natural river systems and artificial canals. Apparently, in 1984 the Bureau of Waterworks Tokyo introduced recycled water into the dried up system. More recently we can see works have been done to try to rehabilitate the water channels and associated ecosystem.[24]

A number of participating actants in this assemblage are brought to the fore: the river Tamagawa, the suburb of Mitaka, the flower *Lycoris radiata*, the season of autumn, a market garden, a harvest of winter melons, an unattended counter, the seventeenth-century Japanese capital of Edo, the Bureau of Waterworks Tokyo, and so on. These objects move fluidly between different spatial and temporal scales, nested within overlapping frameworks of meteorology, urban development, horticulture, and history. The *Lycoris radiata* stands on the banks of the Tamagawa, signaling the arrival of autumn.

The river itself is an artificial water channel made in the seventeenth century to bring water to a growing city. The urban land along the river is used to grow food. The biology of this modified river system has long been in need of rehabilitation and care. This list of things is not unlike Bennett's "theory of distributive agency" that "does not posit a subject as the root cause of an effect. There are instead always a swarm of vitalities at play. The task becomes to identify the contours of the swarm and the kind of relations that obtain between its bits."[25] As readers follow the descriptions, they examine the different types of interactions on different scales, zooming in and out "without ontological hierarchy."[26] A flat ontology grants the material world an autonomy and independence from human pre-conception.

An entry during *Shuubun* (秋分 or Autumnal Equinox) (Figure 8.5) continues the exploration of the urban river system:

> The precipitation probability has again dropped back down to the
> 10 percent mark, with tropical cyclones 0815 slowly dissipating
> and 0817 steering towards Southern China.
>   Whenever it rains, the Kandagawa (Kanda River) around
> Takadanobaba really gushes. The rainwater of the local areas

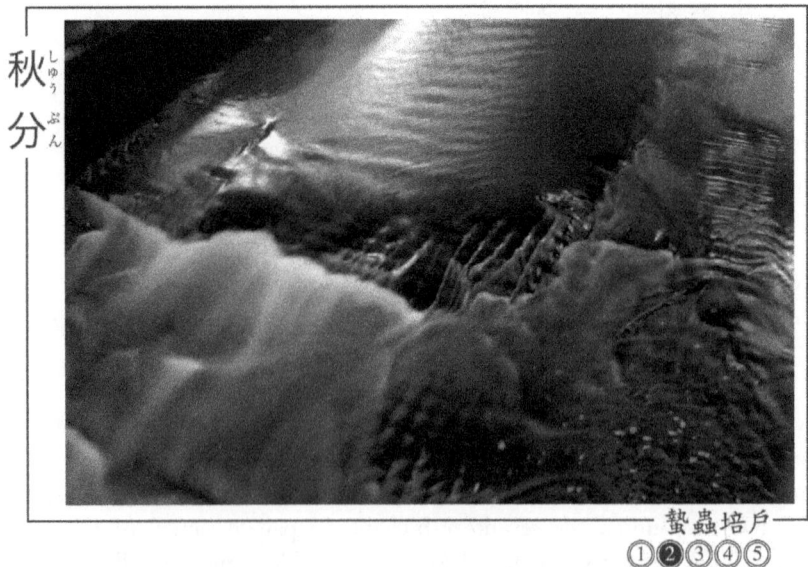

Figure 8.5. Jo Law, "Shuubun: Beetles wall up their burrows / azuki beans ripen 2 of 5," 2008, *The Autumn Almanac of Tokyo*.

drains into the channel, and water flows quite fiercely after heavy rainfall. The Kandagawa acts as a natural dividing line between Takadanobaba and the neighbouring Shima-Ochiai in some parts. We took a walk along the river at night and crossed over to Shima-Ochiai, where at first I thought I saw a brave large street cat crossing a busy road. At closer inspection, as the creature dashed for the bush along the railway—we realized it was a *tanuki*, a raccoon dog.[27]

The rain, the cyclones 0815 and 0817, neighboring China, the Kandagawa, the neighborhoods of Takadanobaba and Shima-Ochiai, rainfall, rainwater, drains and channels, a busy road, the railway, road-side bushes, and the *tanuki* are all actants in this assemblage. The train line is separated from the pavement and the busy road by a fence and planted bushes. The *tanuki* finds shelter in these bushes as its habitats are increasingly encroached by the urban development in Takadanobaba and Shima-Ochiai. The densely built suburbs must have carefully planned drainage to channel away rainwater quickly and to deal effectively with medium and heavy rainfalls, especially during typhoon season. The Kandagawa provides the main waterway to take the rainwater out to Tokyo Bay. In this way, each actant is connected to another in the enmeshed networks, tugging each other, influencing the overall shape of the system. Some are considered alive, some are not, and some are in between. Like the storm drain Bennett witnessed in Baltimore one summer morning, each of these assemblages revealed themselves in a new light where "*objects* appeared as *things,* that is, as vivid entities not entirely reducible to the contexts in which (human) subjects set them, never entirely exhausted by their semiotics."[28] Writing an almanac brings into focus the relationships between parts and wholes within a system, with each part enjoying the same ontological status as the whole; this allows us to perceive how we affect the world and how the world affects us. A complex portrait of the river assemblages emerges from investigations into these interactions.

3.

The more recent project *The Illustrated Almanac of the Illawarra and Beyond* similarly used the Chinese Almanac to explore the rituals and rhythms of the seasons in the Illawarra region, New South Wales, Australia, by collecting observations of phenological occurrences, weather statistics, astronomical information, and anthropogenic events over one calendar. The accumulated data took the form of twelve offset lithographic prints: one for each month of the year. Each design translated material data into everyday narratives of human and non-human activities, and together they present an emergent multidimensional geographic snapshot of place. The lithographs connect the viewer to her environment by threading together materials, objects, human cultural practices, and non-human systems, speculating on how we interact with and within these ecologies. In the May print (Figure 8.6), the viewer's eye is guided through a series of narratives framed by actants at different scales. The story begins on the left with the ancient supercontinent of Gondwana. The tiny hand-drawn arrows denote the convergent and divergent tectonic forces at work, where the dense magma beneath drives some landmasses together and pulls others apart. The eye may be attracted to the bottom of the print to follow the direction of water flow in the underground aquifers in the Sydney Basin. The weather cools in May in the Illawarra, and domestic chickens are observed to molt. The top of the print presents a series of views of a feather under different orders of magnification. A soft feather is composed of tough scales, which are made of beta-keratin. The viewer can also confirm her suspicion that chickens are the closest living relatives of the extinct "terrible lizards." At the center of the print is the spiral periodic table of elements, borrowed here to display the calendar month, moving from left to right, progressing into winter. The twenty-first day of the month marks the solar term "Minor Snow" when "Rainbows Hide." The viewer is presented with Sir Isaac Newton's illustration of the break-up of white light through tiny water droplets suspended in the air, resulting in bands of brilliant colors as observed on land. Above the double rainbow are the lines that stand in for the thin air bubble that cocoons the biosphere, striated into layers. The May print ends with "Winter takes hold" when fires are lit in old cottages with chimneys in the Illawarra. Molecules of carbon dioxide, carbon monoxide, water, and various hydrocarbons draw our attention to the chemical process of combustion. In this way, each print from *The Illustrated Almanac* journeys through stories guided by entities, materials, and actants interacting within intersecting systems, shifting between micro and macro scales and back again. This almanac constructs evolving models of seasons along multiple timelines and spatial scales.[29]

The exhibition of the twelve lithographs at the Wollongong Art Gallery in 2017 invited participants to create a collective almanac. Participants from the Illawarra and elsewhere contributed their observations to the multi-authored environment of Instagram using the hashtag #illalmanac for the duration of the exhibition (Figure 8.7). This collective gathering

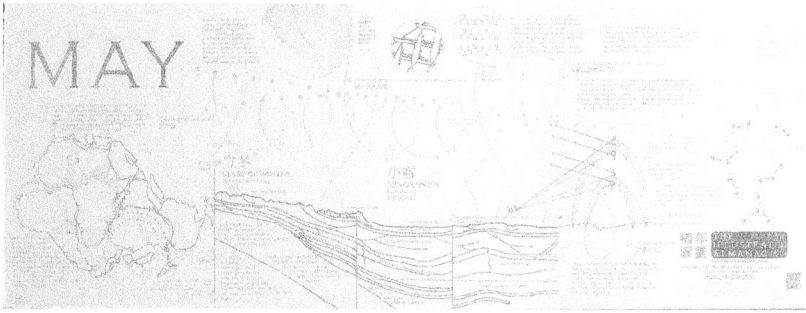

Figure 8.6. Jo Law, *The Illustrated Almanac of the Illawarra and Beyond: May*, offset lithographic print, 76 × 28 cm, 2016.

of observations put in focus the diverse materials, entities, and systems that make up the human and non-human environments. Changing light, evening sky, ephemeral contrails, a fallen wasp nest, Bunya pines, a broken bird egg, and flowering trees are incorporated into the seasonal maps of the Illawarra and elsewhere. In this collaborative act of observation, a photograph or a short video can spark discussions on the materials that made up this changing world.

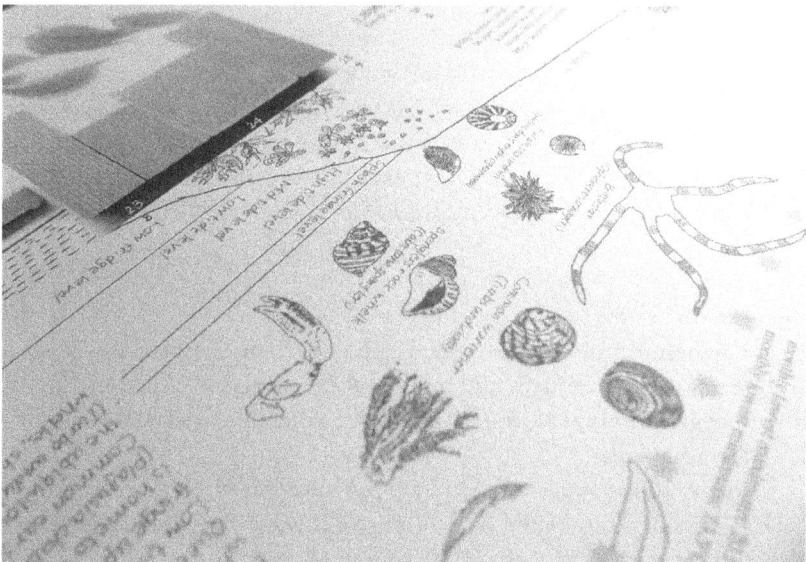

Figure 8.7. Jo Law, *The Illustrated Almanac of the Illawarra and Beyond: January*, detail offset lithographic print, 76 × 28 cm, 2016.

November 2, 2017
jolaw7200
Bundanon Trust

> **jolaw7200** #illalmanac @illustratedalmanac 2 November 2017 Bundanon sky. Bunya pine. Hot sun.
> **alijanesmith5359** Edible seeds?
> **jolaw7200**@alijanesmith5359 True?
> **alijanesmith5359**@jolaw7200 according to the internet. But also can hurt you pretty badly if they fall on you. http://www.happyearth.com.au then search bunya
> **jolaw7200**@alijanesmith5359 Bunya pesto?
> **alijanesmith5359**@jolaw7200 yes please!

October 17, 2017
michele_elliot_artist

> **michele_elliot_artist**. . . . not only bread and water, Coledale evenings (and a dead thing alert in second image) #crow#crowbringsfood #illalmanac #birdboss
> **streetcandypics** Fascinating
> **photosplusart** Wow . . . fascinating Crow stories
> **jolaw7200**@michele_elliot_artist What sort of egg is it? The crow has been busy.
> **michele_elliot_artist**@jolaw7200 very busy! I don't know but quite big, about 5cm. Will check the guide
> **michele_elliot_artist**@jolaw7200 oh I think it is a crow's egg? Makes me wonder if that bird carcass was a baby crow? It had quite big feet and a smallish body. And also explains why the rosemary bush was covered in grey feathers last week.

October 14, 2017
alijanesmith5359

> **alijanesmith5359** Jacarandas beginning. That means we will start seeing Christmas trees any minute. #illalmanac
> **maggycummings** I commented on the same thing today. I think they are a bit early??
> **jolaw7200**@alijanesmith5359 Do you mean the NSW Christmas bush (I posted photo of the ones in our yard with white leaves).
> **alijanesmith5359**@jolaw7200 I mean 🎄
> **alijanesmith5359**@maggycummings I always think November but I generally don't notice things till I'm walking through purple flowers

jolaw7200@alijanesmith5359 I am wondering whether the flowering of the NSW Xmas bush is early too. The leaves usually go red just before Xmas, so a little while to go.

loudirt Beginning and now everywhere, Illawarra Flame Trees are around the corner and it's been nearly five years since we lost Maree. I always remember by the flowering trees xoxo

alijanesmith5359@loudirt Poundin the crete for Maree.

alijanesmith5359@loudirt I think this is a seasonal experience worth emphasising. How certain plants flowering and etc can remind us of past loss and bereavement, in a rather bittersweet way sometimes.

loudirt Totally xx

August 13, 2017
alluvial_fan

   alluvial_fan_ Wasp nest came down in the big winds. #illalmanac #architecture #housing

   girlnagun Maybe 'like' isn't quite the right word for it but still, wow, it's quite impressive. Are there many inhabitants?

   alluvial_fan All gone to find new waspy pastures.

   jolaw7200 Wasp nest. . . . How different is it from a beehive? Does anyone know?

   girlnagun These look like papery cells rather than waxy cells, plus no honey #importantdifference

The method of jotting down observations, the brief exchange of notes, the surfacing of memories and free association present rich avenues for making sense of the material world. Armed with the ubiquitous mobile devices (complete with Global Positioning System), participants are not only able to capture weather observations, but, more importantly, to make sense of them together. The almanac as a medium opens up a space for studying encounters with environmental systems at different scales. It has the potential to make perceptible an inclusive and encompassing ecology that constitutes our multifaceted experience of the seasons. Almanacs can activate a collective capacity to sense complex changes in our bioregions by mapping traces in our environmental systems.

By overlaying an archaic architecture over the almanac projects, my intention is to contrast the perceptions of seasons with their material enactment. Far from imposing a fixed structure over experiences, the ancient almanac gives form to our interaction with the dynamical systems and assemblages that are alive and creative. It does so by recognizing the enmeshed networks of each event or encounter, naming the different actants that are shaping specific assemblages at a point in time, and thereby encouraging the identifications of other actants that may also be at work. Each almanac presents objects and things in a flat ontology: it zooms out to bring into view the nested and overlapping frameworks of the global weather system and the geographic coordinate system as large-scale assemblages; it zooms in to focus on the arrays of actants at play and the series of assemblages that may emerge over the seasons. These assemblages are enmeshed networks of interconnected things: living, non-living, and somewhere in between.

Without an active and creative engagement with the materials that constitute our experience of seasons, we cannot fully appreciate the significance of their occurrences. In the face of extreme weather events, natural disasters, and climate change, we are left with the first and only resort of emotive response. In order to act intelligently, we need different ways of thinking about weather, seasons, and climate. In this paper, I have drawn from a vital materialist perspective to explore the form of an almanac as a medium to enact a vital materialist practice. The almanac projects offer the possibility of providing an inclusive and encompassing way of thinking about the seasons that incorporate a non-human perspective.

Notes

1. Jane Bennett, *Vibrant Matter: A Political Ecology of Things* (Durham, NC: Duke University Press, 2010).
2. Bennett, *Vibrant Matter*, ix.
3. Levi Bryant, "More on Vitalism," *Larval Subject,* October 10, 2011, http://larvalsubjects.wordpress.com/2011/10/10/more-on-vitalism/.
4. Bennett, *Vibrant Matter*, 6.
5. Bennett, *Vibrant Matter*, xiii.
6. Bennett, *Vibrant Matter*, 9.
7. Bennett, *Vibrant Matter*, 9.
8. Bennett, *Vibrant Matter*, 23.
9. Bennett, *Vibrant Matter*, 24.
10. Levi Bryant, "Wilderness Ontology," *Preternatural*, ed., Celina Jeffery (New York: Punctum, 2011), 21–22.
11. Bryant, "Wilderness Ontology," 24–25.
12. *The Autumn Almanac of Tokyo* uses the Japanese translation of the Chinese solar terms. The pentads in the title include both the Chinese and modern Japanese versions translated into English.

13. Liza Dalby, *East Wind Melts the Ice: A Memoir through the Seasons* (London: Chatto & Windus, 2007).

14. The Oxford English Dictionary defines *almanac* as "an annual table, or book of tables, containing a calendar or months and days, with astronomical data and calculations, ecclesiastical and other anniversaries." See *Oxford English Dictionary* (Oxford: Oxford University Press, 1973).

15. Dalby, *East Wind Melts the Ice*, xxiii.

16. Sei Shōnagon, *The Pillow Book*, trans. Meredith McKinney (London: Penguin, 2007).

17. Shikibu Murasaki, *The Diary of Lady Murasaki*, trans. Richard Bowring (London: Penguin Books, 2005).

18. Alexandra Harris, *Weatherland: Writers and Artists under the English Skies* (London: Thames & Hudson, 2015), 166.

19. Aldo Leopold, *A Sand County Almanac* (New York: Ballantine, 1966).

20. Leopold, *A Sand County Almanac*, 239–240.

21. Bryant, "Wilderness Ontology," 21.

22. Bryant, "Wilderness Ontology," 23.

23. Jo Law, *The Autumn Almanac of Tokyo* (Sept. 5–Dec. 5, 2008). http://www.photonicsmedia.net/projects/autumn

24. Law, *The Autumn Almanac of Tokyo*.

25. Bennett, *Vibrant Matters*, 31–32.

26. Bryant, "Wilderness Ontology," 21.

27. Law, *The Autumn Almanac of Tokyo*.

28. Bennett, *Vibrant Matters*, 5.

29. Jo Law, *The Illustrated Almanac of the Illawarra and Beyond* (Sept. 1, 2011–Aug. 31, 2012). http://almanac.photonicsmedia.net.au/

9

The Cycle of Seasons

The Temporal Structure of Fashion

Yvonne Förster

Introduction

The relation of fashion and capitalist strategies is a longstanding topic of philosophical and sociological investigation. The changing of the seasons represents the motor of fashion's productive engine; its cycles have accelerated greatly in recent decades. There is a large volume of research dedicated to the phenomenon of *fast fashion* and questions of sustainability. Fashion brands today produce up to twelve collections, three per season.[1] The production of clothes is one of the most labor- and resource-consuming economic sectors, and it raises many questions about sustainability and working conditions.[2] *Acceleration* of production is one of the central characteristics of contemporary fashion.

I will examine the notion of the seasons within fashion in its conceptual and experiential aspects. The progression of the seasons is and always has been crucial to the dynamics of fashion[3] even if there has been little research undertaken on the theoretical and phenomenological dimensions of the subject. A reflection on the concept of the seasons can clarify underlying ideas of time, including its acceleration, transitory character, and relation to the past, present, and future.

The concept of fashion with its inherent temporality will be considered from a philosophical viewpoint, using phenomenological descriptions and systematic reasoning. I first present basic temporal features of fashion and explain their theoretical impact. Philosophical concepts of time and time-perception are applied to the temporal features identified in relevant theoretical frameworks. Most theories stress the temporal character of fashion without elaborating the concept of time itself. One of the few systematic works on the temporality in fashion is presented by Elena Esposito. She views the transitory character of fashion as crucial to its sociological function; that is, fashion serves as a means to cope with contingency because it gains consistency through change. The *transitory character* is as central to fashion as *acceleration* and an intimate relation to the *past* through constant communication between varying styles.

Fashion exhibits an emphatic notion of the *present* as well as a significant relation to the *past*. It is crucial to fashion, as Georg Simmel noted, to form a "dividing-line [*Wasserscheide*] between the past and the future."[4] I outline this position along with some considerations concerning the acceleration of social life[5] and anticipations or visions of the future in fashion.[6] All of these temporal features have one thing in common: they rely on perception and memory. In doing so, they return our thoughts to the end of the eighteenth century, when the first fashion magazines appeared.[7] These are the initial fashion media, ones that reflected on given styles and their historic development. A sense of time in fashion relies on such media, on images of clothing and styles of presenting fashionable clothing that make the ideas and atmospheres belonging to those objects perceivable for a broad audience.

After outlining the essential temporal features in the concept of fashion and their condition within the sphere of the media, I examine the impact of the seasonal structure of fashion more closely. Features such as fashion's transitory and yet enduring character along with the acceleration that accompanies the pursuit of change and novelty, and fashion's inherent connection to the past and future, can all be addressed in terms of a seasonal structure, including ideas related to seasonal change, the increasing speed of the fashion cycle through intermediate seasons, and the anticipation of the coming seasons. All of these concerns raise another question concerning the seasonal structure of fashion: namely, to what extent it not only represents a pragmatic means to consumerist ends but also suggests a more profound anthropological feature and its contemporary forms of expression.

Basic Temporal Features of Fashion

Fashion has always been considered a temporal phenomenon, and so fashions in the plural are always transient. They change from one season to the next and, even more obviously, from decade to decade. The twentieth century can reasonably be called "the century of fashion" because each and every decade had its own style and exhibited its unique character by means of particular kinds of clothing. It is difficult to think of the 1920s without picturing women with bobbed hair dancing in marvelous sleek and silky dresses, or to imagine the 1960s without miniskirts or the 1980s without wide shoulders and big hairdos. Fashion is one of the most important means of conveying the atmosphere of a particular decade and sustaining it through enduring images. In fact, the specific aesthetic impact of fashion in the twentieth century led Barbara Vinken to coin the term *la mode de cent ans*, the one hundred years' fashion.[8]

Fashions only gain their visibility because they are transient. They are marked by visible differences from their predecessors and successors. Hence, the distinct identity that fashion creates is based on its temporal *transitoriness*. The seasonal production cycle lends this process its rhythm. This transient character was first described by Simmel and later developed by Esposito in *Die Verbindlichkeit des Vorübergehenden (The Obligingness of the Transitory)*. Esposito rests her characterization of fashion on Niklas Luhmann's system theory and elaborates a theory of fashion that originates from two basic ideas: first, fashion is always *changing* and, second, it is a means of *individualization* as well as *integration* or conformity. To perform these functions, it must always generate new styles that enable people to stand out. Standing out through fashion also means being part of a fashionable group. And this entails that fashionable people possess a high degree of individuality while identifying themselves with certain standards and groups as well. Their "standing out" is always backed by a system of styles and personalities, a point that was expressed very early by Simmel.

Change and the quest for novelty are central temporal characteristics of fashion, but simply stating this point does not fully explain its specific temporal quality. The broader picture is far more complex, and the various interpretations of it lead to very different views of history and the cultural processes in modernity.[9] The manner in which new fashions are generated can in fact be regarded as a metaphor for modernity itself or as a functional paradigm of modernity as Veblen, Simmel, or Esposito suggest. The concept of change is especially relevant to the notion of fashion as a functional paradigm, a subject to which we now turn before exploring fashion as a metaphor of modernity.

Change, Novelty, and the Perception of Presence in Fashion

In 1899, at the dawn of the twentieth century, Thorstein Veblen presented his theory of conspicuous consumption.[10] In this framework, fashionable dress serves as a means of expression of social status. Social status and wealth find their expression in a special form of consuming luxury goods, which in turn display their owner's wealth. These luxury goods reveal wealth by being appropriate only for leisure rather than productive work. Furthermore, they are usually displayed not so much by the actual owner but by his staff and family. Fashionable clothes and jewelry are not only expensive but also often not useful for the activity involved in any kind of work. Since fashion is constantly changing, it becomes the perfect medium to display monetary power. The consumption of fashion is expenditure in its purest form because the goods are purchased not to last but only to show—at least according to Veblen's conception.

The "principle of novelty" in fashion derives from a distinct practice of consumption, "conspicuous waste."[11] "Dress must not only be conspicuously expensive and inconvenient; it must at the same time be up to date."[12] The conception of novelty that is applied here is a very simple one because fashion is defined as the product of a certain consumer practice and as a function of social distinction. The simplistic conception of change focuses merely on novelty. It leaves aside the fact that novelty can only be grasped as such in comparison to what has been before. The past is a necessary implication of change.

Veblen limits expression via fashion to the display of social rank. This is the reason why he and his contemporary Simmel hold that fashion is essentially senseless and lacking in any intrinsic logic whatsoever. Striving for novelty leads to strange and futile caprices in fashion: "styles in vogue two thousand years ago are more becoming than the most elaborate and painstaking constructions of today."[13] Veblen's view derives from his functional conception of fashion, which leaves no room for a closer consideration of the objects themselves. The concept of change in fashion equals novelty, but Veblen fails to provide an account of the dimension of the past, which is a necessary aspect of such novelty.

A similar position was asserted by Simmel just two years later, in 1901, in his essay "Fashion," though he does not subordinate fashion as much to a law of consumption. Both Simmel and Veblen take a sociological stance toward fashion and define it as "a product of class distinction."[14] Simmel emphasizes the relationship between the individual and their social class. In this regard, his notion of expression through fashion is more complex than Veblen's account. For Veblen, fashion is merely an expression of social status. For Simmel, fashion serves an intrinsic anthropological need for expressing individuality as well as social belonging. He distinguishes two antagonistic anthropological forces: "The whole history of society is reflected in the striking conflicts, the compromises slowly won and quickly lost, between socialistic adaptation to society and individual departure from it."[15] According to Simmel, fashion is the only social form in which both of these antagonistic demands are met. It allows for adaptation to the masses via imitation as well as provides for differentiation because the adaptation of newest fashions gives the individual a means to stand out. Despite the fact that Simmel's account of fashion is a functional one just as is Veblen's, he sets forth a more elaborate notion of change and conveys a key temporal structure: "Fashion always occupies the dividing-line between the past and the future, and consequently conveys a stronger feeling of the present, at least while it is at its height, than most other phenomena. What we call the present is usually nothing more than a combination of a fragment of the past with a fragment of the future."[16]

There are two temporal aspects specific to fashion, both of which do not apply to the actual objects themselves but only to fashion more generally and to its public perception. What Simmel describes is the advent of the fashionable, which is always a temporal phenomenon, not only in terms of the process but first and foremost in terms of appearing and vanishing. That is why he speaks about the dividing-line between past and future. Fashion can only exist in a small window of time, otherwise it could not be a fashion. New styles make their appearance with the necessary prospect of vanishing soon thereafter. This is the temporal characteristic involved in the perception of fashion. The perception of fashion implies a heightened sense or feeling of the *present*. In Simmel's words, fashion is synonymous with the present, since the present itself is nothing more than a combination of a small portion of what has just passed and the anticipation of what is yet to come. The present itself, therefore, is essentially nothing: it is neither a duration nor an instant. It is just the dividing-line between past and future—a liminal concept of presence, which becomes interesting in Simmel's account when applied to the perception of time.[17] In an analytical sense, the present is the liminal figure. In the experience of the perceiver, the tension between what-has-been and what-is-yet-to-come leads to a heightened sense of presence. Fashion thus becomes a metaphor for time itself because, just as the present, it appears or comes into presence only by the prospect of vanishing soon afterward.

It is an interesting coincidence that fashion as a system of production and consumption emerges roughly around the same time as the modern concept of the *future*. As Lucien Hölscher[18] points out, a notion of the future as a temporal space that has to be filled only develops around 1770, especially in the context of philosophy of history. It accrues more and more significance during the Industrial Revolution and reaches its peak between 1890 and 1950 with the nascent belief in progress and industrial develop-ment. This faith in progress is, of course, put to the test after the Second World War. I refer here to the essentially modern notion of the future as progress in order to contrast it with the temporality of fashion. As Simmel emphasized, fashion is a phenomenon of presence—an emphatic kind of presence.

There are two points that should be added to this picture. The first is that the emphatic presence associated with fashion might be linked to a special form of consumerism: a thought that has been spelled out by Werner Sombart. He connects the rise of fashion and consumption of luxury goods to a modern form of hedonism.[19] According to Sombart, the purchase of luxury goods not only brings social distinction but also a heightened sense of feeling alive. In other words, he equates the sensuous qualities of luxury goods to erotic experience. Without going into too much detail about the theory of consumption, one key idea can nevertheless be made: the extraordinary or emphatic presence in fashion might be two-sided. On the one hand, it is an exemplary material structure of temporality itself. On the other hand, it gains its presence from the enjoyment of those products (setting aside the question whether the indulgence of luxury is implemented upon us by the world of advertisements). The heightened feeling of the present in fashion seems to be linked to an augmented sense of being alive, of enjoying sensuous qualities.

The second critical point concerns the new quality of the concept of the future mentioned above. Two characteristically modern phenomena seem to be incompatible. There is an orientation toward progress and the construction of an ideal future. At the same time, there exists an indulgence in products whose value will soon have disappeared. The enjoyment that comes with fashion is a transient one. It always has to be regenerated by purchasing new goods. This makes fashion the flipside of eternal beauty and happiness, as Baudelaire observed.[20] A tension remains between the concept of the future and fashion's emphatic presence in modernity. Both are paradigmatic temporal structures in the modern world. And they are linked by another one: acceleration.

When the future is to be understood as a temporal void that needs to be filled by progress, then the production of fashion is one way of doing so. Fashion unceasingly generates novelty. That is why anticipation is central to fashion: the anticipation of future desires and tastes is crucial to success in the business. With the orientation toward the future in the transition from the nineteenth to the twentieth century and the wave of technical inventions such as photography, film, electricity, light bulbs, automobiles, and other items, life and fashion have both accelerated. Fashion is changing faster—especially as intermediate seasons are added to the traditional two seasons of fall/winter and spring/summer—and styles are differing more and more. However, even though the fashion cycle has increased in speed, the experience of fashion itself remains similar to what it was before. The purchase and display of fashionable goods retain the character of emphatic presence and hedonistic indulgence. The changing of the seasons becomes the medium of acceleration in production. The seasonal logic allows for short-lived collections because one can always invent a more fine-grained seasonal structure or an activity-oriented collection such as those organized around cruises or travel.

Esposito presents one main feature of modern society as being in contingency: namely, the orientation toward change and novelty. The idea that history is guided by "grand narratives" as Jean-François Lyotard pointed out, has lost its persuasive power.[21] There is no deeper rationale to be found in the course of history. Only the logic of progress or novelty, which is in itself devoid of content, drives developments.[22] Fashion is so important in modernity because it follows the logic of novelty, but it also allows people to identify with a particular group or a style. Fashion is thus a system for orientation that functions on the basis of contingency. Esposito notes that fashion transforms a social difference into a temporal one, from conformism/deviance to continuity/discontinuity.[23] Modern society is thus rooted in paradoxes, and fashion especially represents a very functional paradox. Fashion is devoid of meaning, reason, or justification, but it serves as a structuring moment; it provides orientation without having a sense or reason in itself. It is a way of coping with contingency by giving contingency a positive value, in rendering chance productive.[24]

Let me turn from the functional aspects and their temporal structure to more philosophical aspects of temporality in fashion. As mentioned previously, anticipation is central to the fashion process—and, according to Benjamin, it is one of its most remarkable characteristics:

> For the philosopher, the most interesting thing about fashion is its extraordinary anticipations. . . . Each season brings, in its newest creations, various secret signals of things to come.

Whoever understands how to read these semaphores would know
in advance not only about new currents in the arts but also
about new legal codes, wars, and revolutions.—Here, surely lies
the greatest charm of fashion, but also the difficulty of making
the charming fruitful.[25]

Benjamin reflects insightfully on the objects of fashion. These objects exhibit
a temporal structure because fashionable garments combine stylistic elements
from different times. The anticipations of which Benjamin speaks are expressed
through a combination of elements. These elements are a medium for the
expression of the Zeitgeist, the special atmosphere, attitude, and convic-
tion of a concrete period of time. This form of expression differs from the
expression of social status in Veblen's theory and also from Simmel's idea
of fashion as expression of anthropological needs. The material constellation
of fashion, namely designs, fabrics, textures, accessories, and images, are
themselves expressions of their time and cultural atmosphere. Moreover, they
transmit sedimented time, references to the past, biographical and cultural
memory. In that sense, they *embody* cultural memory, which is not only a
social phenomenon, but also a bodily one. Fashion is always connected to
the body of its wearer; it shapes and orients the body in the private and
social realm and thus is a crucial component of bodily expression. In this
regard, Maurice Merleau-Ponty's theory of embodied cognition as well as
his later ontology of the perceptual world is relevant to fashion theory.[26]

Fashion's inherent connection to the past, which is expressed in its
very own objects, is crucial in at least two intertwined respects: memory
and novelty. Novelty necessarily implies a relation to the past, against which
something can appear to be new. In order to establish this relation between
the past and the present, memory is also necessary. Fashion requires memory
in order to appear as something new and desirable. One needs to notice
the differences between designs in order to appreciate them. This changing
of tastes in fashion is closely tied to its media-based communication. Media
such as fashion photography serve as the material or external memory of
fashion perception.[27]

Another integral topic in Benjamin's material account of fashion involves
its relation to modernity. Benjamin expresses its role in the following way:
"Fashion has the scent of the modern wherever it stirs in the thicket of what
has been. It is the tiger's leap into the past."[28] In this passage, Benjamin
compares history to fashion, a point which makes sense since he advocates
a materialistic approach to history. Both history and fashion are temporal

crystallizations. They represent material structures that are essentially temporal in the sense that they are filled by *now-time*.[29] Yet in their presence they are always referring to the past—a past which is not only repeated but also altered by being implemented in the now-time. The contrast between fashions of different times is not, however, to be misunderstood as an apologetic stance toward progress. On the contrary, Benjamin construes fashion as a limiting term with respect to progress.[30] Henceforth, fashion is also a form of critical practice, which is a perspective to which most theories are oblivious.

Benjamin's image of the tiger's leap has intriguing temporal implications. First, the leap itself implies a connection between two points that are separated by a distance of time and space. The leap is a dynamic motion that connects these points in and through historical time in nearly no quantitative time at all. There is no significant temporal continuity to be found in this picture. The tiger's leap recalls J. M. E. McTaggart's paradox. McTaggart famously argued in 1908 that time cannot exist.[31] A necessary condition for its existence is change. As an essential feature of time, change cannot be understood in terms of "earlier" and "later" (the so-called B-series) because this logic cannot adequately accommodate it. Events viewed on a timeline never change their position; they stay in the exact same position, at least if we argue from the viewpoint of our standard mesocosmic framework of physics (though quantum theory might admittedly provide another vantage on this approach). Thus, change can only be accounted for in the logic of moving from having-been-future to becoming-present and eventually being-past (this is what McTaggart calls the A-series). If we investigate this language, we can identify a problem, a contradiction. If one event is future, it is future in the present and past in the future—hence it possesses all three mutually exclusive properties at once. This is not the appropriate place to engage in detail with McTaggart's paradox. Suffice it to say that the image of the tiger's leap connects at least two of the mutually exclusive temporal predicates: the present and the past.

Second, other than the image of the tiger leap itself, which suggests dynamism, the times connected by the jump appear to be rather static. The tiger's leap figures as a Benjaminian dialectical image, which he defines as a constellation of past and actual times: "It's not that what is past casts light on what is present, or what is present its light on what is past; rather, image is that wherein what has been comes together in a flash with the now to form a constellation. In other words, image is dialectics at a standstill."[32] The term *constellation* here refers to static structure, which nevertheless is in itself temporal because there are elements from different times placed together in one entity. From a temporal perspective, such an entity cannot be a unity but must contain a rupture.[33] I am not using the term "rupture" here in a truly Benjaminian sense but rather to clarify the temporal structure of fashionable objects. These objects are marked by a temporal rupture because their unity supervenes on elements with differing temporal features. Objects of fashion can be described as unities of a temporal manifold. This tension is not only inherent in the material. It also appears in the perception of the objects and, depending on what one sees and remembers, fashionable objects will tell different stories to the beholder.

The Seasons as Temporal Structure in Fashion

After having outlined the central temporal characteristics of fashion, I will investigate fashion as a process of consumption and production, which is governed by the concept of the seasons. The "seasonal" nature of fashion originated in the eighteenth century alongside altered consumption habits and innovations in production means.[34] Prior to that period, fashion changed from year to year.[35] The necessary conditions for changes in fashion in general were the final disbandment of sumptuary laws in the eighteenth century,[36] a new form of consumption, and accelerated media-based communication of the new products. For example, the first fashion journals were published at the end of the eighteenth century; *Das Journal des Luxus und der Moden* began publishing in Weimar in 1787.[37] Apart from these media and sociological changes, the concept of the seasons is interesting from a philosophical standpoint. My considerations here remain tentative. To my knowledge, the issue has barely been discussed until now. The first question that needs to be addressed concerns the conceptions of time that underlie the practices in fashion of trading and consuming.

First and foremost, the changing of the seasons implies a cyclical concept of time. Spring, summer, fall, and winter occur over and over again in the same uniform order. This uniformity differs from the radical quest for change and novelty in fashion. The cycle of the seasons structures time in a very special way. One might assume this is the most natural way to organize time—by the perception of natural cycles in circadian rhythms or, on a larger scale, according to the seasons. As one of the oldest cultures, the Chinese built their conception of time according to such a natural cycle. In traditional Chinese thought, time is closely connected to space, and these phenomena are even treated alike: time is seen as a "compound of seasons or epochs, and space a compound of territories, areas, and orients."[38] According to François Jullien, time is not objectified as an entity or a continuity. It remains a compound, whose diverse parts have distinct affordances or require different ways of living and acting. Every season necessitates its special practices in agriculture and in all other cultural areas.

Jullien stresses that the seasonal structuring of time is accompanied by a specific logic, one that is not theoretical but rather strategic.[39] This way of dealing with temporal cycles is a ubiquitous phenomenon, even when the culture as a whole is structured by other conceptions of time. Seasonal change represents the source of a specific time concept: the time of action—*Handlungszeit*.[40] Karen Gloy differentiates *Handlungszeit* from mental time, which is structured by varying modalities—the memory of the past, the present, and the anticipation of the future. In contrast to mental time, *Handlungszeit* is a temporal structure wholly tied to the present.[41]

By being defined through natural alterations in weather, climate, food supply, and living circumstances, the seasons afford changing ways of self-cultivation and behavior in general. The overall structure induced by seasonal change is cyclical; spring, summer, fall, and winter occur over and over again. The internal structure of the seasons implies yet another temporal structure: the opportune moment (καιρός in Greek mythology and early Greek philosophy). The καιρός (*kairos*) is a wholly different concept from sequential or cyclical time. It is neither continuous nor measurable. The καιρός means a moment in time, which is right for a certain action, deed, or decision. Within the cyclical structure of the seasons there is room for a temporal discontinuity; for the opening up of a temporal slot, which is unique because only then is the right time, the opportune moment. It is the time to sow the crop, to harvest, to gather for a big feast, and so forth. The καιρός can be interpreted in an emphatic sense, as the right time for great deeds, or in a more modest sense, as the right time for things that ought to be done. Jullien explains this temporal dimension within the cyclical concept of seasons by an etymological approach to the French word for season, *saison*, which derives from the Latin *satio* and means *to sow*.[42] "Season" is not originally an abstract or theoretical concept but rather directly related to an action. Jullien provides several examples of the usage of *saison* in French, all of which refer to the right time or moment for something or, alternatively, not the right time or moment: for example, *il est de saison* (the right moment) or *hors de saison* (an unfavorable or inappropriate moment).[43]

Thus, in the seasonal structure of time there are three very different temporal features that are combined and that ought to be discerned analytically: (1) there is a cyclical process, which in its repetitive continuity nevertheless allows for change; (2) the concept of the season can be understood as a compound, whose internal structure at least in part depends on time-structuring activity; and (3) the seasonal structure is not abstract but based in a material reality.

Let me consider these three features in relation to fashion. Earlier, I outlined the temporal features of change/contingency, acceleration, and the emphatic notion of the present (which incorporates the past as a constitutive element) along with its anticipations.

Change and the Cycle of Seasons

Over time, the concept of the seasons applied to fashion becomes more and more abstract. This point can be illustrated by the repetitive structure of the seasonal cycle. Traditionally, the kinds of work and cultural practices that accompany seasonal change had to be repeated from year to year. These practices in combination with the natural conditions can be viewed as the material of cyclical time. Their combination leads to the formation of ages and epochs as well as the evolution of styles in fashion. In fashion, however, the season as a natural condition does not necessarily determine the styles. Even if winter collections will show coats and warm shoes, no seasonal style is thoroughly determined by the seasonal conditions. This is because fashion is a global phenomenon and needs to cater to the needs of people traveling globally. Each season must contain, at least in part, pieces for travel to warmer or colder regions, cruise styles, cocktail styles, and the more uniform business attire. The natural change of the season thus does not determine the creation of fashion as much as it did when people did not travel and buy globally.

A second reason for the thinning out of the natural content of seasons involves the differentiation between the cycles of presentation and the cycles of consumption. The presentation of a clothing collection for a new season occurs well before the actual consumption of these items, so that a spring/summer collection, for example, is presented to the public during the previous autumn. In actuality, two cycles exist. One is anti-cyclical: a cycle of presentation. Another, the cycle of consumption, is slightly different from the actual seasonal cycle. Precisely because the seasons in fashion are not much more than an abstract rhythm, the practices that fill the intervals can vary greatly. Fashion-making certainly focuses on the natural demands and affordances of the seasons, but since the business is global, production is not restricted to that. Seasonal change in fashion is repetitive insofar as there are set dates for the fashion industry and conditions in the Western Hemisphere govern a large portion of design. This centralized character is becoming increasingly diluted by intermediate collections and local designers who produce according to the actual climate in their countries. The schedule of the great shows nevertheless remains stable.

Since production and consumption cycles resemble a kind of pulse generator, they in fact do create space for change. Change in fashion is contingent in the sense that there is no necessity to the nature of its alterations. The designs, colors, or shapes that come into fashion are not dictated by any higher reason than the logic of creation itself—at least not at first glance. The logic of creation in fashion, however, does possess its own regularities and is not completely independent from the Zeitgeist[44] or the temporality of life itself (birth, youth, aging, death). Roland Barthes famously argued that fashion is structured similarly to language, which retains logic or rules that make up one system with different layers.[45] The relationships between the artifacts, their internal material makeup, and their presentation or rhetoric are semiotic in nature and also form a closed system. Yuniya Kawamura likewise argues that fashion in the modern and Western sense is an institutionalized system that as such exists only in some Western cities like Paris, London, or New York.[46] These theories have in common the idea that fashion is detached from something else, be it actual human needs, natural circumstances, or other cultural realms.

I maintain that with respect to seasonal structure the detachment of fashion involves a shift toward imaginative freedom. Two reasons support this claim. First, as mentioned above, seasonal change possesses an internal rhythm that requires change related to natural conditions: There is an objective alteration in outer circumstances such as the climate or cultural habits as when one travels to warmer or colder regions. Such outer circumstances are often arbitrary because a large part of the fashion industry is now globalized. Second, apart from objective or natural implications, the concept of the seasons allows for a huge repertoire of images, emotions, visions, and memories—an imaginative playground, so to speak. This playground of images and associations has its sources in individual experiences and cultural consciousness. Even if there are major parts of clothing collections that make sense only for a limited number of people who have the opportunity to spend a summer in the sunny islands or enjoy skiing in winter, those imaginative dimensions still in some way belong to their objects. With fashion one buys *atmosphere*, not merely function.

Although outdoor clothing lines are part of a large financial market, even those products are not purely functional. They carry a sense of freedom and an association with nature, both of which appear to be attractive to people who do not follow mainstream fashion. As a similar example, clothing items from cruise collections are often purchased by individuals who never actually take cruises. These collections might create the impression of the beauty of a sunny afternoon on a boat traveling, for instance, along the French coast. Such images that make fashionable objects desirable often acquire their associative content from seasonal images that are combined with particular cultural practices or places. Nature and culture are wedded together in these objects. This fusing process is extremely creative because both culture and its relation to the natural world are constantly changing.

ACCELERATION

The seasonal structure of fashion is clearly a motor for novelty and imaginative creation. This accelerated quest for novelty is rooted in urban culture and its rapidly changing social processes. Another significant and contemporary accelerator is the media itself. With the emergence of new media, digitalized information is always close at hand. And consumption of it increases in speed and availability with internet transactions. But is there something in the seasonal structure that supports this phenomenon of acceleration? When we look back at Jullien's interpretation of the seasonal concept of time in ancient China, one noteworthy point stands out: seasonal time is a compound rather than a unified entity. It is a compound not only of epochs or ages but also of smaller portions of time with their respective characteristics involving weather, qualities of light, cultural rituals, and affordances. The portioning of time in this conception has no real limit. Even the number of seasons varies according to the more-or-less fine-grained perception of such qualitative differences. This possibility of increasing the portions of time comprised in the circle of seasons offers fashion greater opportunities for devising designs that fit the various nuances of particular occasions or circumstances. The intermediate seasons that structure time between the two major seasons reflect in turn the subtler differences in the nature-culture interplay.

THE EMPHATIC PRESENT AND ANTICIPATION

The third and last point connects the *emphatic present* and *anticipation* in fashion with the season as a material basis. In the previous considerations, I stressed the tendency toward detachment from the natural traits of the seasons. This tendency is characteristic of fashion in general. However, following Jullien's interpretation of Chinese thought, seasonal structure possesses great explanatory potential. In terms of the emphatic present and the extraordinary anticipations of fashion that follow Benjamin's image of the tiger's leap, there is also a connection to be found in the seasonal structure.[47] The emphatic present resembles the καιρός, the opportune moment, which is an important temporal feature of the seasonal conception, as Jullien argued. The fashionable object is a transient one. With its inherent combination of elements that consist of new parts and references to the past, it has a temporal structure that possesses a strong presence because of its very temporality.

The fashionable object is a material constellation of time that is expressive, one which breathes Zeitgeist. The German noun *Zeitgeist* stands for the atmosphere, culture, lifestyle, and thinking of a singular period of historical time. Its formation is neither detached from the past nor from anticipation or visions of the future. Fashionable objects are materializations of the Zeitgeist. They can figure as such only in a temporal perspective: they express their time in their time. They thereby stand out and eventually become part of a material culture, which preserves them and makes them available for future reintegration in different constellations of temporal materiality. The momentariness of the fashionable artifact resembles the ancient concept of καιρός because there is only one time, which is suited for a certain fashion to appear. In this intimate relation of fashion and time arises the extraordinary form of anticipation that Benjamin praises in his *Arcades Project*. Artifacts in fashion are not only a constellation of the past and the present. Rather, these constellations are also a result of human imagination, and it is precisely the imaginative dimension that opens up the future and gives rise to creative visions of it.

In summary, my explorations of the seasonal structure of fashion and its connection to the temporal features of this subject focus on the relationship and merging of nature and culture. If one underscores the detached character of fashion, the artificiality of products and the needs created by them, then the whole system of fashion might appear only to be a capitalistic maneuver to increase production and consumption. The question then arises as to why people respond to it in the way they currently do. It would be naïve to assume that we all are simply blinded by the "evil advertising" industry; there is more to fashion than mere capitalistic allure. Rather, there is an anthropologically grounded need for expression and similarly an anthropologically based quest for novelty. There is something about the artificial formation of outer appearance that is rooted deeply in our phylogenetic history.[48] One important step toward a broader picture of the fashion system and its anthropological foundations is the inquiry into its temporal features and seasonal structures.

Notes

1. It is necessary initially to clarify the meaning of the seasons in fashion. As opposed to the common differentiation of spring, summer, fall, and winter, fashion systems traditionally discern two broad seasons: spring/summer and fall/winter. The presentation of collections for the coming season typically takes place at the beginning of the current season. For example, the spring/summer collections are presented in September of the previous year. This leads to a dialectic that needs to be considered in order to fully explain the characteristic temporality of fashion.

2. For a detailed account see Kate Fletcher and Mathilda Tams, eds., *Routledge Handbook of Sustainability and Fashion* (London: Routledge, 2015).

3. When I speak of fashion I refer to it in its modern sense. I do not merely refer to the human habit of wearing clothes and ornamenting the body, which also could be called fashion when the concept is used in a more anthropological sense. This usage is widely debated, and I tend to defend it as one possible way of speaking about fashion. In this essay, I nevertheless use the term fashion in its more common form as referring to the system of fashion that started in the nineteenth century in Paris. Cf. Kawamura, Yuniya, *Fashion-ology: An Introduction to Fashion Studies* (Oxford: Berg, 2006).

4. Georg Simmel, "Fashion" [1901], in *The Rise of Fashion* (pp. 289–309), ed. Daniel L. Purdy (Minneapolis: University of Minnesota Press, 2004), 295. The translation of *Wasserscheide* into English presents some difficulties. It could also be translated as "pivotal divide" or "watershed" in its figurative sense.

5. Cf. Hartmut Rosa, *Beschleunigung. Die Veränderung der Zeitstrukturen in der Moderne* (Frankfurt am Main: Suhrkamp, 2005).

6. Cf. Walter Benjamin, *The Arcades Project*, trans. Howard Eiland and Kevin McLaughlin (Cambridge, MA: Harvard University Press, 1999).

7. For a detailed account of the early fashion journals, see Bea Abadas, *Spielball der Mode. Von der ersten deutschen Frauen- zur Modezeitschrift* (Münster: Fischer, 1996); and Astrid Ackermann, *Paris, London und die europäische Provinz. Die frühen Modejournale 1770–1830* (Frankfurt am Main: Peter Lang, 2005).

8. Barbara Vinken, *Fashion Zeitgeist* (Oxford: Berg, 2005), 61ff.

9. For an overview cf. Elizabeth Wilson, *Adorned in Dreams: Fashion and Modernity* (London: Tauris, 2003).

10. Thorstein Veblen, *The Theory of the Leisure Class* [1899], in *The Rise of Fashion* (pp. 261–288), ed. Daniel L. Purdy (Minneapolis: University of Minnesota

Press, 2004), 280. For detailed accounts of consumption in modernity, cf. Collin Campbell, *The Romantic Ethic and the Spirit of Modern Consumerism* (Oxford: Writers Print Shop, 1987); Neil McKendrich, John Brewer and J. H. Plumb, eds., *The Birth of a Consumer Society: The Commercialization of Eighteenth-Century England* (Bloomington: Indiana University Press, 1982); Dominik Schrage, *Die Verfügbarkeit der Dinge: Eine historische Soziologie des Konsums* (Frankfurt: Campus, 2009); and Werner Sombart, *Liebe, Luxus und Kapitalismus: Über die Entstehung der modernen Welt aus dem Geist der Verschwendung* [1913] (Berlin: Wagenbach, 1966).

11. Veblen, *The Theory of the Leisure Class*, 281.

12. Veblen, *The Theory of the Leisure Class*, 280.

13. Veblen, *The Theory of the Leisure Class*, 281.

14. Simmel, "Fashion," 291.

15. Simmel, "Fashion," 290.

16. Simmel, "Fashion," 290.

17. On the distinction between the ontology of time and the experience of time, see Yvonne Förster, *Zeiterfahrung und Ontologie: Perspektiven moderner Zeitphilosophie* (Munich: Fink, 2012); and Yvonne Förster, "Flesh of Time: Conceptualizing Time and Memory in the Digital World," *V!RUS* 2 (2017), http://www.nomads.usp.br/virus/virus15/#.

18. Lucian Hölscher, *Die Entdeckung der Zukunft* (Frankfurt am Main: Fischer, 1999).

19. Sombart, *Liebe, Luxus und Kapitalismus*, 59ff.

20. Charles Baudelaire, "'Beauty, Fashion and Happiness,' 'Modernity,' and 'In Praise of Cosmetics' from *The Painter of Modern Life* (1863)," in *The Rise of Fashion* (pp. 213–221), ed. Daniel L. Purdy (Minneapolis, London: University of Minnesota Press, 2004), 213ff.

21. Jean-François Lyotard, *The Postmodern Condition: A Report on Knowledge* (Minneapolis: University of Minnesota Press, 1984).

22. Elena Esposito, *Die Verbindlichkeit des Vorübergehenden: Paradoxien der Mode* (Frankfurt am Main: Suhrkamp, 2004), 155.

23. Esposito, *Die Verbindlichkeit des Vorübergehenden*, 155.

24. Esposito, *Die Verbindlichkeit des Vorübergehenden*, 173.

25. Benjamin, *The Arcades Project*, 63–64.

26. See Maurice Merleau-Ponty, *The Phenomenology of Perception* (London: Routledge, 1981) and Maurice Merleau-Ponty, *The Visible and the Invisible* (Evanston, IL: Northwestern University Press, 1968), 130ff.

27. See Yvonne Förster-Beuthan, "Perspectives on the Concept of Fashion in Romanticism," in *Australian Yearbook of German Literary and Cultural Studies*, ed. Franz-Josef Deiters, Axel Fliethmann et al. (Vienna: Rombach, 2012), 141–157.

28. From Benjamin's *Theses on the Philosophy of History*, quoted in (a modified translation by) Ulrich Lehmann, *Tigersprung: Fashion in Modernity* (Cambridge, MA: The MIT Press, 2000), 37.

29. Lehmann, *Tigersprung*, 37.

30. Cf. Philipp Ekardt, "Fashion/Time-Differentials: From Simmel's *Philosophie der Mode* to Benjamin," in *Georg Simmel in Translation*, ed. David D. Kim (Newcastle upon Tyne: Cambridge Scholars, 2006), 183.

31. J. Ellis McTaggart, "The Unreality of Time," *Mind*, New Series, 68 (1908): 457–474.

32. McTaggart, "The Unreality of Time," 462.

33. For a detailed interpretation of the term "rupture" (*Zerreißung*) in Walter Benjamin, cf. Andrew Benjamin, *Style and Time: Essays on the Politics of Appearance* (Evanston, IL: Northwestern University Press, 2006), 57ff.

34. Cf. Daniel L. Purdy, *The Tyranny of Elegance. Consumer Cosmopolitanism in the Era of Goethe* (Baltimore, MD: Johns Hopkins University Press, 1998); Campbell, *The Romantic Ethic and the Spirit of Modern Consumerism*; and Schrage, *Die Verfügbarkeit der Dinge*.

35. Cf. Rebecca Arnold, *Fashion. A Very Short Introduction* (Oxford: Oxford University Press, 2009), 51.

36. Esposito, *Die Verbindlichkeit des Vorübergehenden*, 21.

37. Angela Borchert, Ralf Dressel, eds., *Das Journal des Luxus und der Moden: Kultur um 1800*, Heidelberg: Winter, 2004.

38. Francois Jullien, *Über die "Zeit": Elemente einer Philosophie des Lebens* (Zurich: Diaphanes, 2004), 41, my translation.

39. Jullien, *Über die "Zeit*," 49.

40. Cf. Jullien, *Über die "Zeit*," 49 and Karen Gloy, *Zeit: Eine Morphologie* (Munich: Alber, 2006).

41. Gloy, *Zeit*, 73ff.

42. Jullien, *Über die "Zeit*," 62.

43. Jullien, *Über die "Zeit*," 62.

44. Cf. Vinken, *Fashion Zeitgeist*, 41ff.

45. Roland Barthes, *The Fashion System* (West Sussex: University Press Group, 1990).

46. Yuniya Kawamura, *Fashion-ology: An Introduction to Fashion Studies* (Oxford: Berg, 2006).

47. In my interpretation of the temporal features of a seasonal concept, I follow Jullien's view of the seasons in ancient China.

48. The development of species, especially in sexual selection, is not oriented toward a standard of normality or an average. It follows the logic of standing out, of transgression. This is widely discussed in the contemporary debate about evolutionary aesthetics (see Wolfgang Welsch, *Animal Aesthetics* [2004], https://contempaesthetics.org/newvolume/pages/journal.php?volume=2). The aesthetic surplus is not a modern invention; it can be traced back to the earliest stages of life on earth. When it concerns human beings, there is the complexity of subjective experience in an objective world. Humans have an internal world, a first-person experience, that is

constantly shaped and altered by contact with other people and the environment. The body is a means of expression (see Yvonne Förster-Beuthan, "When Fashion becomes Art: Medial Aspects of the Body in Fashion," *The Journal of Humanities* 33, no. 2 [2012]: 263–281). This is the natural part of the fashion process. In order to explain the anthropological aspect of fashion, one has to examine the complex interwoven structure of nature and culture, a dichotomy that is itself artificial. Today, nature and culture have merged with technologies that enter the body itself. For a discussion of fashion and the body with regard to digital technologies, see Yvonne Förster (2018) "From Digital Skins to Digital Flesh: Understanding Technology through Fashion," *Popular Inquiry 2* (2018), https://www.popularinquiry. com/blog/2018/8/30/yvonne-frster-from-digital-skins-to-digital-flesh-understading-technolgy-trough-fashion?rq=yvonne.

DECOLONIZING LITERATURE

10

The Nature and Culture of the Seasons

Homage to Henry David Thoreau

Rod Giblett

All cultures have seasons, an understanding of the cycles of the year, especially the growing, gathering, and hunting periods, and the predominantly hot-or-cold and wet-or-dry times of the year that are related to those periods. Yet the number and nature of the seasons and their physiological and psychological affects varies widely across cultures. The four seasons of spring, summer, autumn, and winter are a European cultural construction of nature. These four seasons were imposed on the antipodean, upside-down world of Australia, and on its climates considered vaguely and inappropriately "Mediterranean" or "temperate." The European exemplars conflicted with the Indigenous seasons—six in the case of some Australian Aboriginal groups, such as the Nyoongars of southwestern Australia. In this chapter I chart briefly the colonization of the seasons in Australia and then call for and begin their decolonization. I do so through a deconstructive reading of some of the writing about the seasons in the European literary canon, especially James Thomson, and through an appreciation of Henry David Thoreau, who was an American dissenter to the tradition. The seasons, however, are not merely a matter of idle historical curiosity nor an interesting antiquarian hobby. They play a much more vital role in contemporary cultural and environmental politics in an age when human-made climate change is disrupting the seasons, both European and Indigenous. Rather than "climate change" or "global warming," I propose "seasonal dislocation" or "seasonal disruption" as better, more precise and poetic ways to describe this phenomenon.

The seasons play an important role in organizing a sense of time, of the progression of the year, of the cycle of the year, and of the years. Their role has also changed over time, especially from Paleolithic hunter-gather societies to Neolithic agricultural ones, and then to modern industrialized ones. The seasons have a history. The term *season* has a history deriving, as J. D. McClatchy points out, from the Latin for "sowing" and so it originally referred only to spring, and to agricultural societies.[1] The names for the seasons also have a history, as it was not until the sixteenth century that their names were stabilized in English, French, and German.[2]

The role of the four seasons in Europe has also changed historically from when sowing, reaping, and fallowing were periods vital for survival in the mainly agricultural society of Neolithic Europe and in its colonial diasporas. In modern, predominantly urban society, and in the globalized world, there has always a growing period occurring somewhere in the world. The four Europeans seasons are a construction of what Cicero called "second nature," of nature worked by agriculture. More precisely, they are a construction of what Alexander Wilson called a culture of nature and of what I have elsewhere called the second culture of nature (drawing on Cicero and Wilson).[3]

By contrast to the four European seasons, the Aboriginal Nyoongars of southwestern Australia have six seasons:

BIRAK: Dry and hot (December/January)

BUNURU: Hottest part of the year, with sparse rainfall (February/March)

DJERAN: Cooler weather begins (April/May)

MAKURU: Usually the wettest part of the year (June/July)

DJILBA: Often the coldest part of the year (August/September)

KAMBARANG: Warmer with longer dry periods (October/November)

These six seasons of two months each were the result of long-term observation and close engagement with local places, whereas the European four seasons of three months each were simply inverted for the Southern Hemisphere and associated with European climates based on cursory observation and minimal engagement with local places.

Yet assigning months to the Nyoongar cycle of the seasons is notional. Colleen Hayward, a senior Nyoongar woman and head of the Kurongkurl Katijin Centre for Indigenous Studies at Edith Cowan University, says the Nyoongar seasons are related to the weather and to changes in the plants, not to the months. The twelve months of the year are based loosely on the lunar cycle in which the moon orbits the earth 13.4 times a year and so the months are largely natural and transcultural in that regard. Yet the names for the months constitute the Julian calendar developed and introduced by Julius Caesar that enshrines his name in July and Augustus Caesar's in August and other months in Latin numerals which are now out of alignment as the Julian calendar was originally ten months. (September, literally the seventh month, is now the ninth; October, literally the eighth, is now the tenth; November, literally the ninth, is now the eleventh; December, literally the tenth, is now the twelfth.) These names for the months are another European cultural construction of nature, another instance of the second culture of nature.

The Australian Bureau of Meteorology, in contrast to the Nyoongars, enshrines the four European seasons in dividing the year in Australia, as in Europe (albeit inverted), into four quarters (and seasons) of three months each. It also divides the seasons in accordance with the months:

in Australia, the seasons are defined by grouping the calendar months in the following way:

Spring: The three transition months; September, October and November.

Summer: The three hottest months; December, January and February.

Autumn: The transition months; March, April and May.

Winter: The three coldest months; June, July and August.[4]

This division says nothing about the driest or wettest months, or seasons, presumably because they vary so widely across Australia. The seasons (and the months) derived from one place and one side of the world are transported and transcribed onto Australia and the other side of the world. The seasons developed from observation and living with the land in a local place by one culture are displaced and superseded by seasons from another place and culture.

The historical, cross-cultural conflict over the seasons in Australia was summarized in the brochure for an exhibition at the Ian Potter Centre in Melbourne. Stephen Gilchrist and Allison Holland state that: "The four seasons of the Northern Hemisphere, transposed to Australia more than 200 years ago, are largely discordant with the antipodean environment. Aboriginal people have developed a highly sensitive understanding of the environment through experiential engagement. Those who had spent a lifetime in its embrace read the subtle variances of shifting seasons."[5] By contrast, those who had *not* spent a lifetime in the embrace of Australia read the European four seasons crudely onto them, and the Indigenous seasons were thereby colonized. Gilchrist and Holland see this merely as a matter of historical fact rather than as concern for contemporary politics about dispossession of place (and distempering of time). For them, the two seasonal systems, and cultures, sit side-by-side in mutual antagonism and incomprehension.

Yet time and the seasons have been colonized, as the preceding discussion of the European seasons, the Australian Bureau of Meteorology, the Nyoongar seasons, and Gilchrist's and Holland's statement indicate. Thus, they need to be decolonized, just as people and places have been and still are. These discussions indicate that the seasons are involved in a cultural politics operating between, and in, nations and people, and that the seasons are a site of struggle enmeshed in power relations over what and how they mean. As colonization of space, time, and the seasons occurred, so decolonization of space, time, and the seasons, needs to occur. This could involve learning, understanding, and using in everyday speech the Indigenous names for the seasons instead of the four European seasons. It would certainly involve valuing an Indigenous understanding of the seasons in Australia.

The seasons have played a role within the cultural politics of nations, especially in what Perry Miller called "nature's nation," the United States of America.[6] Just as settler America colonized space with its fifty states, so it colonized time with the seasons of spring, fall (autumn), summer and winter. Just as it crossed, and closed, a succession of spatial frontiers in pursuit of its "Manifest Destiny" to occupy the area of what is now the lower forty-eight states, so it defined the temporal frontiers of, and between, the seasons, albeit with some condescension to "Indian summer" and with a variation on autumn as "fall," which has a medieval ancestry, anyway.[7] Just as settler America celebrated the West in music, song, word, and image (still and moving), so it celebrated in the same media the seasons, and their passing, and was nostalgic for a time when the seasons were more appreciated, more distinct from each other, and more immediately vital for sustaining life.[8]

Settler Americans, Michael Kammen argues, "blended nature, nationalism, and nostalgia in understanding the seasons,"[9] just as they did in founding and photographing national parks, and in preserving and photographing wilderness areas.[10] The celebration of the seasons provided a nostalgic screen on which to project nationalistic fantasies about nature. For instance, Ansel Adams's famous photograph, *Clearing Winter Storm, Yosemite National Park* (1944), is an illustration of this point.[11] The title combines references to the season (winter), weather (stormy) and place (Yosemite mountains). Each aspect of the title and composition is equally important in the photograph's evocation of the sublime with its affects of awe and terror in the face of monumental objects. These sublime affects relate to other sublime aspects of the photo, including the season of winter, the stormy weather, the mountainous cloudscape and landscape, and the hard and rocky place. Time and place, including season, weather, and mountain, are tied up with each other in Adams's photo.[12] It is the culmination of a long tradition whose medieval manifestations are traced by Enkvist: "Many poetic passages describing [or photographic images depicting] the times of the year are clothed in terms of landscape, whilst most verbal [and visual] pictures of outdoor scenery depict a season."[13] "Wintry storm" is a stock-in-trade device of seasonal description, as Enkvist shows later. James Thomson's "The Seasons," a series of four poems from the eighteenth century, is the exemplar of this tradition of seasonal landscape descriptive imbrication (as we will see shortly) that lives on in much landscape photography, especially on calendars.

The seasons, however, are not simply a subject for historical contemplation. They hold a crucial place in the present-day environmental and social worlds. In the age of human-made climate change, floods and droughts occur more frequently. Floods often occur in dry seasons and droughts in wet seasons. Floods also occur in the middle of droughts. As the seasons in many places are becoming more extreme with wetter or hotter dry seasons and years and drier or wetter wet seasons and years, the distinction between them is increasingly blurred. Paying attention to the seasons becomes more critical in this context as a way of making sense of climate and weather for earthly survival, let alone environmental sustainability. As a part of climate change and global warming, seasonal shift is occurring. Seasons are shifting temporally as the weather associated with one season is experienced in another. Seasons are also shifting spatially as the weather associated with one place is experienced elsewhere. I thus propose *seasonal dislocation* or *seasonal disruption* as better, more precise, and more poetic ways to describe the phenomena referred to as *climate change* or *global warming*. Even *global climate disruption*, proposed by the White House in September 2010, does not acknowledge the seasons as a way of making sense of meteorological phenomena.

Having an appreciation for the cycle of the seasons is a way of connecting the local and the global by acknowledging the current season here and now, and the changes that will take place in the shift from one season to the next with the rotation of the earth. It is also a way of understanding that global warming impacts on local place, the micro-climate, and that local activity affects global weather, the macro-climate. Having an appreciation for the cycle of the seasons is also a way of connecting with the local and resisting globalization by living in bio- and psycho-symbiosis in a bioregional home habitat of the living earth.[14] Developing a richer, more sensual, more embodied appreciation of and for the seasons and local place could involve attending to the sounds of birds chirping and leaves rustling in spring; the sight of browning and dried leaves in autumn; the feel of the sun's heat on the skin or the taste of cold water in winter; and the smell of cooking food or burning wood in summer.

Exemplary in this regard as a thinker about the seasons is the nineteenth-century writer Henry David Thoreau, whom Rick Bass calls "that most American of thinkers and spirits,"[15] and whose most famous book, *Walden,* Lawrence Buell calls "the most famous of all American season books."[16] Thoreau advised his readers to "live in each season as it passes; breathe the air, drink the drink, taste the fruit, and resign yourself to the influences of each. Let these be your only diet-drink and botanical medicine."[17] In other words, eat, drink and breathe locally, merrily and seasonally—not globally and trans-seasonally. One way in which Thoreau advocated an appreciation for the seasons was by having street trees planted that "mark the season . . . Let us have Willows for spring, Elms for summer, Maples and Walnuts and Tupeloes for autumn, Evergreens for winter and Oaks for all seasons."[18] Australians should mark the Aboriginal seasons of their local place by appreciating the native species that flower in succession, often through six months of the year in some highly biodiverse places.

History, geography and culture (or time, place and people) meet in the seasons. The seasons have a cultural history and a historical geography. They are not just a matter of what is called "the natural environment" as a static, immutable construct. They are a dynamic and mutable phenomenon. Nor are they just a matter of the past. An environmental history, or historical geography, of the seasons would be concerned with the seasons in the past. Yet the seasons are operating in the present and will be in the future. With what Paul Carter calls spatial history, "the future is invented" and "travellers and settlers do not so much belong to our past as we belong to their future."[19] Similarly, with what I would call temporal geography, the geography of time (past, present, and future; the cycle of the seasons), the future is invented and, as Carter puts it, "we recover the possibility of another history, our future." Such a future would be marked by an appreciation for the seasons in a political ecology that would include decolonization of the predominant framework and a respect for Indigenous seasons.[20]

History is located in spaces and places; geography is set in time (past, present, and future) including the cycle of the seasons. Spatial history for Carter "begins and ends in language. It is this which makes it history rather than, say, geography."[21] Yet geography, literally "writing the earth," begins and ends in language too, whether it is the verbal language of the explorer's journal about his journey in time through space and between places with his record of his observations of flora through the seasons experienced over the course of his journey, or the visual language of his maps making marks on paper in the scalar grid of latitude and longitude. Time and space come together anyway in longitude, as measuring time is the means to measure space. Temporal geography begins and ends in the language of time, including writing on the seasons of the earth and on the succession of flowering plants through the seasons. Understanding the meanings, metaphors, landscapes, and gender politics of the seasons is part of a better grasp of one's place on earth and one's point in time suspended in the present between a past one cannot return to and a future one cannot know but can invent.[22]

The meanings, metaphors, landscapes, and gender politics are significant in the writing about the seasons in the European literary canon. Decolonizing the European four seasons not only involves a deconstructive reading of this canon but also an appreciation for its dissenter in Henry David Thoreau who developed an embodied sense of the seasonal changes in the world around him. Ideas, attitudes, and values about the seasons that are still very much a part of the European cultural baggage attached to the seasons and transcribed to Australia can be traced back to, and find their culmination and summation in, James Thomson's canonical "The Seasons." This obscure eighteenth-century poem, which today few people know and even fewer have read, provides nevertheless an entry point into the European thought, representation, and tradition of the seasons, from Virgil through

Chaucer to Thoreau and Eliot. The poem also aids in deconstructing and decolonizing the four European seasons.

Spring

Thomson typifies each of the four seasons in quite distinct ways by devoting a long poem to each season. He begins with spring, "When nature all / is blooming and benevolent"[23] coming out of "the faithful bosom of the ground,"[24] and when "Fair-handed Spring unbosoms every grace."[25] The earth in spring is feminized as the good agricultural and horticultural Mother Earth. Spring is the time when "Nature's ample lap" bears fruit.[26] Yet to do this, nature in spring requires the sun. She requires the power of the sun to bloom. The position of the sun in the sky, its angle of inclination due to the angle of inclination of the earth's axis, is the determinant of the seasons. The higher the position of the sun in the sky, the longer the days are, the more energy the earth receives from the sun, and the more productive plants are.

For Thomson, "the bounteous sun" brings forth the bounty of nature to fruition.[27] For him "the penetrative sun, / His force deep-darting to the dark retreat / Of vegetation"[28] penetrates to where "the promised fruit / Lies yet a little embryo"[29] in "the pregnant earth."[30] The sun is masculinized as the active, life-giving force that creates life in the passive, feminized earth. The male sun plants the seed in the female earth who is the mere receptacle. Thomson mentions "the sacred plough"[31] but not the ploughman, sacred or not, nor the sacred earth.

Summer

Thomson also masculinizes summer with "his pestilential heats."[32] As "child of the sun, refulgent Summer"[33] is more precisely son of the sun with his "secret, strong, attractive force."[34] Summer for Thomson is pestilential, especially around swamps in accordance with the prevailing miasmatic theory of disease of his day: "The hoary fen / In putrid streams emits the living cloud of pestilence."[35] Later "the joyless sun, / . . . draws copious steam from swampy fens, / where putrefaction into life ferments / And breathes destructive myriads" and brings forth "the dire power of pestilent disease."[36] According to Thomson, the sun not only brings forth new life out of dry ground, but also brings forth death out of wetlands in accordance with the miasmatic theory of disease in Hippocratic medicine.[37] He is following in the footsteps of Virgil in *The Georgics* in his description of "Land that is breathing out lank mist and volatile vapours."[38]

Thomson, based in a temperate climate, is reproducing Virgil's view based in a Mediterranean climate. Along similar lines to both, the Baroque composer Antonio Vivaldi, in his sonnet "Summer" for *The Four Seasons,* identifies summer as "the harsh season ignited by the sun," when "men and flock languish."[39] As summer is the season of heat, storms, lightning, and "fiery thunder," it has traditionally been associated with the element of fire. Similarly, summer for Hesiod in the late eighth century BCE is the season of fatigue.[40] Vivaldi's and Hesiod's Mediterranean view of summer contrasts with the temperate view of Langland and Chaucer. They indicate some intra-European cultural variability across the climatic zones of Europe, though Thomson attests to the durability of Hesiod's and Virgil's classical view across Europe and its climatic zones. For the medieval Langland in the Prologue to *Piers Plowman,* "A summer season · when soft was the sun" is the time of the year when he goes widely in the world, wonders to hear. This alliterative collocation of "summer," "season," "soft," and "sun" was a typical rhetorical ploy of the Middle Ages; it is found also, for instance, in Chaucer's "Roundel."[41]

Winter

Thomson also masculinizes winter as a time of the "wild" and "waste"[42] and as "the wild season."[43] He repeatedly exploits the medieval and Elizabethan collocation that alliterates winter with wild, waste, and wilderness. He is following in the footsteps of the Elizabethan Edmund Spenser writing in the sixteenth century for whom "thou barren ground, whom winter's wrath has wasted / Art made a mirror to behold my plight."[44] In the mirror of winter he sees "Such rage as winter's reigneth in my heart." Thomson also exploits the pathetic fallacy that poses parallels between the state of nature and the state of the mind-body. When "winter falls, / A heavy gloom oppressive o'er the world" blankets everything.[45] "The soul of man dies in him, loathing life, / And black with more than melancholy views"[46] the soul suffers from "black glooms"[47] and "black despair"[48] in "Dread Winter."[49]

Thomson also draws parallels between the landscape and the mind and body. Unlike the pleasing prospects of spring and summer, winter has a "horrid prospect"[50] of "horrid mountains . . . Cruel as death, and hungry as the grave."[51] Winter for Thomson is "the cruel season,"[52] as it is for the Elizabethan Thomas Sackville, Earl of Dorset.[53] Virgil refers to "cruel winters" in *The Georgics*, the classical urtext on the four European seasons.[54] Yet for T. S. Eliot, in the opening lines of "The Waste Land," mid-spring "April is the cruellest month" as new life is forced out of its comfortable wintry repose:

> April is the cruellest month, breeding
> Lilacs out of the dead land, mixing
> Memory and desire, stirring
> Dull roots with spring rain.
> Winter kept us warm, covering
> Earth in forgetful snow, feeding
> A little life with dried tubers.
> Summer surprised us, coming over the Starnbergersee
> With a shower of rain; we stopped in the colonnade,
> And went on in sunlight, into the Hofgarten,
> And drank coffee, and talked for an hour.[55]

For Chaucer in the opening lines of the prologue to *The Canterbury Tales,* April is also, like for Eliot, the month of burgeoning new life tinged with cruelty:

> When April with his showers sweet with fruit
> The drought of March has pierced unto the root
> And bathed each vein with liquor that has power
> To generate therein and sire the flower;
> When Zephyr also has, with his sweet breath,
> Quickened again, in every holt and heath,
> The tender shoots and buds, and the young sun
> Into the Ram one half his course has run,
> And many little birds make melody
> That sleep through all the night with open eye
> (So Nature pricks them on to ramp and rage)—
> Then do folk long to go on pilgrimage . . .[56]

One Chaucerian scholar has linked these lines from Chaucer's prologue to lines from Virgil's *Georgics,* when:

in spring the swelling earth aches for the seed of new life.
Then the omnipotent Father of air [Aether] in fruitful showers
Comes down to his happy consort
And greatly breeds upon her great body manifold fruit.
Then are the trackless copses alive with the trilling of birds,
And the beasts look for love, their hour come round again:
Lovely the earth in labour, under a tremulous west wind
The fields unbosom, a mild moisture is everywhere.[57]

In other words, and in short, father air inseminates mother earth. In what Rosemond Tuve calls "the marriage of Ether and Earth," "a union of Aether and Earth," and "the Virgilian idea of the union of the fecund earth with ether," the active and seed-bearing father impregnates a passive and receptive mother who is only a fertile receptacle, just as the masculine sun for Thomson planted the seed in a feminized earth.[58] She does not supply an egg for union with his seed, nor carries new life within her for its term before birth. The active role of mother earth in creating new life and the work of the human sower in bringing it forth are obscured in Virgil's account, in which the earth labors and brings forth new life. The same Chaucerian scholar has suggested substituting "*Aprille* for *Aether*" in *The Georgics* as "no less intelligible or appealing to Chaucer's English readers."[59] Equally and conversely substituting *Aether* for *Aprille* in the prologue would give the same Virgilian sense of the activity of father ether and the passivity of mother earth in Chaucer's account. The idea of "sky gods" and "earth goddesses" is an old one that goes back through Hellenic Greek mythology.[60]

Without mentioning (pagan) father ether, for the medieval Christian Alain of Lille/Alanus de Insulis, "winter holds the buried seeds deep in the lap of mother earth, spring sets the captives free, summer ripens the harvests, autumn displays her riches."[61] Earthly and human labor is obscured in plowing, sowing and reaping, and the seasons alone are credited with agency. The earth is even seen as a feminized prison that captivates life, with spring being seen as a liberating force that wrests life from her grasp and sets it free. This line of thought and imagery culminates in the eighteenth century in Thomson's sublime spring that sublimates life into the ether and in Kant's dynamical sublime, an extraterrestrial vector on which to escape from the prison of the earth and count ourselves as independent of nature, and the earth.[62]

Autumn

Autumn for Thomson is the season of "sickly damps and cold autumnal fogs."[63] Autumn for him mixes the qualities of coldness and moistness in the element of air. He does not subscribe to the philosophical theory of the qualities and elements, as autumn in this schema mixes the qualities of coldness and dryness in the element of the earth.[64] The four seasons have been associated traditionally with the four elements of earth, air, fire (or sun) and water: earth with autumn; air with spring; fire with summer; and water with winter.[65] As the mixing of the four qualities of coldness, moistness, heat, and dryness creates each of the four elements, so each of the four seasons mixes these qualities. There is a long tradition, going back at least a thousand years to Byrhtferth's Old English Manual of 1011 CE, that makes the connection between the four qualities, the four elements, the four seasons, and the four humors.[66] These connections build on a much more ancient chain of associations in which the four qualities were mixed to produce the four elements of earth, air, fire and water.[67]

In this schema, winter is the season that mixes the qualities of coldness and moistness in the element of water. Air mixes the qualities of heat and moistness, giving rise to the beneficent exhalations of rain, and is associated with spring. Air in winter, however, can be cold and moist, and gives rise to oppressive and depressive mist and fogs associated with winter, or with autumn as in Thomson, whereas for him in summer extreme heat and excessive moisture give rise to malignant miasma, effluvia, and malaria (literally "bad air").[68] For Virgil in *The Georgics,* "cold moisture" is associated with "early spring,"[69] whereas in the traditional philosophical schema the qualities of coldness and moistness are associated with a watery and wet winter. Yet there is always a blurring between the seasons, and a mixing of the elements in all of them. For Thomson, "sun, and water, earth, and air, / In ever-changing composition [are] mixed" in every season.[70] Rick Bass likewise questions the "neat symmetry of the four seasons" and proposes "the fifth season, the space between winter and spring" which he calls "the mud season."[71] In Thomson's terms, in this season the elements of water and earth are mixed.

Autumn is the time of the changing colors of foliage, though these are not as dramatic in England as they are in New England. In 1859 Thoreau began his essay "Autumnal Tints" by noting that:

> Europeans coming to America are surprised by the brilliancy of our autumnal foliage. There is no account of such a phenome-

non in English poetry, because the trees acquire but few bright colors there. The most that Thomson says on this subject in his "Autumn" [ll. 950–54, p. 166] is contained in the lines:

> But see the fading, many-coloured woods,
> Shade deepening over shade, the country round
> Imbrown; a crowded umbrage, dusk and dun,
> Of every hue from wan declining green
> To sooty dark . . .

The autumnal change of our woods has not made a deep impression on our own literature yet. October has hardly tinged our poetry.[72]

Thoreau goes on to rectify this situation in the remainder of his essay by showing how American autumnal foliage has made a deep impression on him and on his senses—and a first impression on American literature beginning with him, and this essay.

Autumn has made more of an impression in English literature on the mind and mood. Autumn for Thomson is the time and place of "the mournful grove," "the dreary shower," and "the wither'd waste" when "the desolated prospect thrills the soul" and "the Power / Of Philosophic Melancholy comes."[73] These are the places of "vast embowering shades," "twilight groves," "visionary vales," "weeping grottoes," "prophetic glooms" and "the solemn dusk."[74] Autumn made a similarly strong impression on Alexander Pushkin, for whom it is the "season of melancholy."[75] Unlike the homely scenes of spring and summer, autumn for Thomson is an unhomely scene associated with the melancholy and the uncanny. For Keats, in his ode "To Autumn," it is a season of abundance bathed in benign sunlight. Autumn for him is "Season of mists and mellow fruitfulness / Close bosom-friend of the maturing sun,"[76] unlike the harsh sun of summer for Vivaldi.

Aesthetics

Each of the four European seasons has been associated with an aesthetic category or mode. Or, more precisely, nature in each of the seasons presents itself in an appropriate aesthetic mode or fashion. Kammen suggests that for Thomson "nature is . . . beautiful in summer, melancholy in autumn, sublime and terrible in winter."[77] Spring is missing from this list. Unlike

Gerard Manley Hopkins, for whom "nothing is so beautiful as spring,"[78] Thomson views nature in both spring and summer as pleasing and picturesque, while nature presents a desolate prospect in autumn, and a horrid prospect in winter. Winter is associated with the sublime for Thomson for, as Kammen suggests, "the rude mountain and the mossy wild,"[79] "the brooding terrors of the storm"[80] and "the wintry blast of death"[81] all evoke the sublime. For Thomson, spring is also associated with the sublime, or at least its clouds are: "gentle Spring" whose "light clouds sublime"[82] float in its "ethereal mildness."[83] Clouds sublime or sublimate in varying chemical, aesthetic, spiritual, and psychological senses the solid matter of the earth into ether, into air, into gas.[84]

In "Spring" Thomson writes how "From the moist meadow to the withered hill, / Led by the breeze, the vivid verdure runs, / And swells and deepens to the cherished eye."[85] In "Spring" he also writes how, from a height, "the bursting prospect spreads immense around" with "verdant field," "darkening heath," "villages embosomed in trees" and "spiry towns."[86] In "Summer," Thomson writes of "the lawny prospect"[87] of "the surface of the enlivened earth, / Graceful with hills and leafy woods, / Her liberal tresses."[88] In "Summer" he also exclaims, "what a goodly prospect spreads around, / Of hills, and dales, and woods, and lawns, and spires, / And glittering town, and gilded streams."[89] Rather than nature for Thomson being beautiful in summer, it is picturesque in both spring and summer. Spring is the time of the "homely scene"[90] whereas autumn is the time of the unhomely scene. Autumn is arguably an aesthetic experience of the unhomely, or uncanny, a state of fascination and horror, as Freud showed.[91]

Each of these aesthetic modes has a yield of pleasure associated with it. Winter, associated with the sublime, is a state of pleasure bordering on pain. Winter for Spenser in the sixteenth century (without the word *sublime* in his vocabulary) is "the sad season of the year" when "the pleasures" of spring are "buried in the sadness of the dead winter" until they are "worne away" by the sun and "reliveth" in spring.[92] "Winter's sorrow" and "winter's wrath" contrasts for Spenser with "pleasant spring."[93] Spring and summer, associated with the beautiful and the pleasing prospect of the picturesque, are states of relaxed pleasure. Autumn is a state of "blissful pleasure" for Antonio Vivaldi in the "Autumn" sonnet of his *Four Seasons*.[94] Aesthetics has been defined by Michel Serres as "the pleasure of the senses."[95] Most writers about the seasons concentrate on the pleasures of the seasons for the sense of sight. Few write about their pleasures (or pains) for the other senses. Thomson writes about the putrefaction of summer, for instance, but not about what this, or the other phenomena of the seasons, smell like.

Rather than the address of the senses to the other senses besides sight, rather than the impact or influence of the seasons on specific organs of the body, most writers on the seasons are interested in their impact or affect on the mind. As Kammen puts it, there are "the seasons of the mind," or "psychological 'seasons' as states of mind" as he earlier puts it.[96] In the poem "The Human Seasons," Keats writes that "there are four seasons in the mind of man":

> Four Seasons fill the measure of the year;
>   There are four seasons in the mind of man:
> He has his lusty Spring, when fancy clear
>   Takes in all beauty with an easy span:
> He has his Summer, when luxuriously
>   Spring's honied cud of youthful thought he loves
> To ruminate, and by such dreaming high
>   Is nearest unto heaven: quiet coves
> His soul has in its Autumn, when his wings
>   He furleth close; contented so to look
> On mists in idleness—to let fair things
>   Pass by unheeded as a threshold brook.
> He has his Winter too of pale misfeature,
> Or else he would forego his mortal nature.[97]

There are also four seasons in the body of man. Each of the four European seasons has been associated with a time of human life, an "age of man." For the medieval Alain of Lille, the universe "rejoices in the boyhood of spring," "advances in the youth of summer," "matures in the manhood of autumn," and "whitens in the old age of winter."[98] For the Elizabethan Spenser, youth is associated with spring, manhood with summer, "riper years" with autumn, and "latter age" with winter.[99] For Thomson "Flowering Spring" is linked with childhood; "Summer's ardent strength" with youth; "Sober Autumn fading into age" with maturity or middle age; and "pale concluding Winter" with old age.[100] Thoreau goes one step further and associates the seasons with the ages of literary history: "Our summer of English poetry is well-advanced towards its fall, and laden with the fruit and foliage of the season, with bright autumnal tints, but soon the winter will scatter its myriad clustering and shading leaves, and leave only a few desolate and fibrous boughs to sustain the snow and rime, and creak in the blasts of ages."[101] Naturally he places himself in the flowering and fruitful season of summer and prophesizes the fall and frosty winter (of modernism?) to come.

Like Keats, for whom there are "seasons in the mind of man," for Henry David Thoreau there is a season of the soul and "a landscape of the mind" with its seasons across which "a faint shadow flits . . . cast by the *wings* of some thought in its vernal or autumnal migration."[102] In his poem "The Soul's Season" Thoreau relates how:

> A sober mind will walk alone,
> Apart from nature if need be,
> And only its own seasons own,
> For nature having its humanity.

The season of the soul is not necessarily in sync with the season of the earth and sky for:

> Sometimes a late autumnal thought
>   Has crossed my mind in green July,
> And to its early freshness brought
>   Late ripened fruits and an autumnal sky.[103]

A mature, autumnal thought crosses Thoreau's mind belatedly in green, youthful summer and changes the face of summer into autumn. Conversely, what he calls "a dry but golden" autumnal thought crosses prematurely the summer greenness of his mind and makes mature autumnal wisdom linger into green and youthful summer:

> A dry but golden thought which gleamed
>   Athwart the greenness of my mind,
> And prematurely wise it seemed,
>   Too ripe mid summer's youthful bowers to find.

The season of the soul may be out of sync with the season of the earth, yet it is still the season of autumn. In another poem without a title he proclaims, "I am the Autumnal sun" and later, "the winter is lurking within my moods."[104] Thoreau is in no doubt that there is a season of the soul. He is also drawing on a long history of associating the seasons with age, but he upsets the traditional association by dissociating the seasons of the soul, or mind, with the seasons of the earth. Thoreau deconstructs and decolonizes the European cultural construction of the seasons, and the second culture of nature. In this regard, as well as many others, he is an exemplary figure.[105]

Notes

1. J. D. McClatchy, ed., *The Four Seasons: Poems* (New York: Alfred A. Knopf, 2008), 13.

2. Nils Erik Enkvist, *The Seasons of the Year: Chapters on a Motif from "Beowulf" to "The Shepherd's Calendar* (Helsinki: Open Library, 1957), 57, 90.

3. See Rod Giblett, *People and Places of Nature and Culture* (Bristol: Intellect Books, 2011), chapter 1.

4. Australian Bureau of Meteorology, "Climate Glossary." http://www.bom.gov.au/climate/glossary/seasons.shtml.

5. Stephen Gilchrist and Allison Holland, *Shared Sky* (Melbourne: The Ian Potter Centre: NGV Australia at Federation Square, 2009), 22.

6. Perry Miller, "Nature and the National Ego," in *Errand into the Wilderness* (Cambridge, MA: Belknap Press of Harvard University Press, 1956), 201.

7. See Enkvist, *The Seasons of the Year*, 159.

8. Michael Kammen, *A Time to Every Purpose: The Four Seasons in American Culture* (Chapel Hill: The University of North Carolina Press, 2004).

9. Kammen, *A Time to Every Purpose*, 107.

10. See Giblett, *People and Places of Nature and Culture*, especially chapters 5 and 7, and Rod Giblett, *Landscapes of Culture and Nature* (Basingstoke: Palgrave Macmillan, 2009).

11. Ansel Adams, *The American Wilderness* (Boston: Little, Brown, 1990), plate 51.

12. I discuss Adams's photography much more extensively along these lines in Rod Giblett and Juha Tolonen *Photography and Landscape* (Bristol: Intellect Books, 2012).

13. Enkvist, *The Seasons of the Year*, v.

14. See Giblett, *People and Places of Nature and Culture*, chapter 12.

15. Rick Bass, *Wild Marsh: Four Seasons at Home in Montana* (Boston: Houghton Mifflin Harcourt, 2009), 1.

16. Lawrence Buell, *The Environmental Imagination: Thoreau, Nature Writing, and the Formation of American Culture* (Cambridge, MA: Belknap Press of Harvard University Press, 1995), 232. The second most famous American seasons book is *A Sand County Almanac* by Aldo Leopold (1949). For an Australian seasons book following in the footsteps of Thoreau and Leopold and based, like their books, on

a nature journal kept through the seasons, see Rod Giblett, *Black Swan Lake: The Life of a Wetland* (Bristol: Intellect Books, 2013).

17. Henry David Thoreau, *Collected Essays and Poems*, ed. Elizabeth Hall Witherell (New York: Library of America, 2001), 501.

18. Thoreau, *Collected Essays and Poems*, 386.

19. Paul Carter, *The Road to Botany Bay: An Exploration of Landscape and History* (Chicago: University of Chicago Press, 1987), 294.

20. Carter, *The Road to Botany Bay*, 295.

21. Carter, *The Road to Botany Bay*, xxiii.

22. See Giblett, *Landscapes of Culture and Nature*, chapter 9.

23. James Thomson, "The Seasons," in *The Complete Poetical Work*, ed. J. Logie Robertson (Oxford: Oxford University Press, 1908), Sp., ll.9–10, p. 4. I cite "The Seasons" by the poem devoted to a season ("Au," "Sp," "Su," and "W"), line number ("l.") or numbers ("ll.") and the page number.

24. Thomson, "The Seasons," Sp, l.46, p. 5.

25. Thomson, Sp, l.529, p. 23.

26. Thomson, Sp, l.182, p. 10.

27. Thomson, Sp, l.26, p. 4.

28. Thomson, Sp, ll.78–81, p. 6.

29. Thomson, Sp, ll.99–100, p. 7.

30. Thomson, Su, l.1378, p. 104. See also Rosemond Tuve, *Seasons and Months: Studies in a Tradition of Middle English Poetry* (Paris: Librairie Universitaire, 1933), 76.

31. Thomson, Sp, l.58, p. 5.

32. Thomson, Sp, l.320, p. 15.

33. Thomson, Su, l.2, p. 53.

34. Thomson, Su, l.97, p. 56.

35. Thomson, Su, ll.292–294, p. 64.

36. Thomson, Su, ll.1027–1035, p. 89.

37. See Rod Giblett, *Postmodern Wetlands: Culture History Ecology* (Edinburgh: Edinburgh University Press, 1996), chapter 5.

38. Virgil, *The Eclogues; The Georgics*, trans. Cecil Day-Lewis (Oxford: Oxford University Press, 1983), II, l.217.

39. Antonio Vivaldi, *The Four Seasons* (New York: Dover, 1999), xii.

40. Hesiod, *Theogony; Works and Days*, trans. M. West (Oxford: Oxford University Press, 1988), 56.

41. McClatchy, *The Four Seasons*, 74. Enkvist, *The Seasons of the Year*, 84, 86, 95.

42. Thomson, Sp, l.25, p. 4.

43. Thomson, Au, l.64, p. 135.

44. Edmund Spenser, *Shepheard's Calendar: Containing Twelve Eclogues Proportionable to the Twelve Months*. C. Herford, ed. (London: Macmillan, [1579] 1932, 15.

45. Thomson, W, ll.57–58, p. 187.

46. Thomson, W, ll.60–61, p. 187.

47. Thomson, W, l.73, p. 187.

48. Thomson, W, l.289, p. 196.

49. Thomson, W, l.1024 p. 223.

50. Thomson, W, l.281, p. 196.

51. Thomson, W, ll.390 and 393, p. 200.

52. Thomson, W, l.243, p. 195.

53. McClatchy, *The Four Seasons*, 194.

54. Virgil, *The Eclogues; The Georgics*, II, l.373.

55. T. S. Eliot, *The Complete Poems and Plays* (London: Faber & Faber, 1969), 61.

56. https://www.westernacademy.net/poetry-corner/2014/4/15/excerpt-from-the-general-prologue-of-the-canterbury-tales

57. Virgil, *The Eclogues; The Georgics*, II, ll.324–327.

58. Tuve, *Seasons and Months*, 26, 52, 88.

59. Cited by Tuve, *Seasons and Months*, 52.

60. See Rod Giblett, *The Body of Nature and Culture* (Basingstoke: Palgrave Macmillan, 2008), 86–89.

61. Alain of Lille/Alanus de Insulis, *The Complaint of Nature*, trans. D. Moffat (Hamden, CT: Archon Books, 1972), 37.

62. Immanuel Kant, *The Critique of Judgment*, trans. James Creed Meredith (Oxford: Clarendon, 1952), 109, 111.

63. Thomson, Sp, l.329, p. 15.

64. See Noga Arikha, *Passions and Tempers: A History of the Humors* (New York: HarperCollins, 2008), fig. 1, p. 11.

65. Arikha, *Passions and Tempers*, fig. 1, p. 11.

66. Cited by Enkvist, *The Seasons of the Year*, 41. See also the "*Secreta Secretorum*" cited by Enkvist, 187–189.

67. See Giblett, *Postmodern Wetlands*, 156–162.

68. See Giblett, *Postmodern Wetlands*, 103–105.

69. Virgil, *The Eclogues; The Georgics*, I, l.43.

70. Thomson, Au, ll.635–637, p. 155.

71. Bass, *Wild Marsh*, 80.

72. Thoreau, *Collected Essays and Poems*, 367.

73. Thomson, Au, ll.990–1005, p. 168.

74. Thomson, Au, ll.1030–1033, p. 169.

75. McClatchy, *The Four Seasons*, 142.

76. McClatchy, *The Four Seasons*, 123.

77. Kammen, *A Time to Every Purpose*, 69.

78. McClatchy, *The Four Seasons*, 31.

79. Thomson, W, l.98, p. 188.

80. Thomson, W, l.115, p. 189.

81. Thomson, Su, l.581, p. 75.

82. Thomson, Sp, l.30, p. 4.

83. Thomson, Sp, l.1, p. 3.

84. See Giblett, *Postmodern Wetlands*, chapter 2.

85. Thomson, Sp, ll.87–89, p. 6.

86. Thomson, Sp, ll.951–955, pp. 38–39.

87. Thomson, Su, l.53, p. 55.

88. Thomson, Su, ll.130–132, p. 58.

89. Thomson, Su, ll.1439–1440, pp. 105–106.

90. Thomson, Sp, l.786, p. 33.

91. See Giblett, *Postmodern Wetlands*, chapter 2.

92. Spenser, *Shepheard's Calendar*, 11, 14.

93. Spenser, *Shepheard's Calendar*, 25.

94. Vivaldi, *The Four Seasons*, xiii.

95. Michel Serres, *The Five Senses: A Philosophy of Mingled Bodies*, trans. Margaret Sankey and Peter Cowley (London: Continuum, 2008), 329.

96. Kammen, *A Time to Every Purpose*, 169, 153.

97. Cited by Kammen, *A Time to Every Purpose*, 4–5.

98. Alain of Lille, *The Complaint of Nature*, 29; cited also by Tuve, *Seasons and Months*, 21.

99. Spenser, *Shepheard's Calendar*, 84.

100. Thomson, W., ll.1029–1032, p. 223.

101. Thoreau, *Collected Essays and Poems*, 145.

102. Thoreau, *Collected Essays and Poems*, 253. For landscapes of the mind, see Giblett, *Landscapes of Culture and Nature*, part IV.

103. Thoreau, *Collected Essays and Poems*, 560.

104. Thoreau, *Collected Essays and Poems*, 583.

105. See Giblett, "Henry David Thoreau: Patron Saint of Swamps," *Postmodern Wetlands*, 229–239.

11

The Decolonized Pastoral

Kinsella, Thoreau, and the Seasons

Tom Bristow

We wade through senses
we can't name but know are there,

bothering blood.

—John Kinsella, "Spring Pollen"

What's a summer? Time for a turtle's eggs to hatch

—Henry David Thoreau, *Journal* entry, Aug. 28, 1856

Introduction

A recent engagement with American literature and philosophy by the Austra-lian ecopoet John Kinsella develops a syncretic poetics wherein a single form fulfills two different functions: to write out a portable and international sense of place that is attuned to an acute geographic site. This expansive localism is intriguing for its attention to the seasons and the poet's experiments with rhizomic transhistorical and transgeographic connections. Resonating with the volume's emphasis on groupings and comminglings—that work to undermine any sense of isolated, atomic life—a pragmatist emphasis on

the material interactions within these poetically conceived clusters of life
suggests not only that matter is a fundamental substance in nature, but also
that consciousness is a result of interactions within these clusters.

Deliberate Living and Radical Pastoral

Henry David Thoreau's *Walden; or Life in the Woods* (1854) is the result of
an experiment in self-sufficiency. It is America's scriptural call to establish
the foundations of nationhood. John Kinsella's *Jam Tree Gully* is indebted
to Thoreau; twenty of one hundred poems use *Walden* for their epigraphs;
another twenty either take their title from a quotation or paraphrase of
Thoreau; several others demonstrate deep learning from the text and/or
mimicry of Thoreau's Emersonian compression of ideas.

The epic event of America is pregnant with philosophical and political
notions of selfhood. The triumph of principles and latent convictions that
constitute enlightenment within the self signifies progressive formations of
nation and individual. For Ralph Waldo Emerson—America's first public
intellectual and sponsor of Thoreau's solitary dwelling project—this particular aversion to society is at once a rejection of an obsession with "names
and customs" and an endorsement of "realities and creators."[1] There is an
inherent push toward materialism combined with an active imagination as a
mode of reason itself, over and above abstraction. While Emerson envisioned
this project as the clarification of the ways in which the soul is linked to
the divine spirit, Thoreau applies a principled and more practical sense of
selfhood to his reading of the environment, including his capacity to read
the seasons. Thus, an idealized position lived out through practical engagement with the world that is animated by "embodied sensuality"[2] stands as
the founding formulation for American wilderness writing, which has some
purchase on the Australian imaginary today.

In *Walden*, seasons do not come first; human emotion and intellect
precede chronotopic and atmospheric representations. Human autonomy
achieved in this manner, experienced and conceived within the midst of
nature—the central focus of Kinsella's and Thoreau's experiments—offers a
form of Romanticism, a mode of feeling rather than a choice of subject.
Thoreau recounts that "In any weather, at any hour of the day or night, I
have been anxious to improve the nick of time, and notch it on my stick
too; to stand on the meeting of two eternities, the past and the future,
which is precisely the present moment; to toe that line."[3] To write down
the passing of time and to mark its improvements in "any weather" is to

extend consciousness to all seasons regardless of any particular opportunities or difficulties they might present to the human and the environment.

Here, a self-reflective witness of the earth's subjects—humans implicated in the condition of the environment under survey—and the inherent attributes of earth's circadian cycle—night and day—are fused. The literal alignment between the history of events in Concord, Massachusetts, and their relation to the claim of an American national identity, reaches beyond a claim for a new literature.[4] It offers the grist of dialectic, self-placement and identification that extends to the furthest meaning of climate and season. "In any weather" is a subjective interpretation that is a novel perception. It appears to be universal, too, or part of an original intelligence that betrays resonance with a materialist philosophical monism, for Kinsella extends this stance beyond the pastoral frame.

Ecological Empiricism

Thoreau's anarchism is distilled in his literal and metaphorical reading of stable seasons within a philosophical presentation of climate. Kinsella's transference of Thoreau's anarchism from the domain of liberty to the discourse of environmental consciousness enacts a counter-pastoral poetry, moving away from concepts of freedom and autonomy to activist thinking about being and being in ecology. This is traceable through the spatial arrangement of objects in the location, Jam Tree Gully:

> . . . Red ants bite my feet
> and I carefully brush them away. A hawk
> looks for a safe perch to settle for the night.
> Each substance 'inheres,' or is it 'in which
>
> they inhere'? as William James might attribute
> to this wood from the fallen tree, questioning its quality
> of 'combustibility and fibrous structure.'
> I—*we*—manage our days because of those
>
> attributes, those qualities of burn.[5]

Here, the layering of the non-human animal onto the pastoralists' environment via the philosophically acute sense of dwelling situates images within textual events that perceive space as ecological site, namely: "the 'complementarity'

of the animal and the environment."[6] Here the world is perceived in terms
of the spatialized relationships between objects and also in terms of the
possibilities of objects: eucalypt as temporary home for the hawk, sapling as
a host for fungal parasites and phytophagous insects. Objects and referents,
therefore, can be read as concepts that are both "territory" and "event"[7];
they are parts of the physical environment (*terre*) that give rise to other
moments of life in space. These new phenomena and occurrences are most
legible during the collection's heightened depiction of heat, which I shall
return to in full when I offer an in-depth reading of "Survey."

A Darwinian tone here is explicitly amplified by the focus on climate
within the lyric's sincere anxiety. *Jam Tree Gully*'s reading of "harsh winds
and corrosive temperatures"[8] can be raised to near apocalyptic levels: "open
space joins open space . . . on a planet getting hotter day by day, /
with lengthening fire seasons that erase // calendars and equinoxes and cities
like London."[9] The literal displacement of the European model of the four
seasons is paradoxical: in part, it portends a space where the mediating role
of language is dissolved; however, as instanced by the prosaic yet inspiring
phrase "fire seasons," the recourse to abstraction here promotes linguistic
necessity, that is, lyricism undermined to promote the decentered orbiting
consciousness (pastoral) in close relationship to the material events of the
location. This seems to resonate with Gaston Bachelard:

> Metaphors are not simple idealizations which take off like rockets
> only to display their insignificance on bursting in the sky, but
> on the contrary metaphors summon one another and are more
> coordinated than sensations, so much so that a poetic mind is
> purely and simply a syntax of metaphors.[10]

Kinsella's poetic flowering relies upon a synthesis of images that draw from
a sensitivity to heat and to the wake of fire. Such attunement to process
registers an intellectual disposition that negates temporal transcendence of
any still moment or image in view, and yet this observational frame refuses
to stop at the material object: it emphasizes events, properties, and location.

The emphasis on real implications of referents within a lyrical space can
be seen clearly in the representative slice of the dwelling place's ecosystem or
contingent "arrangement" that speaks to the constructed realm and to the
affordance for life within nature's emergence. For Thoreau, this sensitivity
offers an important materialist nuance to transcendentalist intellectualized
skepticism. For Kinsella, it attends to a cultural ecological insight as it
includes humanity's impact on the land.

Figure 11.1. John Kinsella, "Brown-headed honey-eaters on 'great tank,'" April 18, 2009.

Honeyeaters gather around a hairline fracture on the twenty-thousand gallon rainwater tank, gripping the oxidation and lime extrusion to drink, in the hot, dry atmosphere of the place.[11]

> The crack in the curve
> of the great rainwater tank
> brews algae and crusts
> of calcium that foothold
> brown-headed honeyeaters

> tonguing cool water
> up where water shouldn't be;
> not taxidermy,
> nor the dry arrangement
> they're set against: branch, leaves,
>
> an entire stunted tree under a dusty glass
> dome: an arrangement
> for future generations
> to wonder at.[12]

A problem for one species enables a "foothold" for another. This brief moment in *Jam Tree Gully* instances what Kinsella names *anti-pastoral*, a genre "situated in the inability to celebrate without negativity."[13] It is but a simple step to contrast this to pastoral as the control or denial of nature we make for ourselves wherein the nature of good husbandry is defined by "preservation of a nature, of intact environments."[14]

An ecocritical reading would note that "dry" and "dusty" are set against the brewing algae. Process and adaptation are notable as animating devices—attention is drawn to the verbs that blur strict divisions between language and animals while indicating response to climate (the birds are seen "tonguing"). In *Jam Tree Gully* Kinsella scrutinizes landscape with a painterly keenness that imbues each stanza with pictorial clarity that resists sentimentalized or stale images. Here the referent—the water tank—affords life for the honeyeaters. The summer climate is a subtle thread that performs the temporal and spatial dispersion of elements in the poem: the birds in the foreground on the tank in the present moment are set against both the dry landscape and the equally arid historiography of the future; heat conditions the poem to prevent any simple unification of diverse and disparate things, of climate and season.

Season, thus, is a deconstructive texture in that it demonstrates the poem's hidden dependence on the terms (water, refreshment, sustenance) it purports to exclude. Furthermore, the lineation and generative lines react to a sense of tidiness and order that result in a sense of "arrangement" as a highly contingent meeting or contract. This brief moment in the collection should be read within the context of summer heat and autumn dryness that impresses an anxiety for firebreaks, signs of burning, concern for hairline fractures on water-tanks and the use of water-bombs that are fundamental to continued human survival in Western Australia. The impacts of anthropogenic climate change coupled to the damage brokered by winter fronts that "have enough strength / to tear off roofs, annihilate trees"[15]; such attention to seasons and space displaces the human subject, leading to a reading of the landscape as "biosphere" which speaks, with pastoral hues, of loss and escape, "the slow gravitational / urge to find another planetary home."[16]

Rather than a two-dimensional landscape that is animated by space and time, "Arrangement" suggests a theater of images not unlike a nineteenth-century diorama that evokes taxidermy and collection in its slow and still imagery. This is but one example from a series of place-based poems of experimental dwelling within a collection of one hundred poems that deny a comedy's imagined community of poet, birds, and kangaroo. As instanced here, the lyrical lens shoots a material existence that is independent of our thoughts about it, *and yet* it triggers deep human emotions that are hard-wired to our need to find a direction home. I anticipate that some readers will be conflicted as to whether this exemplifies clear objectivity that can be so clearly distinguished from "perceptual subjectivity" wherein the world is open to particular models of sense.

Comportment Toward Nature

Walden ends with a threefold reflection on seasons; "Winter Animals," "The Pond in Winter" and "Spring" reinforce Thoreau's attention to the environment through his discoveries about relations between humans and non-humans, and about the link between observation and sympathy.[17] These now resonate with earlier thoughts on time and labor, particularly inflected by a sense of (human) adaptation alongside Kinsella's phenomenology of more-than-human animals that is highly sensitized to the transitive aspect of world. "Spring" opens thus: "The opening of large tracts by the ice-cutters commonly causes a pond to break up earlier; for the water, agitated by the wind, even in cold weather, wears away the surrounding ice. But such was not the effect on Walden that year, for she had soon got a thick new garment to take the place of the old."[18]

In this observation, supported by pages of analysis of the pond's temperature throughout March, Thoreau is not at all embarrassed by the extension of human technology into the description of the lake; it has enabled him to speak of a body without directly speaking of it—the garment

outlines what is underneath and ironically foregrounds a fresh manifestation
of nature's appearance to the human mind. Moreover, Thoreau's conception
of nature's economy is climatic, essentially stressing a stability that resides
within nature's cycles and the season's fluctuation. The emphasis is on the
energy that prevails and recurs amid variation, global systems, and local
permutations. These rhetorical impulses provide robust cognates for Thoreau's
practice of deliberate dwelling that Kinsella takes to his reading of the six
Nyoongar seasons in Jam Tree.[19]

While clarifying seasonal and resource-based challenges to his home
economics, Thoreau writes, "Man is an animal who more than any other
can adapt himself to all climates and circumstances."[20] While the inclination
to attempt making bread without yeast (in contrast to normal practice)
might indicate his forgetfulness of rules, Thoreau's argument is not one of
individualized, liberated self-reliance but of adaptability to the environment
that operates beyond the locus of his consciousness. Rain might prevent him
from hoeing in the lowlands, yet it would be valuable for the uplands; a
lack of ingredients or a memory failure might afford new culinary practices
that are not less valuable than earlier practices. All events framed historically
offer surety rather than discord. In "Solitude" this is understood as a bond:
"While I enjoy the friendship of the seasons I trust that nothing can make
life a burden to me."[21] Self-assurance here is scaffolded by a world operating beyond doubt, a world underwritten by changes in weather, ecology,
and daylight hours; in this sense the self is seasonal. Conversely, Kinsella is
keen to disown any such sense of security; his response to Thoreau's organic
stability is toxic instability from damage.

Pragmatism as Orientation

Pragmatism is concerned with the relationships between parts and wholes;
in "Survey"—with exception of the first quatrain that is the sole example
of an enclosed sense unit that is syntactically isolated—discrete units (parts)
are modeled in stanzas (arrangements) that are meshed through form and
interlaced through content that betoken angled, almost cubist wholes. A
quick glance at the poem will reveal connected sense units via lineation and
enjambment that portend a sophisticated understanding of the legacy and
ecology of human impact within the context of interactions that afford life.
I claim this as a micro-moment where complementarity between human and
non-human worlds can be detected in the poem's foreground.

The water-trough I fill for kangaroos and other
wildlife in this desiccated habitat is almost
dry and what moisture remains informs a bloom

of algae.[22]

Knowledge that the dead tree limbs cleared by the surveyor will provide
an enclave for ground insects and perches for birds supports a mind that
connects both to the geographical specificity and the literary heritage. It is
indicative of the spatial amalgam that I am indicating in Kinsella's reading
of climate. The climatic pastoral of the vacant block invokes a mental season
where temporality is emphasized by the present participle and the recourse
to verbs: "I work"; "I note"; "I carefully brush." These are self-centered
moments within the nexus of fragility and endurance registered in the seasonal conditions, wherein enjambment illustrates the kinetic potential of the
cusp (running across the third and fourth stanzas at lines 15–16, above), a
structure underlined by vocabulary, the "bloom // of algae."

Abstract seasons in *Jam Tree Gully* are quashed by metonyms for "the
circumvention of quarantine,"[23] how things bleed through the conceptual
containers or categories of larger patterns. Heat in "Survey" is linked to
Kinsella's hot summer surveying of the land at Jam Tree, but it also signifies
the parasitic and symbiotic poem itself, foregrounding its textures and intellectual contexts as one part of an intertextual soup that is the embodiment
of an *international* regionalism.

Returning to the nine lines of "Survey" quoted above (12–20), the
act of the surveyor brushing off the biting ants from his feet signifies the
human response to the environment (in the present tense), which, in this
example, extends to the tentatively anthropomorphic description of the hawk.
Both lines gesture to human emotion and mood in its absence, but this is
sufficiently quashed by the shift to philosophical intertextuality that resonates
with a controlling ambiguity imitating precision, both in the reference to
James and the poet's modification of personal pronoun from singular to
plural. However, the allusion to James's philosophy does not detract from the
poem's facility to instance perceiving relations in space, which is one part of
the idea behind Kinsella's rhizomic international regionalism. Furthermore,
the sense of the heat and the survey site as a home for the (potentially
thirsty) kangaroo (drinking from the speaker's refilled water trough) as an
event in the site, underplays the *assertion* of an event—"the wording of the
world"[24]—and thus dilutes anthropocentrism in the same manner as entailed

in the focus on the image. The quotation the speaker is looking for arrives in the second sense—"in which they inhere" is correct James—emphasizing *participation*. It is complex and significant for the Kinsella reader who is keen to measure this against the ideas of impact and protection around which *Jam Tree Gully* orbits.

Inherent Pragmatism

"Each substance 'inheres,' or is it 'in which

they inhere'?" (lines 15–16).

"Inhere" in *Jam Tree Gully* is a literary critical object in itself: it is the present, active infinitive for "stick in / stick to," and is commonly used as a verb to exist permanently (or essentially) in something. It is a predicate that requires a subject and an object. Facts inhere in substances: the attribute "a safe home" inheres in the hawk while the hawk is said to participate in the attribute of a safe home; storms inhere in winds that move the branches of trees when caught in leaves; "combustibility and fibrous structure" both inhere in the fallen eucalypt branches in "Survey," denoting respective metonyms of potential climate futures and historical genetic makeup.[25] It is an already complex concept that Kinsella mobilizes for ecological effect. To those not versed in early twentieth-century relations between Henri Bergson, William James, and C. S. Peirce, it is undoubtedly esoteric.

Kinsella quotes James's reading of the qualities of wood from the essay "On a Certain Blindness in Human Beings,"[26] which illustrates substance through particulars, "local" manifestations of something deeper and larger. "[C]ombustibility" and "fibrous structure" are predicates and attributes (or *affections* or *accidents* in James's lexicon); they are related to the subject and substance "wood" in the same manner that "whiteness" and "insolubility" are predicates and attributes of the substance "chalk." For James, all we can know of things are the *groups* of attributes by which substance is known.[27] For James, life is dynamically hard-wired to qualities of things in the world and not to static situations; moreover, we make abstractions in language both as entry points to our environment and as non-relations to a richer, more-than-human world (for example, names for flora, fauna, and climate, i.e., seasons). Kinsella accepts the second preposition as an Adamic problem of representation even though he seems dismissive of the first preposition.

The lack of precision with references in "Survey" suggests both an element of disinterest and instinct rather than error. Moreover, it portends that instinct in itself is faithful to thought and feeling *as processes*, and yet the literary rhizome's particular selections from significant moments in American culture (that extend outwards) belie this idea.[28] In taking his cue from Deleuze and Guattari's *A Thousand Plateaus*,[29] Kinsella is indicating something quite specific with respect to identity.[30] Intertextual references in "Survey" suggest neither lineage, nor the anxiety of influence despite the reworking of the pastoral genre, but a move toward the deterritorialization (of the control and order of the *literary terrains*) of pastoral and philosophy. This move heralds multiplicities laid out to show ways to connect to each other despite their distinct disciplines, geographies, and histories: Kinsella to James; Kinsella to Thoreau; Thoreau to James, etc. This decolonized pastoral, or non-hierarchical conglomeration without structure—as embodied by Kinsella's acute sense of inherence—is irreducible to a singularity or an array of multiple events. At times these densely fabricated knots in the lyricism bypass and update the part-whole emphasis in pragmatism. This is a context in which to read the poem's final act of "overbelief" toward the season alluded to in the final line (below).

> I survey
> The block in the relative cool of evening
> While there's still enough light to make things out:
> Shape them individually and as an entirety,
>
> Into a whole that adds up, is as good as might be,
> Kept from larger harm, grouped in those days
> James lectures us about, phenomena of climate
> And gumption to resolve as much as possible.
>
> I entrust to the relative cool of night (lines 24–32).

Overbelief is to give one's mind or reasoning to uncertainty, or uncertain light; to show that we can have faith in a position that is without knowledge, without evidence that is required for clarity and precision. Again, the epistemic modality invites the reader to contemplate whether such faith can be projected on the present, the memory of the past, or the future envisioned in the present (albeit pointing to something beyond us in space or time, or both—climate change, for example).[31] For James's project, it is where knowledge is justified on emotional need or faith rather than evidence. Furthermore, to "resolve" in Kinsella's transference of James's pragmatism, is to entertain a Thoreauvian seasonal mind (disposition) that embodies openness and change, thus provides reassurance to the epistemological blindness or underplayed trust in the validity of one's abilities to perceive the world.[32]

Images and Scale (Interpretative Frameworks)

The late walk in "the relative cool of evening" leads the figure to claim that he "entrust[s]" to the forthcoming "relative cool of night."[33] This follows a leap of faith in the "entirety" that the poem has constructed, a projection of nothing more than the total sum of experience encountered by the speaker and rendered in structured language. It is interesting to note that this fiction is "kept from [larger] harm." At this moment, the poem is drawing from James's Edinburgh lectures "Varieties of Religious Experience" (1902) while the speaker has the blindness essay in mind.[34] In "Varieties" James notes that a common human disposition is to speak of *groups* of days.[35] Kinsella appears alert to James' desire to sensitize readers to processes of abstraction while bringing out the relationship between empirical enquiry and spiritual judgment.

The psychic reality of the cartographic poem "Survey" takes place within (or inhabits) the closing hours of daylight that reflect upon the comprehension of a day in Jam Tree. It parallels the amount of time given to "Four Scenes," a collection of unraveled images that detail action within the landscape. The third of these is of use when considering the "set" of images that the poet places only a dozen pages earlier in the collection:

> We've been through two seasonal cycles here
> but the seasons don't add up; I can't co-opt
> the Nyungar six seasons either. Dry is the word
> it all pivots on, if I want to convey what it's like.[36]

No season name is offered, only dryness as a phenomenological language construct within an autobiographical moment. The intervention of consciousness here negates any tendency toward somnolence. Such anxiety is replayed in the manner in which the substance inheres in seasonal dryness: this anxiety is likened to "Perverse comfort" (line 7), a weariness in the body that eliminates resources being drawn to the mind. This results in an emptiness that can be filled by the night. Here, rather than a law, the resistance of the world to the speaker's half-intention to "co-opt" the climatic cycles instances oneiric temperament, that is, the orientation of the imagination by the seasons that is the concentration of an ecological psyche.

While "Four Scenes" affords a view of the surveyor moving through the landscape—with the lyrical timeframe animating the encounters so that the reader can observe relations—time is deleted in "A Set of Images Makes the Day," leaving the reader wishing to "read through" images, to draw out a metaphor or realize symbolic value due to the heady compression of the text. These compressions are worth contemplation as they invoke Emerson's prose and focus on spirit; furthermore, they too do not conform to any unit, to an array that can be trusted to "add up." Much like the seasons— European and Indigenous—they run on into each other but are free from that which precedes them. These moments in Kinsella appear to be closest to Bachelard in the impulse to return to phenomena themselves.

Spring and Images

Kinsella's sense of place as a location for humans interacting with animals within a changing climate is most obvious in the poem "Spring Pollen" that leads from Thoreau's final contemplation of metonymy in "Spring."[37] It takes the following two sentences for its epigraph: "Thus it seemed that one hillside illustrated the principle of all the operations of Nature. The Maker of this earth but patented a leaf";[38] it is married in Kinsella's sly acknowledgment of his compressed aesthetic and *Jam Tree Gully*'s playfulness with respect to scale and allegory: "The valley is the microcosm you'd expect."[39]

Rather than comparing geographies and biochemical patterns (pollen), "Spring Pollen" is indicating simultaneous understanding across the texts and the hemispheres. Here, metonymy acts as synecdoche, both referring to the larger earth from the view of the hillside (*pars pro toto*), and the operations within Nature viewed in compressed replica and manifestation of the leaf (*totum pro parte*). This dialogue is reworked in yet another collation of ideas that vibrate within a fascinating set of six tercets in "A Set of Images Makes the Day":

2. In ground tough as flint
objection sparks steel of shovel;
and yet, damp bloody soil."

. . . .

6. Shaky with work, the parrots' tonguey
chirrup becomes a piping: I am their
movie: they shimmer more when still.[40]

For Bachelard, like James, knowledge always involves an object of knowledge and a knowing subject. The interplay between these two poles, which gives rise to the grounds of knowledge, is first triggered in *Jam Tree Gully* by the physicalist, tactile, embodied subject working within the landscape. Most often, as exemplified above, the reader finds an array of sense experiences running parallel with the speaker's goals, which in turn instance the speaker's ability to step outside of the self to view the world from the position of another subject.

Here, the external world does not exist as anything other than a world conjoined to human experience. The perceived image entails a function of reality, that is to say Kinsella's images offer a psychological realism as understood by Bachelard in addition to complementing what he has elsewhere termed *intensivism*: a form where the small place acts as an anchor point for international communication.[41] This mode of realism argues that "it is the *perception* of images which determines the processes of the imagination"—a world that runs short of accommodating unreality in its preference to adjust the mind to a reality marked by social values: "We begin by seeing things, then we imagine them; we combine, through the imagination, fragments of perceived reality, memories of experienced reality, but there is no question of ever reaching the domain of a fundamentally creative imagination."[42] Thoreau learned to see well, for he prepared his senses by adjusting the season in his mind. Kinsella plays off from here, noting that to rely upon a Kantian attunement of the mind to the world overshadows other advice to dream well.

"Spring" ends *Walden* with an exit into summer and an image of Thoreau's departure from the scene. The penultimate sentence of the penultimate paragraph develops the American's observation of the pitch-pine's pollen covering the pond, stones, and wood along the shore: "This is the 'sulphur showers' we hear of."[43] The meteorological metaphor signifies not only the phenomenon of pollen carried by the wind over great distances; it also alludes to the ancient garden remedy or control for foliar fungi and mites. The allusion is transparent, as Thoreau deploys quotation marks and drops a reference to Calidas, the fifth-century Indian poet whose fluvial geomorphology was as accurate as the American's. This departure at the end of *Walden* suggests something larger than biochemical processes as a referent of change and interconnection. Thoreau, it seems, precedes Kinsella in his international regionalism here. This is no mere allusion to spiritual consciousness: sulfur is an essential element for all life.

What ends one text of 1847 ignites another of 2011. Kinsella's "Spring Pollen" begins with an epigraph taken from "Spring," and its opening stanza continues the pragmatist nature writing tradition into the twenty-first century:

Yellow overwhelms, satiates,
blocks out the picture of hillside: leaves
wave in mild suns, searching out
attention.[44]

Ecopoetics attends to the operations of nature from a position that is not reduced to the human senses, as Kinsella has imagined above. In "Spring Pollen" the viewer is not required to make the scene complete if we are sensitive to lineation: "attention" stands out to register the cognitive process of concentrating on one aspect of the environment, selectively; thus the careful examination and penetrating aspect of the pollen invoke a consciousness that is clearly delineated and yet is not independent from the wind. This understated interanimation—a mutual relation between environment and human subject (amplified by unique and repetitive seasonal manifestations)—indicates the Thoreauvian isomorphic allegory or "principle of all the operations of Nature" ("Spring") that is fully developed in Kinsella's singular attentiveness to seasons in *Jam Tree Gully*:

. . . screenprints of pollen,
dusted cuffs come out of black centres,
not yellow petals.

. . . Grandparents
might say: we feel it in our waters,
our noses tingle before the flowering.[45]

The second movement of the poem brings together a technological conception of the environment ("screenprints"), ecological accuracy with respect to floral structure and reproduction (stamens containing pollen within the corolla), and a familial-mythical narrative on how we anticipate our physical responses to changes in the seasons. Kinsella's broad canvas is used to detail a singular natural phenomenon quite distinct from the emissions of odors and dust from manufacturing plants of the human world. The assault upon the senses in "Spring Pollen" bothers "blood" (line 14), which indicates genetic makeup over lineage to denote something deeper in our human faculties than family trees; with forefathers—elders, Indigenous and white—adumbrated to a thin trace or watermark throughout *Jam Tree Gully*, biological phenomena such as tree and flower pollen can disclose themselves more readily *to our minds*.

Here, the Jamesian overbelief in "Survey" that might relate to pastoral quietude or Romantic negative capability, is shot through with "irritation" and fluidity (as with the images from "A Set of Images," above), particularly an open ecological vulnerability, which instances a poetics of withdrawal, decolonizing the pastoral mode. Such reactionary and changeable ideas portend a mood that is less easily contained or uniformly mannered than Thoreau might have us believe. Spring itself might be easily determined and defined, but the movements *within* spring (i.e., pollen) are less easily accountable, as suggested by Kinsella's form that keeps a distance from pastoral yet acknowledges its consequences. The strongest rhyme occurring at a line end is between "centres" and "waters" (second to this is the link between "flowering" and "wresting," below): stability and fluidity conjoined to unpack Thoreau's metaphorical sense of season as a concrete, disciplined, and learned spiritual disposition.

Conclusion

Stanley Cavell has argued that *Walden* depends on the tradition of topographical poetry: "Nothing can outdo its obsession with the seasons of a real place."[46] Seasons dictate the dweller's attitude to planting, growing, and harvesting; however, Thoreau reads them as acts of nature, rather than acts of humans, that is, nature confiding in us, in its largest moments and most significant arrangements. Thus, each action betokens an allegorical event in the text. Cavell's understanding of the philosophical work of British and American skepticism acknowledges "some mass of anxieties, desires, and concepts from which everything verbal or pictorial or otherwise formal is drawn." Allegory, in this reading, "is not merely one of the ego's more specialised mechanisms of defence"—perhaps a sublime intellectualization of world affairs. Rather, as Timothy Gould argues, it is "one of the human's mechanisms of edification," that is an opportunity "for civilization to defeat the drive towards stasis and death."[47] At times we notice Kinsella nuance his perception of landscape to suit either his mental climate or the mood of the poem. Rather than positioning the speaker within a moral framework, each subject is motivated by an attention toward the vicissitudes of history that are held in moments of contemplation. This motivation situates the poem in proximity to the confessional mode and to the intimacy of autobiography. These images offer different meanings and evoke reverie while also aspiring to new imaginings. In effect, these events in the text are a response to a spatial stimulus, which has brought into relief microevents—referents with ecological contexts—that herald a literary material tropism. Any irreducibility or ambivalence in these moments of turning indicate freedom that is secured by a Kantian reflective attitude that puts forth our *comprehension* of images, rather than securing the meaning of an image on the way to unifying or consolidating a pictorial array. Thus, the external world of Jam Tree promotes the singing of the inner signs of active lyricism wherein a subterranean growth springs forth as a resting, thoughtful mind that dwells: a "tonus even to our physical life."[48]

Notes

1. Ralph Waldo Emerson, *Essays: First Series* [1841], reprinted in *Selected Essays and Lectures*, ed. Joel Porte (New York: Viking, 1983), 261.

2. John Charles Ryan, "Recalling Walden: Thoreau's Embodied Aesthetics and Australian Writings on Place," *Journal of Ecocriticism* 3, no. 2 (2011): 43–45.

3. Henry David Thoreau, *Walden; or Life in the Woods* [1854] (London: Penguin, 1984), 1, 23.

4. Thoreau's experiment commenced on the fourth of July, 1845.

5. John Kinsella, "Survey," in *Jam Tree Gully Poems* (New York: Norton, 2011), 82, lines 13–20.

6. James Gibson, *The Ecological Approach to Visual Perception* (Boston: Houghton Mifflin, 1979), 127.

7. M. Bonta and John Protevi, *Deleuze and Geophilosophy: A Guide and Glossary* (Edinburgh: Edinburgh University Press, 2004).

8. Kinsella, "Language generates nothing as whole trees fall," *Jam Tree Gully Poems*, 78, line 2.

9. Kinsella, "Urban Attitudes in the Bush," *Jam Tree Gully Poems*, 86, line 9, lines 11–13.

10. Gaston Bachelard, *The Psychoanalysis of Fire*, trans. Alan C. M. Ross (Boston: Beacon Press, 1964), 109.

11. Photograph and words by John Kinsella.

12. Kinsella, "Arrangement," from the sequence "A Jam Tree Gully Sheaf," in *Jam Tree Gully Poems*, 107.

13. John Kinsella, *Contrary Rhetoric: Lectures on Landscape and Language*, ed. Glen Phillips and Andrew Taylor (Fremantle: Fremantle Press/Edith Cowan UP, 2008), 153.

14. Kinsella, *Contrary Rhetoric*, 159.

15. Kinsella, "Battening Down," *Jam Tree Gully Poems*, 134, lines 6–7.

16. Kinsella, "Reading," *Jam Tree Gully Poems*, 40, lines 24–25.

17. Thoreau's diligent account of the seasonal temperatures of Flints,' Goose, Walden, and White ponds around Concord is recorded in "The Ponds," and in "Spring" (*Walden*, 230–231, 347–367).

18. Thoreau, *Walden*, 347.

19. The Nyoongar peoples are Australian Aboriginals that have six distinct seasons. Their calendar is one determined by weather patterns that indicate when specific plant and animal resources are plentiful; seasons also correspond to habitat movements and feeding patterns (regarding the availability of seasonal foods). The author directs the reader to "The Qualities of Sadness" in *Jam Tree Gully* to compare the pragmatic attitude of the laborer, George, to generalizations made about Indigenous cultures (as above).

20. Thoreau, *Walden*, 106.

21. Thoreau, *Walden*, 176.

22. Kinsella, "Survey," 82, lines 13–16.

23. John Kinsella, *Disclosed Poetics: Beyond Landscape and Lyricism* (Manchester: Manchester University Press, 2007), 135.

24. Stanley Cavell, *The Senses of Walden* (New York: Viking, 1972), 43.

25. Kinsella first refers to Empedocles' idea that qualities of matter come from relative proportions of elements entering into a thing.

26. William James, *Talks to Teachers on Psychology and to Students on Some of Life's Ideals* [including "On a Certain Blindness in Human Beings" and "What Makes a Life Significant"] (New York: Henry Holt, 1899).

27. James calls this the "cash-value" of our actual experience. Note that James extends this paradigm to non-matter: the predicates and attributes, "our thoughts" and "our feelings," relate to the subject and substance "several souls" which make up the primal substance of "spirit." Substances do not signify "things," they signify bare cohesion, i.e., phenomenal properties that do not adhere in names; they only adhere or cohere with each other. In response to rationalism's emphasis on universals, James argues that there is no "invisible cement" that supports cohesion

between parts of a mosaic; we must drop this idea (James, *Talks to Teachers on Psychology*).

28. The apparent laziness here might indicate a looseness that could be read in concordance with the disposition at line 5: "The difference here; the difference elsewhere." This clearly indicates a distinction between observation (empiricism) and action (preservation) in lines 1 to 4 (see above). However, the vagueness that resides in the opening line of a new sense unit suggests less particularity to the Jamesian context. Thoreau: "I shall never find in the wilds of Labrador any greater wildness than in some recess in Concord." (Henry David Thoreau, *The Journal of Henry David Thoreau*, vol. 2 [New York: Dover, 1962], 33.) This position is underlined by Cavell (in his outline of water as metaphor for the promise of a world yet to come, a baptism or immersion in words): "The water of Walden Pond is unique, but so is every other body of water, or drop, or place; and as universal" (*The Senses of Walden*, 17). Intertextuality, allusions, and intellectual contexts that resonate throughout *Jam Tree Gully* promote understanding as a matter of orientation (survey), not comparison nor relativism.

29. Gilles Deleuze and Felix Guattari, *A Thousand Plateaus: Capitalism and Schizophrenia* (London: Continuum, 1988).

30. The use of the botanical term *rhizome* ("mass of roots," Greek), explicitly refers to sending out roots from nodes, a paradigm that is opposed to an arborescent conception of the root/tree dualism and binary.

31. William James, *Varieties of Religious Experience: A Study in Human Nature* [1902] (Oxford: Oxford University Press, 2012). It is valuable to note here Richard Poirier's summary of the labor of the poet in the American tradition. To clarify a line of literature that works through a post-Puritan sense of reading signs in the world, Poirier refers to James on "truth": "In most circumstances 'nothing but eventual verification' . . . [poets] insist that his or her own writing, even as it emerges on the page, is the epitome of what work can best accomplish" (Richard Poirier, *Poetry and Pragmatism* [London: Faber, 1992], 123). See also William James, "Pragmatism's Conception of Truth," reprinted in *Essays in Pragmatism*, ed., Alburey Estell (New York: Hafner, 1948). The author wishes to stress that his georgic inflection to Kinsella's "post-Pastoral" is entirely intentional.

32. The author uses the word *blindness* here in sympathy with James's essay (above) while indicating a sense of willed refusal of human world-making (conscious orientation and place-taking) over a form or mode of ignorance.

33. Kinsella, "Survey," 83, line 29.

34. William James, *Varieties of Religious Experience*.

35. Cf. William James, "Some Metaphysical Problems Pragmatically Considered," Lecture 3 of *Pragmatism: A New Name for Some Old Ways of Thinking* [1907], reprinted in *Essays in Pragmatism*, 33–48.

36. Kinsella, "Four Scenes," *Jam Tree Gully Poems*, 141.

37. Thoreau, *Walden*, 347–367.

38. Thoreau, *Walden*, 356.

39. Kinsella, "Past Tense," in *Jam Tree Gully Poems*, 77, line 13. Thoreau's "Spring" is used as an epigraph for "Pressure at the Boundaries (of Jam Tree Gully)," too to foreground a human sense of inheritance of land (rather than history) that extends to "plastic emotions" (line 9) meeting "quasi-scientific" desires (line 22), which are detailed against a backdrop of an orange crowned hill and the overwhelming death of trees: "groundwater vanquished / And surface evaporated" (lines 11–12). This use of Thoreau as a platform for Kinsella's pastoral negativity is worth comparison to the American's chapter "The Ponds," which anticipates his seasonal chapters at the close of *Walden* in its contemplation of smooth surfaces and no disturbances as metaphor for a relatively cool mind, albeit animated and excited by the apostrophe to spring: "The thrills of joy and thrills of pain are undistinguishable. How peaceful the phenomena of the lake! Again the works of man shine as in the spring. Ay, every lead and twig and stone and cobweb sparkles now at mid-afternoon as when covered with dew in a spring morning. Every motion of an oar or an insect produces a flash of light; and if an oar falls, how sweet the echo!" (Thoreau, *Walden*, 235).

40. Kinsella, "A Set of Images Makes the Day," *Jam Tree Gully Poems*, 127, lines 4–6; 16–18.

41. Kinsella, *Disclosed Poetics*, 137–138.

42. Gaston Bachelard, *On Poetic Imagination and Reverie*, trans. Colette Gaudin (Indianapolis: Bobbs Merrill, 1971), 12–13.

43. Thoreau, *Walden*, 367.

44. Kinsella, "Spring Pollen," *Jam Tree Gully Poems*, 64, lines 1–4.

45. Kinsella, "Spring Pollen," 64, lines 6–8, lines 14–16.

46. Cavell, *The Senses of Walden*, 21.

47. Timothy Gould, "The Literal Truth: Cavell on Literality in Philosophy and Literature," in *Stanley Cavell: Philosophy, Literature and Criticism*, ed. James Loxley (Manchester: Manchester University Press, 2012), 150–151.

48. Bachelard, *On Poetic Imagination and Reverie*, 20.

Suggestions for Further Reading

Bass, Rick. *Wild Marsh: Four Seasons at Home in Montana*. Boston: Houghton Mifflin Harcourt, 2009.

Bosco, Ronald A., ed. *Nature's Panorama: Thoreau on the Seasons*. Amherst: University of Massachusetts Press, 2005.

Buell, Lawrence. *The Environmental Imagination: Thoreau, Nature Writing, and the Formation of American Culture*. Cambridge, MA: Harvard University Press, 1995.

Chenowith, Helen Stiles. *Pageant of Seasons: A Collection of American Haiku*. Rutland, VT: Charles E. Tuttle Co., 1970.

Clarke, Philip. "Australian Aboriginal Ethnometeorology and Seasonal Calendars," *History and Anthropology* 20.2 (2009): 79–106.

Dalby, Liza. *East Wind Melts the Ice: A Memoir through the Seasons*. London: Chatto & Windus, 2007.

Enkvist, Nils Erik. *The Seasons of the Year: Chapters on a Motif from "Beowulf" to "The Shepherd's Calendar."* Helsinki: Open Library, 1957.

Giblett, Rod. *Black Swan Lake: The Life of a Wetland*. Bristol: Intellect Books, 2013.

Hatley, Jim. "Wild Seasons and the Justice of Country: Dreaming the Weathers Anew in Hebraic Midrash." *Environment, Space, Place* 5, no. 1 (2013): 171–200.

Heinrich, Bernd. *Summer World: A Season of Bounty*. New York: HarperCollins, 2009.

Heinrich, Bernd. *Winter World: The Ingenuity of Animal Survival*. New York: Harper Collins, 2003.

Kammen, Michael. *A Time to Every Purpose: The Four Seasons in American Culture*. Chapel Hill: University of North Carolina Press, 2004.

Lensing, George S. *Wallace Stevens and the Seasons*. Baton Rouge: Louisiana State University Press, 2001.

Leopold, Aldo. *A Sand County Almanac*. New York: Oxford University Press, 1949.

Mauss, Marcel and Henry Beuchat. *Seasonal Variations of the Eskimo: A Study in Social Morphology*. Trans. James J. Fox. Boston: Routledge & Kegan Paul, 1979.

McClatchy, J. D., ed. *The Four Seasons: Poems* (New York: Alfred A. Knopf, 2008).

Prober, Suzanne M., Michael H. O'Connor, and Fiona J. Walsh. "Australian Aboriginal Peoples' Seasonal Knowledge: A Potential Basis for Shared Understanding in Environmental Management." *Ecology and Society* 16, no. 2 (2011).

Rose, Deborah Bird. "Rhythms, Patterns, Connectivities: Indigenous Concepts of Seasons and Change, Victoria River District, NT." In *A Change in the Weather: Climate and Culture in Australia*, ed. T. Griffiths and L. Robin, 32–41. Canberra: National Museum of Australia, 2005.

Ryan, John Charles. "The Six Seasons: Shifting Australian Nature Writing Towards Ecological Time and Embodied Temporality." *Transformations* 21 (2012).

Shirane, Haruo. *Japan and the Culture of the Four Seasons: Nature Literature, and the Arts*. New York: Columbia University Press, 2012.

Tetsuro, Watsuji. *Climate and Culture: A Philosophical Study*. Trans. Geoffrey Bownas. New York: Greenwood Press, 1988 [1961].

Thomson, James "The Seasons," in *The Complete Poetical Works*, ed. J. Robertson. Oxford: Oxford University Press, 1908.

Tuve, R. *Seasons and Months: Studies in a Tradition of Middle English Poetry*. Paris: Librairie Universitaire, 1933.

Vivaldi, Antonio. *The Four Seasons*. New York: Dover, 1999.

Wright, Katherine. "Rethinking the Seasons: New Approaches to Nature." *Transformations* 21 (2012).

Contributors

Joseph Ballan holds a PhD from the University of Chicago Divinity School. His publications include essays on Søren Kierkegaard, W. E. B. Du Bois, and W. G. Sebald. He currently works within the field of adult education for the city of Helsingborg, Sweden.

Tom Bristow has published *The Anthropocene Lyric* (2015), co-edited *The Cultural History of Climate Change* (2016), and undertaken a fellowship at the ARC Centre of Excellence for the History of Emotions at the University of Melbourne (2014–2017). Tom is editor-in-chief of *Philosophy Activism Nature*, series editor for Environmental Literature, Media and Culture at Routledge, and Roderick Research Fellow at James Cook University.

Paola-Ludovika Coriando is professor of philosophy at Innsbruck University, Austria. Her areas of specialization include phenomenology (Husserl, Scheler, Heidegger), metaphysics and critiques of metaphysics (Kant, Nietzsche), anthropology, and philosophy of religion. She is the author of four books that investigate phenomenological and metaphysical themes. Her book *Affektenlehre und Phänomenologie der Stimmungen: Wege einer Ontologie und Ethik des Emotionalen* (2002) elaborates an ontology of affects, which draws on the writings of Heidegger, Scheler, Aristotle, Rilke, and Hölderlin. She has written numerous articles and edited a number of books, including several volumes of Heidegger's complete works (*Gesamtausgabe*).

Luke Fischer is a philosopher and poet. His authored books include *The Poet as Phenomenologist: Rilke and the "New Poems"* (2015) and the poetry collections *A Personal History of Vision* (2017) and *Paths of Flight* (2013). His co-edited works include *Rilke's "Sonnets to Orpheus": Philosophical and*

Critical Perspectives (2019) and a special section of the *Goethe Yearbook* (2015) on Goethe and environmentalism. He is an honorary associate of the philosophy department at the University of Sydney. For more information, visit www.lukefischerauthor.com.

Yvonne Förster teaches philosophy at Leuphana University Lüneburg (Germany) and is appointed as foreign expert at Shanxi University (China). She has taught aesthetics at Bauhaus University Weimar and been awarded senior research fellowships at two Institutes for Advanced Studies (*Media Cultures of Computer Simulation* at Leuphana and *Cultural Sciences* at University of Konstanz). Her research focuses on human-machine relations, posthumanism, the future of technology, theories of embodiment, and fashion as art. Her latest projects focus on the aesthetics of technology and its impact on experience and ethics of technology. For more information, visit www.yvonnefoerster.com.

Rod Giblett is the author of *Black Swan Lake* (2011), in which he traces the life of a wetland through the seasons—both the four European seasons and the six local indigenous seasons. His latest books are *Environmental Humanities and Theologies: Ecoculture, Literature and the Bible* (2018); *Environmental Humanities and the Uncanny: Ecoculture, Literature and Religion* (2019); and *Psychoanalytic Ecology: The Talking Cure for Environmental Illness and Health* (2019). He has also published several environment-friendly and animal-friendly retellings of stories and legends about dragons. He is honorary associate professor of environmental humanities in the School of Communication and Creative Arts, Deakin University, Australia.

Craig Holdrege is co-founder and director of The Nature Institute in Ghent, New York, which is dedicated to research and educational activities applying phenomenological, contextual methods. He is a leading researcher in the empirical approach known as Goethean science and has written widely on plants, animals, ecology, and environmental topics. He holds a PhD in sustainability education from Prescott College, Arizona. His books include *Do Frogs Come from Tadpoles? Rethinking Origins in Development and Evolution* (2017), *Thinking Like a Plant: A Living Science for Life* (2013), *Beyond Biotechnology: The Barren Promise of Genetic Engineering* (co-authored with Steve Talbott, 2008), and *The Giraffe's Long Neck: From Evolutionary Fable to Whole Organism* (2005).

Jo Law is an artist and researcher whose works investigate the transformative potential of art, science, and technology in response to changing the sociocultural, political, and natural environments. Her publications include the book *100 Atmospheres: Studies in Scale and Wonder* (2020), the journal article "Materials Science, Slow Textiles, Ecological Futures" (2021) in *Leonardo: Art Science and Technology*, and "Enchanting Materialities: e-textiles installations for an ecosophic world" (2020) for ISEA: Montreal. Her artworks have been exhibited at the Museum of Applied Arts & Sciences, Sydney, and the Sheila C. Johnson Design Center, New York. She teaches at the University of Wollongong, Australia.

Alphonso Lingis is an American philosopher, writer, and translator. He is currently professor emeritus of philosophy at Pennsylvania State University. His areas of specialization include phenomenology, existentialism, modern philosophy, and ethics. He is the author of many articles and books, including *Excesses*; *Libido*; *Deathbound Subjectivity*; *Abuses*; *Foreign Bodies*; *The Imperative*; *Dangerous Emotions*; *Trust*; *Body Transformations*; *Violence and Splendor*; *Contact*; and *Irrevocable*.

David Macauley is associate professor of philosophy and environmental studies at Penn State University, Brandywine. He previously taught at Oberlin College, Emerson College, and New York University and was a Mellon Fellow in the Humanities at the University of Pennsylvania. Macauley is the author of *Elemental Philosophy: Earth, Air, Fire, and Water as Environmental Ideas* (SUNY Press) and the editor of *Minding Nature: The Philosophers of Ecology*. He has published articles on environmental philosophy, aesthetics, political theory, philosophy of technology, ancient Greek philosophy, and Continental thought. He is currently completing a book entitled *Walking: Philosophical and Environmental Foot Notes* (Indiana University Press) and putting together a collection of philosophical parables, myths, and allegories entitled *Re-storying Wisdom*. For more information, visit https://www.brandywine.psu.edu/person/david-macauley.

John Charles Ryan is adjunct associate professor at Southern Cross University and adjunct senior research fellow at Notre Dame University, Australia. His interests include critical plant studies, Aboriginal Australian poetry, and Southeast Asian ecocriticism. He is the co-editor of *The Language of Plants* (2017) and *Australian Wetland Cultures* (2019). His book *Plants in*

Contemporary Poetry (2018) examines the role of botanical life in the work of Les Murray, Mary Oliver, Joy Harjo, and other major poets. His latest collection of poetry is *Seeing Trees: A Poetic Arboretum* (2020).

Index

Nind, Scott, 125, 126, 127
nomad/nomadism, 9, 19, 144, 147,
    159, 161
Northern Hemisphere, 2–3, 7, 9, 53,
    86, 88n2, 121, 127, 133, 226,
    255
Norway, 19, 144–147, 152, 159,
    160–161
Nyoongar, 19–20, 114–118, 120,
    124–133, 223–226, 250, 260n19

Oates, Joyce Carol, 39
objectification, 5–6, 94, 117, 118, 211
Ono, Yoko, 45
ontology (being), 6, 34, 47, 55, 64,
    81, 87–88, 93–98, 103, 106,
    107–108, 116–118, 119, 132,
    170, 182, 184–185, 188, 192,
    193, 198, 208, 245
orgasm, 145

painting, 15, 32, 35, 37, 149, 159
Passover, 9
past, 5, 38–39, 43, 106, 120, 173–
    174, 188, 201, 202, 204–205,
    208–209, 211, 212, 215, 229,
    244
pastoral/anti-pastoral, 22, 85, 245–249,
    251, 253, 258
Peirce, Charles Sanders, 252
periodicity, 3, 7, 17, 19, 21, 27, 29,
    33, 37, 38, 41, 42, 44, 49, 59,
    61, 62, 86, 120, 127, 131, 146,
    151, 166, 168, 187, 208, 223,
    224
phenology, 115, 131–132
phenomenology, 5, 17–19, 36, 44–45,
    54–55, 64–65, 69–92, 93–95,
    97–98, 105–106, 115–119, 125,
    128–129, 131–133, 201–202,
    249, 254–255

place, conceptions of, 5–6, 15, 17, 19,
    27–28, 30, 33–34, 38–39, 43–44,
    47, 48, 49, 53–54, 115–117,
    118–119, 120, 121, 125, 129,
    132–133, 144, 159–160, 168,
    175, 194, 224–229, 235,
    243–244, 246, 249, 254–256,
    258–259
plant development, 4, 8, 17, 29, 30,
    35, 36, 53–66, 75–76, 77, 81,
    84, 85, 86–88, 113, 128, 131,
    132, 156–157, 225, 229. See also
    metamorphosis
Plato, 38, 44, 46, 73, 79, 80, 94
Poe, Edgar Allan, 146, 152
poetry, 5, 9–13, 16, 18, 21, 31–32,
    38, 46, 69–92, 97–111, 165, 167,
    173, 175, 187, 224, 227, 228,
    229–239, 243–262
polar regions, 7, 19, 40, 53, 144–163,
    165–178. See also Arctic, Antarctic
polarity, 75–76, 84, 86, 87
pragmatism, 22, 243–245, 250–254,
    257, 256, 258
presence/emphatic presence/present, 20,
    33, 34, 39, 44, 77, 95, 98, 101,
    105–106, 116, 117–118, 119,
    125, 126, 127, 129, 133, 173–
    174, 185, 191, 198, 201–212,
    214–215, 229, 235, 244, 248,
    251, 254, 255
Proust, Marcel, 72, 73
psychology, 6, 9, 11, 13, 21, 28, 71,
    77, 78, 79, 80, 83, 99, 118, 223,
    236, 237, 256

rationality/reason, 5, 18, 43, 94–95,
    97, 103, 107–108, 127, 145, 244,
    260n27
reindeer, 19, 147–150, 153–154, 156,
    158, 160

www.ingramcontent.com/pod-product-compliance
Lightning Source LLC
Chambersburg PA
CBHW030343270326
41926CB00009B/940